Economic Reform in China and India

Economic Reform in China and India

Development Experience in a Comparative Perspective

Joseph C.H. Chai

Associate Professor of Economics, School of Economics, University of Queensland, Australia

Kartik C. Roy

Associate Professor of Economics, School of Economics, University of Queensland, Australia

Edward Elgar

Cheltenham, UK • Northampton, MA, USA

Published by
Edward Elgar Publishing Limited
Glensanda House
Montpellier Parade
Cheltenham
Glos GL50 1UA
UK

Edward Elgar Publishing, Inc.
136 West Street
Suite 202
Northampton
Massachusetts 01060
USA

A catalogue record for this book
is available from the British Library

ISBN-13: 978 1 84064 987 1
ISBN-10: 1 84064 987 9

Printed and bound in Great Britain by MPG Books Ltd, Bodmin, Cornwall

MANA

Contents

Contents

Introduction

WHY CHINA AND INDIA?

There are several important reasons why we need to study China and India. To begin with, China and India are the world's most populous countries. The Chinese population ranks number 1 and the Indian population ranks number 2 in the world. The combined population of China and India make up almost 40 per cent of humanity. Second, both economies are among the largest in the world. Chinese gross domestic product (GDP), adjusted for purchasing power parity, ranked number 2 after the USA since 1999, whereas Indian GDP, adjusted for purchasing power parity, ranked number 4 after Japan. The combined real GDP of both countries accounted for more than one-quarter of world gross output. Third, over the last two decades both countries have experienced an accelerated rate of economic growth. The Chinese rate increased from between 5 to 6 per cent during 1949–78 to about 10 per cent during 1980–2004, whereas the Indian rate also jumped from about 3 per cent a year during 1950–79 to between 5 to 6 per cent a year during 1980–2004. If both countries could sustain their present rate of growth in the future, they are likely to overtake other large economies in the world in the 21st century. In fact, according to the World Bank's calculation, China is poised to overtake the USA and become the world's largest economy in 2020.

Finally, and not least, there are many similarities between the two countries in their development patterns. Both have an ancient and prestigious cultural heritage; both suffered from European domination and humiliation prior to their modernization drive; and both initiated their modernization drive more or less at the same time, namely in the early 1950s. The initial conditions of both countries were similar with low income per capita, and an economy based on agriculture using traditional technology and facing severe land resource constraint. Both are under the influence of the Soviet model and initially pursued similar development strategies; namely, central planning and rapid industrialization. Later on, both deviated from the Soviet model and adjusted their development strategy to suit their unique resource conditions by giving more emphasis to agricultural development and the adoption of traditional technology as well as the development of small and medium-scale enterprises. Of late, after years of

1

frustration with the inefficiency of the Soviet model, both have embraced economic reform and liberalization – China in the late 1970s and India in the early 1990s. Yet after almost half a century of development, the results of the two countries' modernization drive are strikingly different.

As mentioned earlier, the rate of growth of pre-reform China was around 5 to 6 per cent; whereas that of pre-reform India was only 3 per cent a year. After the reform, the gap between the two countries' rates of growth widened with China's rate twice as high as that of India. The upshot is that while China and India started with more or less similar per capita income in the early 1950s, by 2002 the real GDP per capita adjusted for purchasing power parity of China was almost 72 per cent higher than that of India. China outperforms India not only in terms of economic development but also social development. In terms of the United Nation's human development index, China is years ahead of India. Though India lags behind China in terms of social and economic development, it is well ahead of China in terms of political development. So what went wrong with India? Why has China been able to perform better?

The answer to these questions is crucial to other developing countries with similar conditions to those of China and India, as these countries can learn a lot from their experiences. This book is an attempt to do just that.

There have been quite a few comparative studies of China and India in the past (see for examples, Bardharn 1969; Bhalla 1992, 1998; Dreze and Sen 1989; Eckhaus 1995; Garnaut 1996; Lal 1995; Malenbaum 1959, 1982; Rosen 1992; Sen 1995; Srinivasan et al. 1993; Swamy 1973, 1989; Weisskopf 1980), but most of them were undertaken more than ten years ago. Hence their findings were somewhat dated. Moreover, they were mainly carried out by an Indian specialist who was severely handicapped by a dearth of statistics on China due to the statistical blackout in China during this period. In recent years, an increased amount of statistical data has been released by both countries' governments as well as international agencies. But unfortunately there have been few studies to take advantage of the increased information available. Most of the recent studies are undertaken piecemeal as they focus either on certain features or certain epochs of China and India's development process. The book aims to fill in this important gap.

This book differs from others in several respects. First, this book presents a comprehensive comparison of the development experiences of China and India. This book covers not only economic but also social, political and environmental aspects of China and India's development. Second, it is policy orientated. This book attempts to draw specific policy conclusions, which are useful for China and India as well as other developing countries to solve their current development problems. Third, to enhance the objectivity of the study, quantitative analysis is used as extensively as possible in this book.

THE STRUCTURE OF THE BOOK

Chapter 1 compares the initial conditions and the development strategies of the two countries. It begins by comparing the most important initial resources for development in the two countries – human resources, energy and transport, and communication networks – and then the goals and objectives of development and the evolution of the development strategy in the two countries since the early 1950s are reviewed.

Chapter 2 examines the institutions for control and allocation of resources in both countries to implement their alternative development strategies. It contrasts the ownership system between the two countries and the relative role of central planning and market mechanism between the two countries during both the pre- and post-reform era.

Chapter 3 looks at agriculture. Rapid growth in agricultural output is a prerequisite for modern economic growth in large countries like China and India. This chapter analyses the role of agriculture in development in both countries, and compares and evaluates the agricultural development policies adopted by both countries.

Chapter 4 focuses on industrial and technology policy. Modern economic growth is achieved through industrialization and technological progress. This chapter examines in detail the industrial policy undertaken by both countries. It compares their policy objectives and tools as well as their effectiveness.

Chapter 5 considers the foreign sectors of the two economies. Modern economic growth is accompanied by increased internationalization of the economy. This chapter compares the role of foreign trade and capital in both countries' development, and assesses the foreign trade and investment policies adopted by both countries.

Chapter 6 considers the growth of capital stock in both countries. Modern economic growth is achieved not only through rapid structural change but also through rapid increase of strategic production factors, especially capital. This chapter examines how investment was financed and how surplus was extracted from the agricultural sector to finance the industrialization. It also looks at the rate of investment and investment efficiency in both countries.

Chapter 7 considers labour resources in both countries. Modern economic growth in countries like China and India is not constrained by worker shortage but by overpopulation and surplus labour. This chapter contrasts the policies undertaken by both governments to solve these problems and their relative effectiveness.

Chapters 8–11 consider the social and political development strategies as well as the environmental policy of the two countries, and evaluate the results of half a decade of developments in both countries in terms of such criteria as growth, equity, standard of living, women's empowerment, democratization and environment degradation.

The final chapter reviews the earlier comparisons between the two Asian giants and summarizes the major findings of the study. It also attempts to answer the question of (a) whether India would be able to catch up with China in the growth race; and (b) what policy reforms India needs to introduce in order to narrow its growth gap with China.

1. Initial conditions and alternative paths to economic development

China and India have adopted two distinctive paths of development over the last 50 years. This chapter compares the goals and objectives of development in the two countries and gives an overview of the evolution of the development strategy adopted by the two countries since the early 1950s.

INITIAL CONDITIONS

The development strategy of a country depends very much on its initial conditions (Ishikawa 1986, pp. 2–3). China and India have a lot in common in their initial conditions. But there are also significant differences between the two countries. These differences go a long way in explaining the two different strategies adopted by the two countries and their varying performance.

Similarities

To begin with, both countries have achieved a high level of economic development in the past as both were once the world's largest economies and richest countries. According to the estimate of Maddison (2001, pp. 261 and 264), China's and India's GDP per capita were among the highest in the world around the year 1000 and their purchasing power parity (ppp) adjusted GDP ranked number 1 and 2 in the world respectively from 1500 to 1870. Second, both had failed to modernize in the past and, as a result, by the mid-20th century both were among the poorest countries in the world with a per capita income of only 20 to 30 per cent of the world average. Third, both suffered from heavy population pressure with limited arable land. China's population topped the world in 1952, accounting for almost one-quarter of humankind, whereas it has only 5 per cent of the world's cultivated area.

India's population ranked number 2 in the world in the early 1950s and the land holding of its peasants was also among the tiniest in the world. Finally, not least, the external environment facing both countries was almost identical. Both suffered from Western domination for a considerable period of time. India was under British colonial rule for almost 200 years. Though China was never fully colonized by a Western power, a large chunk of Chinese territory was ceded to a Western power or succumbed to Western influence after the opium war in 1842.

Differences

The first difference is that China was more backward than India in the mid-20th century. Chinese income per capita in terms of 1952 US$ was only 83 per cent that of India. The weight of the primary sector in China was also larger than that of India in the early 1950s. In 1952 84 per cent of the total workforce in China was engaged in the agricultural sector, whereas in India only 72 per cent of the workforce was engaged in agriculture. India also had a larger modern sector than China in the early 1950s. According to Wrigley (1988, pp. 5–6), the modern economy is distinct from the traditional economy in the kind of energy it uses. The traditional economy is known as an 'organic' economy, which relies on organic materials as the main source of energy. Since the supply of organic raw materials in the long run is constrained by the fixed production factor of land, growth and productivity of the traditional economy are bound by the availability of land. Once the land frontier is reached, diminishing returns set in and the traditional economy stagnates. Both China and India have encountered this phenomenon – known as the 'high-level equilibrium trap' – in the past (Lal 1995, pp. 1477 and 1489).

The modern economy, in contrast, is a mineral-based energy economy which utilizes stock of stored energy represented by fossil fuels. Through the development of the steam engine the fossil fuels provide an unlimited supply of mechanical energy for the modern economy. As a result, the productivity and growth of the modern economy is no longer bounded by the fixed factor of production-land. Thanks to the British influence India had a head start in the transition from a traditional to a modern economy. Under British rule, modern industry was introduced into India beginning with cotton textiles in the mid-19th century and diversifying into many other industries such as jute textiles, sugar, cement, steel by the first half of the 20th century (Weisskopf 1980, p. 40). Modern industry was also introduced from the West in the mid-19th century in China; but it was not until the first quarter of the 20th century that it started to experience a rapid growth. Despite its rapid growth, China's nascent modern industry was relatively small as it accounted for only 1.3 per cent of China's employment in the early 1950s as compared with 2.6 per cent of India; and the output level of major industries such as steel, cement and cotton cloth remained well below those of India (Table 1.1).

Table 1.1   China and India: initial conditions

	China 1952	India 1950/51
1. Population, million	567	357
2. Population density, sqkm per capita	58	110
3. GDP per capita, ppp-based, 1990 US$	537	623
4. Crop area per farmer, acres	0.5	1.67
5. Grain output per capita, kg	272	281
6. Agricultural share of employment	84	72
7. Industrial output per capita		
Coal, kg	96	97
Pig iron, kg	2.8	5
Crude steel, kg	2	4
Cotton spindles, units	0.01	0.03
Cement, kg	4	9
8. Railroad, km per million population	43	160
9. Electric power, kw per capita	0.005	0.01
10. Literacy rate	20	19
11. Primary school enrolment	49	21
12. Tertiary students per 100 000 population	330	118

Sources: Chen and Galenson 1969, p. 35; Maddison 2001, p. 304; SSB 1985, pp. 143 and 171; Weisskopf 1980, pp. 54, 81 and 82; World Bank 1983a, p. 43.

Apart from modern industry, India was also well ahead of China in terms of modern infrastructure development. In transport, for instance, China's rail coverage per million people was only 43 km in 1952, whereas the corresponding figure for India in 1951 was almost quadruple that of China. In communication, there was only six telephones for every 10 000 people in 1952 in China (SSB 1984, p. 91). The corresponding figure for India, in contrast, was one telephone connection for 2149 people in 1950–51 (CSO 1977; GOI 1992). In electricity generation, electric power per capita in India in 1950 was 0.01 kw, whereas the Chinese figure in 1952 was only half of that of India (Table 1.1).

The second difference between the two countries is their differing resources, cultural and institutional endowments. First, in terms of resources endowment, China was poorer than India in terms of land resources. The land–person ratio of China in 1950 was 58 sq km per capita as compared with 110 sq km per capita of India (Table 1.1). In agriculture, for example, the average Chinese farmer had only half an acre of farm land to cultivate; whereas the corresponding figure for India in 1950 was 1.67 acres.

China was also poorer than India in terms of capital resource. Unlike India, China was relatively isolated in the international community in the early 1950s because of its communist ideology. It has limited access to foreign capital, with the exception of that of the Soviet Union and other communist countries in Eastern Europe. Hence most of its capital formation had to be sought internally in the form of 'primitive capital accumulation' through the extraction of agricultural surplus during its early industrialization drive. However, the potential for agricultural surplus extraction in China was more limited as compared to India. Due to China's larger population and lower agricultural labour productivity, the per capita availability of food grain was lower than that of India, hence, the size of agricultural surplus which can be extracted to finance industrialization was also much less as compared to India.

However, in terms of human resources, China was better endowed than India in the early 1950s. Not only was the Chinese population larger than that of India, but its population was also healthier and better educated than that of India. The average Chinese in the early 1950s had a life expectancy 28 per cent longer than that of India (Weisskopf 1980, p. 5). The Chinese literacy rate was 20 per cent as compared to the 19 per cent of India (Table 1.1). The primary school enrolment rate of China in 1952 was 49 per cent, whereas the corresponding figure for India in 1950 was only 21 per cent. China was also well ahead of India in tertiary education enrolment. There were 330 tertiary students per 100 000 population in China in 1952. In contrast, the corresponding figure for India was only 118.

Moreover, the kind of subjects taken by Chinese tertiary students were more technical and skill orientated as compared to India. The percentage of students taking science and engineering subjects reached 40 per cent in China in 1952 (SSB 1985, p. 150), whereas the corresponding figure for India was less than 1 per cent (see Chapter 8, Table 8.7).

Second, in terms of cultural heritage, mid-20th century China inherited a culture which is more conducive to modern economic growth as compared to that of India. Culture here refers to a system of basic common values that help shape the behaviour of the people in a given society. McClelland (1983) demonstrates that there is a close correlation between national rates of economic growth and their level of n-achievement. This n-achievement is not hereditary but, rather, instilled in people by their parents and school systems through the use of stories or school texts. Mid-20th century China inherited a unique value system known as Confucianism. Kahn (1979) finds that there is a close relation between Confucian ethic and n-achievement. Average Chinese children are taught in the school and by their parents to be thrifty, diligent and commit to their group, and to place a higher value on education and desire for accomplishment in various skills. The cultivation of these values is evidenced from the stories or textbooks used in traditional Chinese schools. The recent World Values Survey also provides direct empirical evidences to support the Kahn hypothesis. Granato et al. (1996, p. 264) construct an index of n-achievement based on the result of this survey for 25 countries, which shows that on a scale from 125 to −125, the Chinese index stands at 87.5 and is among the highest in the world. In contrast, India's index is −44.

India's value system has been deeply influenced by India's culture, which in turn has been greatly influenced by India's main religion, Hinduism, which asks followers to try to achieve spiritual perfection and the unification of the individual with the supreme soul. This automatically rules out a desirable objective in life, accumulation of savings, wealth, achieving success in life, pursuit of material well-being, and so on.

Hindu philosophy instilled among Hindus the spirit of individualism which made them fiercely individualistic in their day-to-day activities willing to submit themselves only to the supreme authority – God. Hence the Indian state could not command the same total obedience from its citizens as the Chinese state or the other East Asian states under Confucian cultural values have been able to do. Also, Hinduism's division of human life into four stages under which the first 15 years of a person's life are spent at the teacher's house and the last two stages of life are spent in forests away from family life and family members, after reunification of all earthly possessions to strive for the liberation of the soul or the attainment of 'Moksha', cannot inspire the nation to work hard to increase material wealth, to sacrifice consumption in the present for the gratification in future and to achieve high economic growth.

While the green colour of the tricolour Indian national flag is the symbol of a young nation, the saffron colour is the symbol of 'sacrifice' or reunification of all earthly possessions. Hence, if a young nation's philosophy is 'reunification', then how can that philosophy inspire people to accumulate capital, achieve high growth (Clark and Roy 1997). Ghandi's development philosophy also did not support accumulation of wealth (Roy 1986). When the British established the empire, the administration instilled discipline among the people by force and the Indians submitted to the British authority because of fear of punishment and also of the lure of future promotions and rewards. Also Indians working as employees of the administration, became used to receiving salaries at the end of every month and maintaining a relatively assured standard of living without taking risks and uncertainty to generate wealth. Then, in the post-independence period, Nehru adopted a system of federal state with multiparty democracy in a country in which the literacy rate in 1951 stood at only 18.3 per cent (GOI 1992). Nehru's government allowed the formation of trade unions to protect workers' rights: from the mid-1960s over a period of more than 20 years the union power established a reign of terror in India's industrial arena. Since the Hindu society used to look down upon communities engaged in trade, commerce and industrial activities, the Parsees and Marwics, being blocked minorities, had to excel in these activities. Hence Hagen's theory of blocked minorities can explain why the level of achievers was much lower in India than in China.

Third, mid-20th century China inherited a social structure which is more conducive to modern economic growth than that of India. Chinese traditional society is not a feudal society. Unlike India there is no caste system in China. Traditionally, the Chinese population is separated into five different groups according to their social status and occupation: (1) literati, (2) peasants, (3) artisans, (4) merchants, (5) soldiers. The class distinction, however, between these five groups is not fixed by heredity but is fluid. Everybody in China can raise their status as long as he or she performs. Hence the vertical mobility of Chinese society is very high. For instance, even though merchant is the lowest class in traditional Chinese society, successful merchants often became gentry through either purchase of an academic degree or by financing their son's study to obtain a degree (Ho 1962). Chinese society is also more homogenous than that of India. Though China has about 56 ethnic groups each with their distinctive culture and traditions, China is essentially dominated by the Han people, who comprise 92 per cent of the total population.

The caste system in India was a social division of labour under which a person born in a caste was required to discharge his or her caste-specific duties. The primary reason for the creation of the caste system was to enable people belonging to a particular caste to gain specialization in the area of their work and to ensure a continuous supply of personnel from every caste into the entire society. But people of the lower caste were mistreated by people of the upper castes for generations and prevented from achieving social mobility through hard work and enterprise. But the rigidity of the old system has weakened considerably through inter-caste marriages and improvement in the economic status of same members of the lower castes. Nevertheless in a few backward provinces, the members of untouchable families are systematically tortured and killed by members of upper castes under any flimsy pretext. But although the presence of the caste system did impede India's economic and social progress, a coalition government in the 1980s increased the percentage of places reserved for members of disadvantaged communities, accounting for about 24 per cent of the total population, in all public sector undertakings to 56 per cent of the total vacancies. Such a policy, formulated and implemented primarily to buy votes at elections for the party in power, acted as a positive discrimination against the majority of the population. Such a policy, still in practice, will continue to impede the country's rate of growth and development.

Mid-20th century China also inherited a unique political system which is characterized by a long history of unified rule under a centralized state dating back from the Qin dynasty in the third century BC. The legacy of political unity has several implications for the modern economic growth of China. First, it fosters social cohesion. Though Chinese society is a multi-ethnic society like India, it has a common written and spoken language, namely, Mandarin. The tradition of unity and cohesion ensures not only political stability, which is one of the prerequisites for high economic growth, but also facilitates organizational unity, meaning the mobilization of the populace for the pursuit of national goals. Last, but not least, the legacy of a long history as a centralized state endowed China with skill and experience in control and management of complex organizations which are one of the main features of the modern economy.

Compared with China, India has inherited from the British a modern political institution with a system of rule of law and a constitutional democracy. By 1950–51 when India initiated its First Five Year Plan, it had already experienced almost a century of industrial expansion, growth of industrial entrepreneurship, social overheads and financial institutions. At the same time, India had inherited from the British an efficient civil service, responsible administration, parliamentary democracy, an efficient judiciary and a law enforcement system capable of enforcing the rule of law. The Indian state was federal but significant powers were delegated under the Indian constitution to provinces and the centre had no control over such vital areas as education, law and order, and agriculture. Such distribution of powers made Indian federalism more centrifugal than centripetal (Clark and Roy 1997). Although India followed the British system of parliamentary democracy it opted for a multiparty system with no restriction placed on the maximum number of political parties that can be legally formed and no restriction on the freedom of an elected representative of a political party to cross the floor of the house and join another party or several other parties whenever self-interest justified such moves.

While Nehru's party enjoyed an absolute majority at the federal parliament and most of the provincial legislatures for many years, the Congress Party's rule also allowed rent-seeking activities to develop. In later years, particularly in the 1980s and the 1990s as the hold of the Congress Party in power loosened, groups of non-Congress parties began to assume power at the centre and at the provincial level. The primary objective of these coalition governments was to stay in power by any unfair means to allow the parties in power and their supporters to collect as much rent as they could. These activities received a strong boost under a burgeoning public sector and as the police force was made corrupt by the political parties in power. Hence, the index of achievement in India had to be significantly lower than that of China.

Accordingly, in 1948, of the three business communities which remained as the dominant force in India's industrial and trading sector in the Bombay Province, the Gujarities who were Hindus, controlled 24.5 per cent of total paid-up capital and 18.5 per cent of gross assets, the Marwics who were Jains, controlled 14.3 per cent of paid-up capital and 7.3 per cent of gross assets and the Parsees (immigrants from Persia) controlled 36 per cent of paid-up capital and 46.5 per cent of gross assets (Myers 1958).

DEVELOPMENT STRATEGY: CHINA

The Pre-reform Period

The Feldman Paradigm

The goal of the Chinese development strategy during the pre-reform period from 1952 to 1978 was threefold. The first goal was to achieve rapid economic independence from the outside world. This objective was driven by security considerations. China was relatively isolated in the international community in the early 1950s due to a Western embargo because of its participation in the Korean war. At that time, the only outside link China had was that with the Soviet Union and its Eastern European allies. After the Sino-Soviet split in the late 1950s, China's isolation from the international economic community was almost complete. Hence, to ensure economic survival in such a hostile international environment, it had no other choice but to build up an independent industrial system as rapidly as possible. The second objective was the rapid catch-up with the Western world in terms of per capita income and living standard. This objective of the Chinese government was understandable in view of the humiliations which China had suffered from Western imperial power for more than half a century. Finally, being a communist regime, the third goal of Chinese government was to build a socialist society with a high degree of egalitarianism.

The strategy China adopted to realize the above three objectives is the Feldman Development Paradigm borrowed from the Soviet Union. This strategy, formulated by Feldman in the 1920s during the Great Industrialization Debate, is essentially an unbalanced growth strategy which emphasizes the investment allocation ratio in the heavy capital goods sector. The rationale behind this strategy had been that machines could produce more machines and, in the process, industries using machines would grow downstream at an accelerated rate; this not only maximizes the rate of long-run growth of the economy, but also generates a maximum stream of consumption for the entire population.

There is little doubt that China consistently adopted the Feldman Paradigm during the pre-reform period. This is borne out by the fact that throughout this period the heavy industry sector received the lion's share of state investment at the expense of the light and agriculture sector. On average during 1950–79 the allocation coefficients for the three sectors were 53.2, 5.2 and 12.4 respectively (Ma and Sun 1981, table 1). This sectoral distribution of state investment demonstrates that the Chinese government was determined to outdo its Russian counterparts in speed of industrialization, as over half of Chinese state investment went to the industry. In contrast, Soviet industry received only 40 per cent of state investment during its First Five Year Plan (Chen and Galenson 1969, p. 39).

The implementation of the Feldman Paradigm necessitates a system of state-controlled resources allocation in order to mobilize and allocate resources from the rest of the economy to finance such a heavy dose of investment in the heavy capital goods sector. Hence, in the early 1950s, China initiated the wholesale transplant of Soviet institutions and policy into China, in particular the system of collectivized agriculture; the centralized planning; the use of price scissors to extract agricultural surplus to finance heavy industrial development and the adoption of the autarky policy in international trade.

The Maoist paradigm

The Feldman Development Paradigm was designed to suit the Soviet environment in the 1920s, which differed significantly from that of China in the early 1950s. Thus, the transplant of the Soviet development strategy into a Chinese environment necessarily generated a great deal of conflict and tension which required the Chinese government under Mao to introduce new policies to resolve these conflicts. The resultant new policies have come to be known as the Maoist approach.

Emphasis on agriculture

The Maoist approach differs significantly from the Soviet approach in a number of important aspects. First, the Maoist approach gives more emphasis to agriculture in its development strategy. One of the prerequisites of the Soviet model of rapid industrialization is the existence of an agricultural surplus which can be extracted through price scissors to finance industrialization. On the eve of industrialization in 1928, the Russians did not suffer from population pressure; and both its per capita availability of farm land for rural population and its per capita grain output were twice those of China (Chen and Galenson 1969, p. 35).

Consequently, while the Russians were in the position to extract as much agricultural surplus as possible to finance its industrialization, the Chinese peasants were living close to the margin of subsistence and there was very little agricultural surplus left over for financing industrialization. As a result, the Chinese industrialization drive constantly ran up against the wall of inadequate food supply. To soften this agricultural constraint the Chinese government at first adopted a self-reliance approach towards the promotion of agricultural development, under which, the increase in agricultural output relied on the mobilization of local labour and materials.

Two measures were initiated during the Great Leap Forward period (1958–61) to achieve this objective. One was the introduction of the commune. The government hoped that by the creation of a larger collective such as a commune more surplus labour could be mobilized for agricultural capital investment (for example, flood controls, irrigation projects, and so on) and current production (for example, via accumulation of farmyard manure, increase of multiple cropping index, and so on). The second was rural-based industrialization, the aim of which was to stimulate the productive use of local resources otherwise left unused or underused to produce modern industrial inputs to support agricultural production. Both policies failed to achieve their objectives.

The first policy failed to increase agricultural yield and total output. The grain yield, instead of increasing, actually declined from 98 kg per mou in 1957 to 81 per mou in 1961 and the grain output also declined from 195 million tons to 147.5 million tons during the same period (SSB 1989a, pp. 146–7). There are many factors behind the decline of agricultural output during this period, but undoubtedly the utilization of surplus labour for capital investment had not significantly increased the effective capital in the farm sector as many flood controls and irrigation works were hastily carried out and the works were substandard and became unusable after a while. Worse still, some irrigation works destroyed natural irrigations and ruined farm land by raising the underground water level. The utilization of surplus labour for current production had not been productive either. The labour-intensive cultivation technique had been adopted and pushed to the limit by Chinese peasants in the past. Further intensifying the use of labour not only ran up against the soil and climatic constraint but also led to diminishing, if not negative, labour productivity.

The second policy of rural-based industrialization also produced little result, as the industrial products from the rural small industries were of such poor quality that they were unusable. The failure of the self-reliance policy coupled with the exceptional poor weather conditions and the withdrawal of Soviet aid and technicians resulted in the Great Famine of 1961which wiped out 16.5 to 43 million people (Riskin 1998).

After the Great Famine, the Chinese approach to softening the agricultural constraint changed. Agriculture had been elevated to 'the foundation of the national economy' and began to attract centrally mobilized resources leading to a reverse transfer of resource from industry to agriculture, which assumed several forms. First, to lessen the extent of agricultural surplus extraction from farmers, the government started to divert precious foreign exchange to finance imports of food grain. Starting from the mid-1960s the government lowered the prices of industrial goods sold in the countryside. This combined with a mild increase of grain procurement prices improved the commodity terms of trade in favour of agriculture (SSB 1984, pp. 115–16). Last but not least, realizing that traditional inputs could no longer be relied upon to boost agricultural output, the government began to direct the centralized industrial sector to produce modern inputs for agriculture, which included chemical fertilizers, pesticides, pump sets, mechanical threshers, tractors and power tillers, and so on.

All in all the above measures brought about some diversion of resources from industry to the agriculture sector. Nonetheless the extent of resources transferred to the agriculture sector was still very limited. To minimize the amount of resources diverted from the centralized industrial sector to agriculture, the agricultural sector was forced to continue to rely on local resources as its main source of growth. The commune system continued to be relied on to mobilize surplus labour for agricultural capital investment and current production. The government continued to promote the development of small rural industries, in particular the so-called five small industries, which utilized local materials to produce modern inputs such as iron and steel, chemical fertilizer, coal and electricity, cement, and agricultural machinery to support agriculture.

'Walking on two legs' policy

The Maoist approach also differs from the Soviet approach in its choice of technology. Another problem brought about by the transplant of Soviet industrialization strategy into the Chinese environment is unemployment. The Soviet approach emphasized the development of large-scale, capital-intensive and urban-based industrial plant utilizing modern technology. This strategy is designed to suit the Russian factor endowment. Unlike China, the Russians did not suffer from population pressure and the surplus labour problem. The Russian population in 1928 was equivalent to only one-quarter of the Chinese population in 1952 (Chen and Galenson 1969, p. 35). There was no large pool of surplus labour which could be tapped for an industrialization drive. In fact the Russians were forced to move millions of people from the country to the cities during the 1930s (Chen and Galenson 1969, p. 37). In contrast, on the eve of its industrialization drive, China had a huge mass of labour. Its population grew at an annual average rate of 2 per cent during 1949–52 (Ishikawa 1983, p. 249). Both unemployment and underemployment were widespread among its rural and urban workforce (Howe 1971). Industrialization via the capital-intensive route meant relatively few new jobs were opening up in the modern industrial sector and aggravated the problems of unemployment in the Chinese economy. Facing the increased seriousness of unemployment problems the Chinese government was forced to adopt a series of drastic measures.

First, agriculture was forced to absorb both the urban and rural surplus labour. To achieve this objective, strict control of rural urban migration was initiated; urban educated youths were sent down to the countryside; the capacity of agriculture to absorb surplus workers was enlarged through the intensification of cropping practice and the emphasis was on capital-saving and labour-using farm activities.

Second, to provide more job opportunities in the industrial sector, the government adopted the policy of 'walking on two legs' in the choice of technology in the industrial sector which stressed the importance of development of a small-scale, labour-intensive rural-based industrial plant using intermediate technology alongside large-scale modern industrial plant in the cities.

Egalitarianism

The egalitarian policy pursued by Mao marked another difference between the Soviet and Chinese approaches towards development. There was serious conflict between the Soviet industrialization strategy and the Maoist goal of building socialism which emphasized specifically achieving greater equality in Chinese society. The Soviet approach, with its heavy emphasis on the development of industry, especially the heavy industrial sector at the cost of agriculture, implied an urban-biased development which widened the urban rural gap which Maoists sought to eradicate. Similarly, to strive for greater efficiency the Soviet model adopted the 'capitalist' system of management, which emphasizes expertise rather than inexperience in the hiring of staff and workers, and the 'capitalist' system of work incentives which stress the principle of remuneration of labour according to work rather than need. These practices increased social stratification leading to greater inequality and contradicted what Mao wanted to achieve.

The Maoist response to this conflict was the introduction of a series of measures to contain the increased inequality generated by the Soviet strategy. First, to narrow the urban–rural gap, urban wages were frozen from 1956. Educated youths were sent to the countryside to experience the rural way of life. Rural-based industrialization was promoted to provide not only modern industrial inputs to support agriculture, but also employment opportunity and industrial experience for the rural residents. Second, to reduce absolute inequality or poverty, an enterprise-based social welfare system was established which provided basic needs such as food, shelter, education, health care, unemployment benefits, old-age pension, and so on for the rural and urban poor. Third, to narrow the social division between the mental and manual workers, cadres in an enterprise were encouraged to participate in manual labour and workers to participate in management. Fourth, to narrow the pay differential between staff and workers, bonus and material incentives were scrapped. In their place, moral incentive was introduced. Attempts were also made to narrow the wage gap between the top administrative and technical workers and those of ordinary workers.

Post-reform Period

Much has been written about China's reform and open-door policy but relatively little on its development strategy since the late 1970s. Ishikawa (1983, p. 21) suggests that in the post-reform period, 'the previous development policy of high growth and high investment, which gave top priority to heavy industry, is being replaced by a new one which aims at securing a steady increase in personal consumption and in which investment is weighted in favour of light industry and agriculture'. This view, however, proved to be premature. It is true that since the reforms the Chinese government no longer emphasizes heavy industry and stresses instead improvement of consumption standard, in particular the increase of wage goods (light industry and agriculture) as the goal of its development strategy. However, it is certainly not true that the government has abandoned its high-growth and investment strategy. To begin with, if the government is no longer interested in high growth, it is difficult to explain why the government continues to extol the doubling of its gross national product (GNP) every ten years as its goal for a long-term development plan (Wu 2000). Second, the allegation that the Chinese government no longer pursues a high investment policy does not square with the fact that the rate of capital formation recorded during the reform period, averaging 37 per cent, is significantly higher than that of the pre-reform period of 29 per cent.

Lin et al. (1996) suggest that China has emulated other East Asian countries by adopting the comparative advantage doctrine as its new development strategy during the post-reform period. This view is also problematic. It is true that during the reform period China has embraced the doctrine of comparative advantage and adopted an export-orientated trade strategy as one of the ingredients of its overall development strategy. But the Chinese post-reform development strategy is different from the East Asian model as the comparative cost doctrine is not strictly adhered to as, alongside the export-orientated strategy, China still maintains its import substitution strategy (Naughton 1996). Moreover, the comparative doctrine is ill suited to serve as a theoretical guide for a country's growth strategy as this doctrine aims at maximizing efficiency not necessarily growth. As Thirlwall (1989, p. 186) demonstrates, the theory of growth suggests that the resource allocation pattern is significantly different from that derived from the theory of the comparative doctrine. For instance, if growth depends on per capita investment and technological progress, it will be unwise to channel all investment resources into activities which are labour intensive where the income generated is mostly consumed and very little is saved, or where there is little scope for increasing returns.

What then is China's new development strategy during the post-reform period? To begin with, the goal of the Chinese development strategy has changed. Following the death of Mao, the objective of building socialism, though not abandoned, has been placed on the back burner, and economic modernization is being elevated as the single most important goal of China's new long-term development strategy. Second, the specific target of economic modernization has changed due to changing external and internal environments. Externally, China finds itself in a more peaceful environment after the establishment of diplomatic relation with the Western world in the early 1970s and the reintegration of the Chinese economy into the world economy. Hence, the goal to achieve rapid economic independence by building up an independent industrial system through fostering the development of heavy industry has become obsolete and been abandoned. Internally, after three decades of heavy industrial development, the rapid growth of consumption as predicted by the Feldman Development Paradigm had failed to materialize and the living standard gap between the mainland Chinese and the overseas Chinese living in Taiwan, Hong Kong, Singapore, Malaysia and other parts of Southeast Asia had widened significantly. Hence pressure was building up for the Chinese government to bridge this gap urgently in order to prevent the social and political upheaval which struck other former communist countries before their downfall. Thus, the raising of the consumption standard of the Chinese population had become an important goal of China's new strategy. Third, the goal of high growth in order to catch up with developed countries' income per capita had not changed. This is borne out by the targets set in China's long-term development plan for 1980–2010, under which a three-step strategy will be adopted to catch up with the developed world. The target set for the first step was to double the GNP of 1980 by the year 1990; that for the second step, to double the 1990 GNP by the end of the 20th century; and for the third step to double again the 2000 GNP by the year 2010. The doubling of national income every ten years implies an annual average rate of growth of 7 per cent (see Wu 2000).

However, the goals of high growth and increasing the immediate consumption standard are mutually inconsistent. As demonstrated by Thirlwall (1989, table 7.1), given the amount of resources, to increase immediate consumption necessitates a reduction in the rate of investment, which may impair growth. Striving for rapid growth necessitates an increase in the rate of investment which cuts into present consumption but will provide greater output and consumption in the long run. China's approach to this dilemma is to diversify the sources of its growth.

In the past, Chinese growth has been mainly achieved through an injection of a high dose of capital. During the reform period, the government emphasized the importance of the growth of total factor productivity as an additional source of growth alongside the high rate of investment. To boost the increase of total factor productivity, reforms and the open-door policy were initiated. Reforms were introduced to rid the Chinese economic system of its inefficiency. The open-door policy was adopted in order to enable China to (a) participate in international division of labour so as to increase its static and dynamic efficiency, and (b) transfer foreign technology into China through foreign direct investment (FDI) so as to accelerate the rate of technological progress in China.

In the past, a high rate of investment was mainly financed by domestic savings. During the reform period, to enable a diversion of resources for increased consumption, foreign investment was increasingly relied on to boost China's rate of investment under the open-door policy. This is evidenced from the increased share of FDI in China's fixed capital investment which shot up from almost nil in 1978 to 9 per cent in 1998.

More recently, the Chinese government initiated several new policies as ad hoc responses to the changing external and internal environments. One of the new policy initiatives is the Western development policy, in response to the increased regional inequality generated by the reforms and open-door policy (see Chai 1996). To bridge the widening income gap between the Eastern region and Western region of China the government diverted investment resources to improve the infrastructure facilities of the Central and Western region so as to entice more domestic and foreign investment into these regions. Another new policy initiative is the development of high-technology industries. Upon the entry of China into the World Trade Organization (WTO) in the late 1990s, Chinese industries faced increased foreign competition. In an attempt to create a new industrial structure that could survive this competition the government fostered the development of high-tech industry. Last but not least, due to the increased importance of the new economy, the government of late also targeted the service industry as a point of development. In particular, the government plans to foster the development of information, education, tourism, social services and inter-mediary service industries (Wu 2000).

DEVELOPMENT STRATEGY: INDIA

Pre-reform Period

India followed a similar Feldman-type planning strategy but for reasons different from those of China. India was not isolated from the rest of the world and India never had the aspiration to catch up with the West. Unlike China, India adopted socialism purely due to the overriding dominance of Nehru in India's policy-making body. The reasons are summarized below.

In March 1931, the Congress (the political party which led India to inde-pendence from British rule) at its Karachi Session passed a resolution to the effect that the state should own or control key industries and services, mineral resources, railways, waterways, shipping and other means of trans-port. This resolution, drafted in consultation with Gandhi, was described by Nehru as 'a step, a very short step in the socialist direction' (Paranjape 1964, p. 1; Roy 1986). He was quite certain that Khadi[1] (the symbol of Gandhi's self-reliant development) was an out-of-date form of production as it was incapable of raising the wealth of the country high enough for the state to be able to create employment for the masses and thereby alleviate poverty and raise the standard of living of the masses. While Nehru was not completely opposed to the involvement of private capital in India's development, he felt that the expansion of private sector investment in India's development would lead to the concentration of capital in fewer hands, thereby preventing the distribution of income to the poor. Hence to him, economic development in India was synonymous with socialism, state ownership of means of production and large-scale industrial development of the Soviet type. Also, he assumed that by socializing the means of pro-duction, the country would be able to get rid of the evils of capitalism. In shaping India's state-sponsored socialism and national planning, Nehru was greatly influenced by Fabian ideas which emanated from the traditions of English utilitarianism, empiricism and classical economic thought. Fabian reformism in the political sphere was adopted in India in the form of parliamentary democracy.

Nehru and Mahalanobis (the architect of India's planning model) believed that, due to the paucity of capital goods, the establishment and expansion of large-scale manufacturing units to generate employment, the primary goal of planned development (Bose and Mukherjee 1985;

Clark and Roy 1997), would take time. Hence, a diffuse sector consisting of small-scale and village industries, as well as agriculture, would be needed in the short run. However, the support of Nehru and his government to small industries was limited to facilitating institutional change, spread of education, improvement of communication and so on. Also, an increase in agricultural output was to be achieved not by an increase in provision of modern inputs, but by undertaking land reforms, consolidation of land holdings and the establishment of village co-operatives (Bose and Mukherjee 1985).

The strategy to develop India by expanding the modern sector and a dual economy at the same time, to prevent the concentration of wealth in a few private hands, led the government to direct the planning to achieve a broad parity in the level of production and of living standards in different regions of India violating the rules of the comparative advantage for determining the location of industries, and also to achieve a reduction in inequalities in income among different income groups. Hence the principal goals of India's development strategy were to substantially expand employment opportunities to alleviate poverty and raise living standards of the masses, to reduce inequalities in income and wealth between the rich and the poor, and to achieve parity in the distribution of economic power among different regions of the country.

These development goals were to be realized by achieving a sizeable increase in national income through rapid industrialization of the country, with particular emphasis on the development of basic and heavy industries first and consumer goods industries later (GOI 1956).

To realize such goals, the public sector share of the total investment was to be raised continuously, and management of the economy and heavy industries were to be established by the state following the pattern of Soviet-style expansion of heavy industry under centralized planning. Indian policy-thinking before the implementation of the development strategy was dominated by the view that distribution of income could not be altered very much by distributive measures of fiscal type (Desai and Bhagwali 1975). Thus, a regime of autarky was established, which was to make use of substantial targeting and of more comprehensive industrial and concomitant import licensing than before, to control and divert the level and composition of industrial wealth and power within a small group of families and groups. However, the expansion of private sector investment was not completely stopped and the inflow of foreign assistance for investment was sought and welcomed, although a sizeable part of total foreign assistance came from the Soviet Union and other Soviet bloc countries.

The resulting Indian development strategy was of a mixed economy type within which modern and growing non-agricultural sectors were subject to growing public investments and production, while the agricultural sector, still contributing half the net domestic product, was subject only to comparatively modest attempts at control rather than radical transformation of the prevailing land tenure system.

Thus there were considerable similarities between the Chinese and Indian development strategies in the pre-reform period. Both adopted the Soviet system of centralized planning and the modern industrial sector was bought under closer control. But in China the agricultural sector was also subjected to state control, whereas in India it remained within the private sector and a part of the growing industrial sector also remained within the private sector.

Emphasis on agriculture

As already mentioned, in the early days of India's planned development, the measures to promote agricultural development were confined to modest land reforms aimed at (a) security of tenancy, (b) abolition of absentee landlordism, (c) land ceilings to encourage co-operative farming, marketing, extension of the area of cultivation and irrigation, and community development programmes as opposed to radical nationalization of land for state farms, like the large collectives in China, or the redistribution of surplus land to landless labourers, as in Taiwan and South Korea. However, since agriculture was within the jurisdiction of provincial authorities, there was no uniformity in the implementation of even these modest land reform measures.

Despite the limited nature of land reform in India, these reforms may well have increased the annual rate of growth of food grain production from 0.11 per cent in the pre-independence decades to 2.5 to 3 per cent during the first two Five Year Plans from 1951 to 1961 (Clark and Roy 1997; Mellor 1976). Indian leaders, however, thought it best to treat agriculture as a 'bargain sector', a sector with large unexploited potential which can provide the requisite surplus with relatively low investment in a comparatively short time after, of course, a certain minimum infrastructure has been developed (Chakravarty 1987). This line of thinking among policy-makers in India was similar to that among policy-makers in China.

However, the poor performance of agriculture towards the end of the Third Five Year Plan (1961–66) exposed a serious weakness in the government strategy of treating agriculture as a bargaining sector. A substantial shortfall in food grain production forced the government to import large quantities of food grain to tide over the crisis. A substantial proportion of the food import came from the USA under its PL480 and PL666 food aid programmes at virtually no cost to the Indian government. This food aid, instead of undermining the future performance of India's agricultural sector, allowed the planners to contain the rate of inflation to prevent mass starvation and to maintain on adequate supply of food to the army engaged in war with Pakistan in 1965.

At the same time, the shortfall in food production, alongside the growth in output under the Intensive Agricultural District Programme (IADP) launched in 1961, made the government realize that

1. the output in the agricultural sector depends on a timely monsoon season, and the bumper crop during the First Five Year Plan (1951–56) was primarily due to such timely monsoons;
2. the low productivity in agriculture was a result of real constraints faced by farmers rather than their ignorance; and
3. significant advances in agricultural productivity are possible only with provision of five complementary inputs (a) improved seeds, (b) fertilizers, (c) pesticides, (d) controlled and adequate irrigation, and (e) knowledge of the proper use of these inputs.

The government launched the High Yielding Varieties Programme in 1966, heralding the onset of the era of 'Green Revolution and technological change' in Indian agriculture (Clark and Roy 1997).

However, neither in the pre-reform nor in the post-reform period has Green Revolution technology been implemented fully and properly throughout the country, due to the following factors:

1. The controlled and adequate irrigation facilities were to be made available mainly to India's wheat belt states, particularly Punjab (now also Haryana) and parts of Uttar Pradesh, but vast areas of India's rice belt stretching from Tamil Nadu and Karuataka in the South to Mizoram State in the North East bordering Burma, continued to depend on timely monsoons to achieve adequate rice production (Roy and Lougheed 1979).
2. Well-trained extension agents were not available in sufficient number to the peasants and labourers, and their knowledge of the proper use of these inputs were limited.
3. The Green Revolution technology largely bypassed the landless female agricultural labourers who were by far the largest visible workforce in India's agricultural sector in terms of both the development of appropriate technology for female labourers and providing adequate training to them in the use of inputs.

Such deficiencies in agricultural policy implementation continued to persist throughout the second half of the 20th century, resulting in the application of an inappropriate input mix (larger amount of fertilizer with less water) in rice fields with its attendant adverse consequences for sustainable increase in production and land fertility.

Although agriculture remains primarily within the domain of the private sector, the state nevertheless intervened in the determination of input price and producer and consumer prices of agricultural output. Per unit cost production of fertilizer at old public sector plants using very old technology were different and quite high. Furthermore, the price of imported fertilizer was also different from the cost of production in public sector enterprises. Hence, the government fixed affordable prices for the domestically produced and imported fertilizer but paid a very large subsidy to the producers, which in turn contributed to the enlargement of budget deficit.

On the producers' side, the government introduced the 'issue price', which is in reality the 'support price'. The next is the 'procurement price' which the government's procurement agency, the Food Corporation of India (FCI), pays to the mill owners for procuring surplus food grain collected by mill owners from dealers or peasant families. Hence the issue price is usually slightly higher than the procurement price.

Then the FCI sells to the poor the food grain and food, through the public distribution system (PDS), at a very low subsidized price. Again the size of their subsidy has been very large and continuously rising. Finally, there is the free market price for agricultural output. However, the effective implementation of such a complex and cumbersome price policy has been very difficult in the absence of adequate state-owned storage facilities, with the result that the peasants in years of bumper crops have been forced to dump a substantial portion of their output on the free market thereby forcing the free market price down to a level at which the per acre cost of cultivation has not been recovered.

The rural labour market in India has historically been free of state intervention, contrary to the situation in China. Labour has moved freely from one region to another in response to market demand and market forces have determined the wages of agricultural labour. However, respective states during the past two decades have enforced an informal minimum wage for rural labour in the rural sector and on cultivators, and have imposed informal restrictions on the movement of labour from village to village. But such a system of wage fixation has raised the cost of production and made it more difficult for the land holders to raise the level of accumulated surplus and thereby raise the level of investment in the economy. However, the rise in rural wages may have helped reduce the rural urban wage differential for unskilled workers. Unlike the attempt made by China to establish small-scale industries in the rural sector to absorb unemployed rural labour, India in both the pre-reform and post-reform periods has made very little attempt to establish small-scale industries.

The presence of considerable underemployment and disguised unemployment in the rural sector has encouraged the migration of rural labour families to the urban informal sector, which absorbs most of the migrant labour. Hence the agricultural sector in India was not forced to absorb urban surplus labour as happened in China. While the cropping practice in India's agriculture has also intensified, an attempt to meet the need for additional labour has been made by increasing the supply of family labour through increasing the rate of reproduction in land holder families.

Egalitarianism

Following the Soviet approach to development, India laid considerable emphasis on the development of the industrial sector with particular reference to the heavy industrial sector, which created an urban bias in India's development and this widened the urban–rural gap during the early part of the pre-reform period. In regard to the appointment of personnel in India's industrial undertakings, India did not follow the Maoist egalitarian policy. Positions of technical personnel were filled by people with appropriate qualifications in public sector enterprises (PSEs) as well as in private sector enterprises. However, the interference in the process of appointment of technical as well as semi-skilled and unskilled personnel by leaders of the political party in power, trade union leaders and senior bureaucrats has continued unabated during pre-reform (Desai and Bhagwati 1975) and post-reform periods. The authorities of most PSEs were pressured to overstaff the enterprises with unskilled and semi-skilled personnel to a level at which the cost of labour was significantly higher than was necessary to efficiently run the enterprises and earn a reasonable return on investment. The pressures of militant trade unions since the mid-1960s forced the PSEs, which were the largest providers of employment in urban India, to raise wages, thereby further widening the rural–urban disparity.

The central government, to reduce absolute poverty in the rural and urban areas, established the public distribution system (PDS) through which essential food and fuel have been sold to poor families at prices substantially lower than the free market price. Primary education has been made universal and available to every family free of charge. Public health centres have been established in rural areas to provide health care to the poor free of charge. Apart from these the central government also made provision for the creation of short-term employment generation for the rural poor by undertaking some public works such as the construction of roads and other infrastructure. The grants (public transfers) to the state (provincial) governments from the central government to undertake such welfare-orientated activities reached Rs 337.9 billion, accounting for 13.6 per cent of revenue expenditure of the central government, in 2000–01 (GOI, *Economic Survey*, 2003–04). However, due to widespread corruption, inefficiency and lack of the administrative apparatus governance, the centre failed to produce a perceptible impact on the level of poverty in the rural sector.

Post-reform Period

In the pre-reform period, although the development strategy was heavily biased towards the building up of heavy and capital goods industries, consumer goods industries continued to grow, albeit slowly, under private sector investment. In the post-reform period, the strategy has been to improve the efficiency of the economy and the international competitiveness of the industrial sector by dismantling quantitative restrictions which crippled the capacity of the PSEs and of the economy to grow (Clark and Roy 1997).

Regarding the heavy industrial sector, which has been built by the public sector, the approach has been to make heavy industries more efficient by forcing them to operate more like private sector enterprises, to face international competition, to disinvest a certain portion of their capital which is not earning reasonable returns or is making losses, and to reduce the size of overstaffing in most PSEs. Thus the government's policy has generally been to improve the operational efficiency of PSEs, but not to dismantle them.

While China may have followed the principle of comparative advantage in determining the location of industries and in selecting the type of industries to be built, India has rarely followed this policy. The states with greater political influence have continued to attract industries to their territories, even if they do not possess the same level of comparative advantage in the availability of factors of production as the other states with lesser political influence. This trend was very strong in the pre-reform period (Desai and Bhagwati 1975; Roy et al. 1992), but does not appear to have diminished greatly in the post-reform period.

Improving the consumption standard of people has also been the objective of the Indian state but not for the same reason as in China. Indians living outside India are spread throughout the world and are not so heavily concentrated in a region close to the boundaries of India as is the case for China. Hence, the difference in living standards enjoyed by non-resident and resident Indians is not so obvious to India's illiterate and fatalist poor, most of whom live in India's rural hinterlands still unaware of the consumption standards of non-resident and rich resident Indians. However, since consumption standards cannot be improved without alleviating poverty, in the post-reform period the government of India has placed greater emphasis on the need for achieving a higher rate of economic growth. But it wants growth to be accompanied by social justice and equity (GOI 1999a).

But Indian leaders never set a similar target to that of China of doubling GNP within ten years. Furthermore, while Chinese leaders wanted the per-capita income of China to equal the average per capita income of Western countries, India's leaders never set such a goal in the pre-reform nor post-reform periods. Also, Indian leaders' obsession with achieving equity simultaneously with growth would have made it difficult for the government to raise the rate of growth to as high a level as that of China.

Domestic saving as a proportion of GDP in India has not been very high, hence foreign capital was actively sought to increase the level of total investment. Although in the pre-reform period Indira Gandhi's draconian nationalization policy, other restrictions imposed on foreign companies operating in the private sector in India and the mayhem caused by trade unions in the industrial sector drove foreign capital out of the country, in the post-reform period relatively liberalized rules regarding foreign investment led to the resumption of the flow of foreign capital into the country.

Nevertheless, India's policy towards foreign capital is still not very proactive as India still remains a relatively closed economy compared with China and other East Asian countries. The size of total capital inflow to India during the first decade of the post-reform period is about the same as the average annual foreign capital inflow in a year in China in the post-reform period (GOI, *Economic Survey*, 2003–04).

However, India's services sector, particularly the information technology (IT) industry and the newcomer, bio-technology industry, has been growing very rapidly compared with the same sector in China. Thus, while India and China followed similar paths to development, their approaches to achieving their goals became different as time went by due to a number of factors, prominent among these being the differences in the style of political regime, of leadership in political institution, labour market institutions and in respective cultures.

NOTE

1. 'Khadi' symbolizes the Gandhian plan of self-reliant development under which a number of villages together were to form a self-sufficient village community producing most of their consumption requirements within the villages and at home by using simple hand-made tools. Some of the most important necessities of villagers such as salt, sugar and iron were to be purchased from the town within the rump economy and consumption of goods requiring complex machineries for their production at home or importation from other countries were to be avoided. 'Khadi' refers to cotton cloth handwoven at home by villagers with the help of handmade tools such as 'charka' for their own use. In the early 1900s, Gandhi inspired the whole Indian nation to wear 'Khadi' as a means of saving the

village republics and as a protest against the British policy of allowing imports of cotton clothes from Lancashire mills, which led to the demise of India's village textile industry. Thus, on the one hand, 'Khadi' represented the essence of the Gandhian plan of rural-based development with non-complex technologies and, on the other, it was a main plank in Gandhi's political movement against the British imperial power. For more details on the issue of import of Lancashire mill clothes into India, see Roy (1988).

2. The economic system and its reform

This chapter begins with a survey of the basic features of the pre-reform system in both countries. Then, it proceeds to trace the origin of and to identify the approach of the reforms which have been carried out in both countries in recent years. It ends with an assessment of the progress of these reforms. The discussion in this chapter focuses primarily on domestic economic reforms. The reform of external economic relations of both countries will be examined in Chapter 5.

THE PRE-REFORM SYSTEM

China

The Chinese pre-reform economic system is based on the Soviet model. It has the following features: (a) collective farms in the agricultural sector; (b) state-owned enterprises in the non-agricultural sector; (c) central planning; and (d) widespread bureaucratic control of the economy by the government. However, there are significant differences in the pre-reform Chinese system from the Soviet model, such as the formation of the commune, the principle of self-reliance, the emphasis on egalitarianism, decentralization in planning, and so on. These deviations can be explained partly by Chinese special conditions and its learning from Soviet past mistakes, and partly by Maoist ideology.

Collective agriculture
Chinese collectivization was preceded by land reform in 1949–52, under which land and other agricultural resources were expropriated from landlords and rich peasants and distributed to the poor and middle peasants. The objective of the land reform was not purely economical. It was undertaken to consolidate the political power of the Chinese Communist Party in the rural area by isolating the rich peasants and elimination of the landlords, and by putting the poor peasants in command of the political powers in the countryside (Ash 1976).

Collectivization was launched after the land reform with the formation of agricultural producers' co-operatives. After the land reform, agricultural output growth slowed. To stimulate agricultural growth, the government was faced with two options. One was the technical transformation of Chinese agriculture. This option would require a significant diversion of investment resources from agriculture to industry and cause a slowdown in industrial growth, and hence was not acceptable to the government. The only other alternative was the institutional transformation of Chinese agriculture, which did not require any significant diversion of investment resources from the industrial sector. In the end, the government opted for the latter and hoped that through the creation of the co-operatives the vast pool of underemployed labourers in the rural areas could be mobilized for rural infrastructure construction and labour-intensive cultivation techniques in order to boost the crop yield.

Another important factor which prompted the government to accelerate the collectivization movement in the mid-1950s was the crisis in the supply and control of surplus food grain (Walker 1966). After land reform, the government encountered difficulty in mobilizing sufficient grain to fund its rapid industrial programme in the cities as peasants increased their self-consumption of grain. Collectivization facilitated government control over the surplus grain as the disposal of surplus grain was in the hands of a collective management committee rather than individual peasants.

Through the formation of the commune in the late 1950s, Chinese collectivization went beyond the Soviet model. The establishment of the commune reflects the ideological difference between the Maoist and the Soviet approach to building socialism. The Soviet Union adopted a sequential approach based on the orthodox Marxist doctrine that advanced 'production relations' cannot be established prior to the development of an advanced 'productive force'. Maoism adopted a simultaneous approach in the belief that the concurrent development of productive relations and forces are necessary in order not only to avoid the bureaucratization of the society, but also to speed up the rate of socialist development (see Van Ness and Raichur 1983). During 1958–60, Mao launched his Great Leap Forward (GLF) and later, during 1966–76, his Cultural Revolution (CR) campaign to put his idea in practice. During the Great Leap Forward, the commune was introduced to speed up the transition to communism by experimenting with the principle of income distribution according to need instead of work.

The introduction of the commune is also partly motivated by increased agricultural output. It was thought that the commune which was much larger than an agricultural producers' co-operative would enable Chinese agriculture to reap the economies of scale and speed up the adoption of new technology as well as to utilize more surplus labour for rural construction projects.

Initially, the commune, which consisted of 3000 households on average, was the basic accounting unit in the countryside, meaning that the organization of labour and the distribution of income were carried out at the commune level. However, the ensuing difficulty in effectively managing such a large farming operation and in motivating its labour force partly contributed to the Great Famine of 1959–61. Consequently, the government was forced to devolve the basic accounting unit to the level of a production team which consisted of only 30 households on average. This modified commune system remained more or less intact until the eve of the reforms in 1978.

State enterprise
In the non-agricultural sector, the basic pre-reform institution was the state-owned enterprises (SOEs). These enterprises were initially formed by the nationalization of the large enterprises owned by the former Nationalist government and foreigners. Later, through a system of buying off private shares, other private enterprises were also absorbed into the state sector (Chen and Galenson 1969, pp. 145–6). The dominant position of the state sector can be seen from Table 2.1. On the eve of the reforms, SOEs accounted for almost 80 per cent of the industrial output, 84 per cent of the retail business, 98 per cent of the transport volume and 64 per cent of the construction output of the country.

Table 2.1 *Share of SOEs in China's non-agricultural sector, 1980 and 2003 (%)*

Sector	1980	2003
Industry (Output)		
SOEs	78.7	37.5
NSEs	21.3	62.5
Retail trade (turnover)		
SOEs	84.2	14.7
NSEs	15.8	85.3
Transport (volume)		
SOEs	98.1 (1975)	NA
NSEs	1.9 (1975)	NA
Construction (output)		
SOEs	63.7 (1975)	26.3
NSEs	36.3 (1975)	73.7

Note: SOEs refers to state-owned enterprises and sole state-funded corporation and NSEs to non-state enterprises.

Sources: Chai 2003, p. 239; *ZGTJNJ* 2004, pp. 518, 577 and 692.

The management of an SOE was modelled on the Soviet model which featured a one-man management system emphasizing the absolute authority of the director, and the privileged role of the experts and specialists such as the engineers and the accountants. During the Cultural Revolution, however, one-man management was dismantled and replaced by a mass participation-in-management system (see Andors 1977, p. 82) , the objective of which was to eradicate the social division of labour in order to speed up the rate of socialist development.

Central planning
The resource allocation mechanism in pre-reform China was based on central planning. Planner's preferences largely determined what, for whom and how everything was produced. The balance between demand and supply was achieved mainly through a system of interlocking materials balance drawn up by the planner. To implement the plan, obligatory input and output targets were issued to the enterprises (see Rawski 1975). The system was copied from the Soviet Union in the early 1950s (Howe and Walker 1989). However, compared with the Soviet Union, the Chinese planning system was less centralized. This was due partly to the relatively underdeveloped Chinese economy and partly to the Maoist simultaneous approach towards the building of socialism. In industrial planning for instance, the absolute number of products covered by central planning in China was much fewer than that of the Soviet Union. In China on the eve of the reforms, this stood at 120 whereas the corresponding figure in the Soviet Union was over 30 000 (Gregory and Stuart 1990, p. 175). The number of material balances drawn up by the planners numbered only 500–700 in China compared with over 10 000 in the Soviet Union (Rawski 1975). The number of obligatory targets received by the enterprises from the planning authorities was also many fewer in China. On the eve of the reforms, Chinese enterprises received only eight targets (see Chai 1997, p. 53); in contrast, the number of targets received by the Soviet enterprises normally ranged between 20 and 30 (Gregory and Stuart 1990, p. 148). Last but not least, from the regional perspective, the Chinese system of planning was also much more decentralized than that of the Soviet model. In the late 1950s and again in 1970 a large number of enterprises was delegated from central to local government control. By the late 1970s, central authorities control merely 2 per cent of all industrial enterprises (Chai 1997, p. 32).

The incentive system adopted by the government to implement its plan is also somewhat different in China as compared to the Soviet Union. As in the Soviet Union, two kinds of incentive exist for Chinese enterprises: one for the enterprise as a whole and one for its staff and workers. The incentive system provided for the enterprise is its profit share. Initially, China adopted the Soviet system, under which enterprise was entitled to a certain amount of its profit depending on the degree to which the enterprise had fulfilled its obligatory targets (Chai 1997, p. 66). This entitlement was fed into an enterprise fund which could be used by the enterprise to finance the construction of a canteen and workers' housing as well as being a source for bonus payments for workers.

The main incentive provided for the workers was incentive pay in the form of a bonus and an above-norm piecework wage (Chai 1997). China, unlike the Soviet Union, did not rely on a bonus to motivate the managers. The pay of managerial staff had no variable element and their main material reward for successful performance was promotion (Eckstein 1977, p. 104).

Under the influence of the Maoist simultaneous approach to building socialism, the enterprise fund, bonus and other material incentives for the enterprise and its workers were scrapped during the GLF and CR. Instead, moral incentives in the form of non-monetary awards, publicity in the press, social benefits, and so on were introduced. It was not until the late 1970s that material incentives were restored.

Factor allocation and the role of price

The allocation of labour and capital in pre-reform China were mainly effected through planning. There was no labour market. Enterprise demand for labour was determined by planning. Each SOE was assigned a labour quota which was derived from the planned output target multiplied by the labour coefficient representing the amount of labour required per unit of output. Labourers were administratively assigned to the enterprise by the Labour Bureau. The mobility of labour was restricted. The spatial mobility was regulated by the household registration system. Inter-enterprise mobility of labour was also restricted as workers, once hired, became tenured labour which the enterprise could not dismiss even if they were found to be unsuitable or redundant (Liu 1980, p. 23).

The capital market was also non-existent. Both the mobilization and allocation of the investment fund was mainly executed through the government budget. The supply of the investment fund was largely under the control of the government as the government was the main saver. Government saving assumed two forms: budgetary and SOE savings. These two types of saving accounted for 97 per cent of national savings on the eve of the reform (Chai 1997, p. 118). Budgetary savings were mainly determined by the government budgetary revenues. The main sources of government revenues were state enterprise profit, the turnover tax and the sale of government bonds. Hence, the government could adjust the level of government revenues by manipulating the enterprise profits, the turnover tax rate and the amount of obligatory government bonds purchased by households and enterprises. Enterprise savings were enterprise retained profits. The level of enterprise profits was manipulated by the government through adjusting prices and wages facing the enterprise. For instance, to ensure high profits of industrial enterprises the government adopted a compulsory agricultural procurement system under which peasants were obliged to deliver to the state a given quota of output at an official price which was set low in relation to cost. The low price of agricultural products translated into a low cost of agricultural raw materials and a low wage for the workers in the industrial enterprises. Similarly, the government, using its monopoly power as the sole supplier of industrial goods, deliberately set the prices of industrial goods sold in the rural areas high to ensure high profits for industrial enterprises.

Enterprise demand for investment funds was also plan determined. The planners applied a capital-output norm to derive the amount of investment necessary to produce the planned output and authorized the investment fund for the enterprises. Some investment could also be financed by enterprise retained profit; but the amount was very limited as most of the enterprise's profits were siphoned off to the budget. Most producer and consumer prices were set by the government. As in the Soviet Union, prices did not reflect relative scarcities and only played a very limited allocative role. They were used mainly for other functions such as measurement, revenue control and manipulation of the distribution of income.

Control of inflation

Inflation was controlled by the planners by balancing the supply (S) and demand (D) for consumer goods:

$$D = wL + PaQa - Sa \qquad (2.1)$$

$$S = PcQc \qquad (2.2)$$

where w = wage rate
L = number of workers
Pa = state purchase price of farm products
Qa = quantity of farm products bought by the government
Sa = household saving
Pc = price of consumer goods
Qc = quantity of consumer goods available.

In equations 2.1 and 2.2, all the dependent variables were under the direct control of the government. Hence excess demand for consumer goods could be easily avoided, theoretically. However, in practice, wage bill (wL)

and/or the value of state purchase of farm products may be larger than the amount of consumer goods available. In that case the excess demand or inflation pressure may either assume an overt form with the rise of consumer goods prices, such as in the famine harvest years of 1960–62, or take the form of depressed inflation with an increased accumulation of involuntary household saving deposits.

India

Agricultural system
After India's independence from British rule in 1947, under the provisions of the Indian Constitution, the agricultural sector was included in the list of subjects under the jurisdiction of states. Hence, it was the primary responsibility of the states to initiate and implement agricultural programmes. All states adopted similar reforms which broadly consisted of the abolition of functionless intermediaries, protection to tenants, nationalization of different systems of land tenure, imposition of ceilings of land-holdings and consolidation of holdings. In West Bengal, the Marxists after assuming power went a step further in land reform by extending the provision of protection to tenants to share croppers by implementing a scheme known as 'Operation Barga'. Although, due to the deficiencies in the formulation and implementation of the land ceiling laws, they could not be strictly enforced on land holder families in West Bengal, surplus lands nevertheless were collected from most land holder families and distributed to the poor and, as a result, the system of absentee landlords was virtually eliminated. Land reform measures, similar to the 'Rejotwari' system undertaken in their provinces led to the greater convergence of ownership and management of agricultural land. However, in states other than West Bengal and Kerala large land holder families continued to be present even after some form of agricultural reform was introduced.

In the pre-reform period, during the first 15 years of planning, there was no nationwide comprehensive programme for agricultural development other than completion of some irrigation schemes, supply of manures and fertilizers, production and distribution of improved seeds, land reclamation and improvement, and plant protection measures. Since much of the assistance from the central government had to be channelled through states, the success in the implementation of the programmes depended very much on the respective states' institutional capacities and genuine desire to implement programmes effectively. Those states which did not have these, did not achieve good results.

Due to a lack of adequate attention paid to the agricultural sector by both central and state governments, the agricultural sector grew at a very low rate in the pre-reform period and its adverse impacts were felt on the supply of food and raw materials for industrial production and, consequently, on price levels and the inflation rate. The average annual growth rate of GDP from agriculture from 1950–51 to 1990–91 remained at only 2.5 per cent (Bhalla 2000–01).

In 1967–68 the government implemented the Green Revolution technology in agriculture, primarily with the objective of achieving self-sufficiency in food production and supply. The government's stated intention had never been to make the agricultural sector strong and vibrant so that it could generate surplus which could be used to finance the industrialization of the country, as happened in China. This is supported by the fact that the Green Revolution programme was adopted by a relatively small number of medium to large land holder families who were able to generate surplus. Hence the size of the surplus was not large (Vyas 2001–02).

In the pre-reform period many controls and restrictions were imposed on agricultural activities. There were zonal restrictions in the movements of agricultural goods, particularly food grain. The highly restrictive trade and industrial policy regime virtually shut off all sectors of the economy, including agriculture, from facing foreign competition. For several commodities, including cereals, there was a minimum support price to ensure that producers got a fair price.

Restrictions were placed on exports of several agricultural products such as vegetable oils and oil seeds, ground nuts and ground nut oil, jute manufacturers, tea, cotton textiles, raw cotton, raw wool, coffee, manganese ore, hide and skins. To maintain price stability in the domestic markets, in some years outright bans were imposed on exports of vegetable oils and ground nut oil. On similar grounds, exports of onions and raw cotton were also banned. Such actions adversely affected the agricultural exporters and agro-based industries. The government sacrificed the export market for the sake of domestic consumption. In the 1960s there were taxes on traditional exports. One World Bank study (World Bank 1996) estimated that during 1970–85, agricultural policies disprotected agriculture as a whole by 4 per cent, which turned to positive protection at the rate of 7 per cent during 1985–91. But the effects of non-tariff barriers via quantitative restriction and monopolization (canalization of trade by state enterprises) on Indian agriculture continued to be far more significant than tariffs during the pre-reform period (Srinivasan 2000).

Although the government expenditure on agriculture as a proportion of agricultural GDP was much higher than in other Asian countries (World Bank 1996), it was greatly skewed towards subsidies which were not effectively targeted towards the poor and against growth-enhancing investment in operation and maintenance of existing stocks of capital needed to improve the quality and reliability of delivery of inputs (Srinivasan 2000). Thus the distributional objective of subsidies, to ensure that poor farmers could use the inputs to a greater extent than in the absence of subsidies, were not met.

Overall, while Indian agriculture is dominated by small and medium-sized family farms, in the pre-reform period, on the one hand, restrictions on the movement of commodities across and within provinces imposed mostly to subserve the interest of political power groups within individual states, kept it fragmented within the country. On the other hand, numerous quantitative restrictions imposed on exports and imports of agricultural products prevented internal prices from being aligned with international prices, thereby preventing agriculture from being integrated with the global market.

State enterprises
Under Nehruvian socialism, the public sector enterprises (PSEs) were to dominate the commanding heights of the economy, and the private sector was to continue to play an important role in the rest of the industrial sector. Gradually over the years, the PSEs' areas of operations were extended to other areas of the manufacturing and services sectors through nationalization of private enterprises and creation of public sector units.

At the time when economic reform measures began to be implemented, there were more than 1000 PSEs of which 700 were owned by states (provinces) and the rest were owned by the centre. This included departmental enterprises such as railways, post and telecommunications, financial institutions such as the State Bank of India, the Industrial Finance Corporation of India (IFCI), the Unit Trust of India (UTI), Industrial Development Bank of India (IDBI) and departmental enterprises or government companies or corporations either incorporated under the company law, such as the Steel Authority of India Limited (SAIL) and the Indian Petro-Chemical Corporations Ltd, or created under statute by Acts of Parliament, such as Coal India, Air India, Indian Airlines and the National Thermal Power Corporation. Non-departmental enterprises account for 75 per cent of value added, more than 50 per cent of gross investment and about a third of the total employment in PSEs. The PSEs contribution to the total output of petroleum, lignite, copper and primary lead was 100 per cent; to the total output of zinc, 98 per cent; to the total output of coal, over 90 per cent; to the total output of steel and aluminium, more than 50 per cent; to the total output of fertilizer close to 40 per cent and to total electricity generation, it was close to 100 per cent (GOI 1992). The PSEs' contribution to the retail trade turnover was small.

Non-departmental PSEs have dominated infrastructure and basic industries such as transport, energy and communications. The PSEs also operate in diverse service sectors such as international trade, consultancy, contract and construction services, hotels and tourist facilities, and so on.

The traditional Indian Administrative Service personnel (IAS) holding the position of chairman or managing director, but with very little technical knowledge and expertise in the area of operation of respective enterprises, has been managing these enterprises. Excessive interference in the operation of these enterprises, by departmental bureaucracy, ministers and other powerful political leaders, severely undermined the capacity of these enterprises to improve their efficiency (Bhagwati and Desai 1971). Ministers in charge of enterprises and highly organized militant trade unions contributed to overstaffing of unskilled labour and payment of higher average unskilled wages than in the private sector. The tight regulations and procedures for investment and restrictions on functional autonomy of the enterprises, particularly in respect of price, labour and wage policy, have long placed severe constraints on the operational efficiency of these enterprises.

Central planning

In India, too, resource allocation particularly in the first two decades of development, was based on rigid central planning. The investment allocations among public sector enterprises were naturally subject to direct planning in both choice and implementation, but the private sector's investments were also directed by the state through physical controls and detailed target-setting of outputs. Such detailed targets were derived without reference to notions of costs and benefits in a systematic manner. In the early days of planning the attempts at matching demand and supply at the industry level were made in a very simple manner so that estimates and targets were meant to serve as the basis for guiding the process of industrialization through industrial licensing.

In reality these targets were not just indicative, but were treated as full-scale targets with regard to which the Industrial Licensing Committee operated and lapses from which were considered, even by government agencies, as failures of planning (Bhagwati and Desai 1971).

The product coverage under central planning was quite extensive as it included private sector industries. However, the rigidity of the planning in terms of fulfilment of expenditure and output targets began to be relaxed in the 1970s as the gap between the capacity licensed and capacity achieved and resource constraints affecting the fulfilment of targets continued to persist for many products. Hence from the late 1980s the Planning Commission began to set an overall growth target for the economy, instead of production targets, for the successive plan. Also, in India many enterprises operated under state control and alongside central planning, and state planning continued to operate for regional development.

To achieve plan targets the incentive schemes in the form of profit-sharing in enterprise management did not exist in India. Employers, including management personnel, in the private sector received performance-based bonuses and in the public sector everyone received a monthly allowance to compensate for the rise in the cost of living.

Factor allocation and the role of prices

Under comprehensive centralized planning of the Soviet type, production targets determined expenditure allocation and subsequent factor allocation. But under a free market price mechanism, for a particular level of control, with a given budget, the allocation of factors depends on production which in turn depends on the relative factor prices. However, given India's poverty, Nehru, a socialist profoundly influenced by the giant stride made by the former Soviet Union in industrialization through centralized planning, decided to implement India's development programme by developing heavy and large-scale industries in the public sector, the decision regarding the choice between the capital-intensive and labour-intensive method of production did not arise. In a free market developing economy with a large unskilled labour force, the price of labour is expected to remain low and the price of capital high, thereby providing the incentive for investors to choose labour-intensive methods of production.

But in India, free market forces were not allowed to play their normal role in labour and capital markets during the first three decades of Indian planning. The price of capital used in PSEs was kept lower as a substantial part of the capital came under the foreign aid programme made available at the nominal interest rate. The PSEs were also granted interest holidays and a moratorium on loan repayments. Apart from capital inflow, part of the expenditure of PSEs was also financed from domestic resources such as balance from current revenues; profits of PSEs; issue of bonds and debentures by PSEs; market loans; small savings; and some loans from financial institutions (GOI, *Economic Survey* 1991/92). The PSEs under the control of state governments continued to incur heavy losses. For the allocation of labour to PSEs, the price of labour had virtually a limited role to play. In the matter of selection and employment of all categories of labour (skilled, semi-skilled and unskilled), the political interference in the recruitment process of employees contributed to considerable overstaffing.

This trend was more serious in PSEs under the control of the respective states. However, since all PSEs, whether under the control of the central government or of respective state governments, had to be located within the jurisdiction of individual states, local political masters and militant trade unions affiliated to various political parties flexed their muscles to overstaff all PSEs with unskilled and semi-skilled labour belonging to their unions to subserve the political interests of political leaders and parties. As a result, on the one hand, overstaffing contributed to the declining productivity of labour, on the other hand, organized union power kept the wages of unskilled and semi-skilled labour at a level which was considerably higher than the wage rate would have been under a competitive labour market (Bhagwati and Desai 1971). Hence, purely political considerations had affected the working of the PSEs, leading to overstaffing and other inefficiencies. This trend was most prominent in West Bengal under Marxists' rule.

Products of PSEs which were used as inputs by other PSEs and private sector enterprises were underpriced under explicit price control. This resulted in the excessive allocation of these resources to the user industries, compared with the use of other inputs where choice was available. Hence economic theory and free market prices of factors had a very limited role to play in their allocation to Indian PSEs and private sector enterprises. This trend continued throughout the 1970s and into the 1980s.

Control of inflation
Inflation in India was sought to be controlled by taking measures to match supply with demand for goods and services. The main elements of the anti-inflationary policy are: augmentation of aggregate supply through higher production, better capacity utilization, imports of essential commodities in short supply and regulated exports of those needed domestically; curbing the activities of hoarders, speculators and black marketeers; and constant monitoring of availabilities and prices of essential commodities.

The public distribution system (PDS) has been incorporated in the supply management policy framework with a view to relieving the adverse impact of inflation on society. At the same time the monetary policy stance has been reasonably restrictive to prevent the accumulation of excess liquidity in the system while also satisfying the legitimate credit requirements of enterprises for productive activities. The fiscal policy, on the other hand, had aimed at encouraging saving and investment and keeping the budget deficit within reasonable limits.

Overall, up to 1980, the conservative demand and supply management policies helped to maintain reasonable stability in price level, thereby keeping the rate of inflation within a manageable level. However the reckless fiscal expansionism of the 1980s led to serious fiscal imbalances (Buiter and Patel 1992; Joshi and Little 1994; Srinivasan 2000) which, combined with supply and demand imbalances in sensitive commodities and rising deficit in balance of payment, contributed to the build-up of inflationary pressures in the immediate pre-reform period.

REFORMS

Origin

China

The immediate trigger of Chinese reforms was undoubtedly the change of leadership in the late 1970s (Harding 1987). Following the death of Mao in 1976 and the subsequent fall of his followers, the 'Gang of Four', the reformers' faction of the Party, led by Deng, rose to power. Under the new leadership of Deng, economic modernization was given the priority over the building of socialism. As a result, the stage was set for a complete overhaul of the Chinese economic system. However, the main cause of Chinese reforms has been the increased dissatisfaction of the Chinese with their existing economic system. The old system has not delivered what the Chinese wanted: a strong and prosperous China. Chinese economic growth has slowed down significantly since 1957. China's real national income grew at an annual average rate of 9 per cent during the First Five Year Period (FYP), but after 1957 it slowed down to only 5 per cent during 1957–78 (Chow 1993, table 1).

The growth slowdown increased the income gap between China and other neighbouring Chinese societies under the capitalist economic system. Real GDP growth in Taiwan, Hong Kong and Singapore, for example, approached almost 10 per cent a year in the 1960s and 1970s (James et al. 1989, p. 6), whereas that of China was only half as high. Consequently, the ratio of per capita income based on purchasing power parity changed. This ratio between China and Taiwan declined from 0.5 in 1960 to 0.18 in 1980 (Maddison 2001, table C3-c).

The main factor behind the slowdown in China's economic growth was poor productivity performance. From 1952 to 1980, 'technical progress' or growth of total factor productivity (TFP) was virtually absent in China (see Chow 1993). Growth during this period can be fully explained by a high rate of capital accumulation. In a neoclassical growth model, in the absence of technical progress, increased capital accumulation inevitably lead to growth slowdown because of diminishing returns on capital as capital–labour ratio rises. Chinese growth slowdown since 1957 was also partly caused by the Maoist radical strategy. Chow (1993) finds that the disturbance of GLF cost China almost one-third and the CR another 12–23 per cent of its total output. Without these two social upheavals, the Chinese growth rate would have been significantly higher during the pre-reform period.

Apart from growth slowdown, China's technology development has also stagnated. A World Bank delegate sent to China in the early 1980s observed that Chinese industrial equipment produced in China was 20 to 30 years behind the best international practice (World Bank 1983a, p. 158). Chinese technology stagnation was caused by many factors, but the indiscriminate application of the Maoist self-reliance strategy in international economic relations and the absence of price and income incentive for China's enterprises to innovate under central planning undoubtedly played an important role.

India

The immediate reason for India's economic reform was a severe balance of payment crisis that the country was engulfed by in 1990. The crisis was accentuated by the Gulf War of early 1991 which raised India's oil import bill and lowered workers' pay. Furthermore although the rupee continued to depreciate, the repatriation of receipts from exports was delayed as exporters temporarily left their earnings overseas with the intention to bring their receipts home after further depreciation of the rupee in the near future. At the same time import payments were brought forward for fear of further depreciation of the rupee. Hence, the resultant alarming decline in the country's foreign exchange reserve left the government with just enough foreign exchange to make payment for two weeks' imports of goods and services (Teja 1992).

But the origin of the Indian economic crisis of 1990 can be traced back to the centralized planning, overriding dominance of the public sector over the economy, pervasive economic and social controls over the private sector and the political institution generating rent-seeking activities since 1956–57 stunting economic growth. The centralized planning imposed strict controls on the establishment of industries through licensing, restrictions on capacity expansion, controls covering monopoly and even normal non-monopoly trade practices, price and distribution controls, labour market and employment controls, comprehensive external sector controls including import licensing and prohibitive tariffs, and direct control over foreign exchange allocation and utilization (Kamath 1993b; Roy et al. 1992). The operation and management of this regime of controls led to the unrestrained growth of a bureaucratic state. Athukorala (2002) comments that by the late 1960s, India was one of the most inward-orientated and regulated countries outside the Communist bloc.

The enormous expansion of the heavily subsidized and unproductive public sector led to the growth of a caste system of politically determined entitlements to income streams created by past state controls over enterprises (Lal 1995), as other means of financing them such as taxation could not be successful because of corrupt state apparatus and economic growth was stunted by the adverse impact of state control on the economy. The high level of expenditure to support entitlements had to be financed from borrowing. While we agree with Lal's comments that dirigisme was the most important factor that contributed to India's crisis in 1990–91, this dirigisme was the product of India's political system led by Nehru. Since Indira Gandhi's regime, corruption permeated India's entire institutional set-up, and the creation of newer provinces by bifurcating the larger ones to satisfy political interests has led to an alarming rise in expenditure by provincial governments, a rise in the corruption level in provinces and a concomitant rise in public transfer from the centre.

Between 1980–81 and 1990–91, while revenue receipts grew at a rate of 16.6 per cent, expenditure grew at 17.1 per cent of GDP. Hence fiscal deficit had to emerge. These expenditures undertaken by both the central and state governments also increased due to rising interest payments on burgeoning loans, payment for subsidies and rising balance of payment deficits. Hence due to the productivity damaging effects of dirigisme during the 40 years (1950–51 to 1990–91) of India's pre-reform period, per capita income grew only at an extremely low average annual rate of 1.41 per cent (Bhalla 2000–01).

Economic reform agenda – phase I: major items   India's major economic reforms were included in the 1991–92 budget and announced in the Indian Parliament in 1991 (Crompton and Rodriguez 1992; GOI 1992). The budget announced a policy shift from centralized planning of the economy and heavy public sector involvement in industry to a more market-orientated system.

Phase I (beginning July 1991):
1.   The government aimed to reduce the budget deficit which stood at 8.4 per cent of GDP in 1991 to a more sustainable level of 3–4 per cent in 1992;
Industrial and trade sector reform
2.   The government also announced in July 1991 a New Industrial Policy which improved the efficiency of domestic industries through reduced public sector regulation and increased exposure to foreign competition. The New Industrial Policy removed government licensing requirements for virtually all industries. The system of endorsement of capacity expansion under modernization/renovation was discontinued for most industries. Small-scale industries engaged in the manufacture of delicensed items were exempted from obtaining Carry on Business (COB) licences to upgrade their status to medium-scale industries. Controls on corporate behaviour were eliminated. Oil exploration and refining and the power sector were thrown open to private sector investment.

3. A simplified and less restrictive trade policy was introduced to make imports of inputs cheaper and more accessible for industry and to expose a large segment of Indian industry to international competition. Most import items were removed from the restricted list.

Fiscal and monetary policy reform

4. The budget of 1992–93 announced the partial convertibility of the rupee under which exporters were allowed to convert 60 per cent of foreign exchange earnings at market exchange rate and the remaining 40 per cent at the lower government-set official exchange rate. Consequent to this, imports of all raw materials, components, and capital goods for use in manufacturing industries were freely allowed, if the importers obtained the required foreign exchange from the market. All intermediate goods, raw materials, components and spare parts are now on the Open General Licence.

5. The EximScrip was introduced to enable importers to access duty-free imports to the value of 30–40 per cent of total exports of the firms.

6. Also in the 1992–93 budget, the Export Promotion Capital Goods (EPCG) Scheme made capital goods importable at 25 per cent and 15 per cent duty as long as the importers agreed to fulfil a stipulated export commitment.

7. The floor level of interest rates on commercial bank advances was reduced by 2 per cent in 1992.

8. The capital market was liberalized and government control over capital issues were withdrawn. The Office of the Controller of Capital Issues was abolished. The Securities and Exchange Board of India (SEBI) was converted into a statutory empowered body to regulate the activities of the capital market and stock exchange.

9. With a view to improving the incentive for private sector resource flow towards the industrial sector, taxation of capital gains was restructured to allow for inflation accounting. Also, double taxation of partnership firms was abolished and financial assets such as equities and debentures were exempted from wealth tax.

Foreign investment and policy reform

10. The Foreign Investment and Promotion Board was created to encourage foreign participation in industrial development.

11. The permissible foreign ownership level in industrial undertakings was increased from 40 per cent to 51 per cent with 100 per cent ownership allowed in power, coal mining and several other sectors.

12. Automatic approval of the Reserve Bank of India for raising equity up to 51 per cent was to be granted to companies engaged in expansion programmes in high-priority industries and in companies

engaged in high-priority industries to raise equity base without an expansion programme.

13. The Foreign Exchange Regulation Act (FERA 1973), which was substantially liberalized in January 1993, removed all restrictions in FERA companies relating to borrowing funds or raising deposits in India as well as taking over or creating any interest in business in Indian companies.

14. Investment by non-resident Indians (NRI) up to 100 per cent of full convertibility was allowed in export houses, trading houses, hotels and tourism-related industries as well as in high-priority industries.

Other reforms: the government also aimed to achieve reduction in agricultural subsidy as well as subsidy to loss-making PSEs, to initiate and expedite the process of privatization of public enterprises and to initiate labour market reforms.

The second generation of reforms in the new millennium   During the first phase of the reform process, the industrial sector has been deregulated; trade has been considerably liberalized; income tax reform has been undertaken and the financial sector has been liberalized. The full convertibility of the rupee on the trade account has already been achieved. The 'peak' customs tariff on non-agricultural goods has been reduced to below 20 per cent in 2005. The size of the budget deficit was reduced to a level well below 8.4 per cent of GDP. During the new millennium the government has to aim to continue the reform process in sectors included in the 1991 reform agenda and to initiate reforms in the following areas.

Reform of the infrastructure sector
1. Infrastructure includes roads, seaports and airport facilities, railways, other transport networks, power and telecommunications. While achieving high growth in manufactured exports requires substantial reform in all components of the infrastructure sector, achieving high growth in service export is greatly dependent on substantial reform of the telecommunications sector. There has been only limited progress in the telecommunications sector since the early 1990s. The monopoly of the Videsh Sanchar Nigam Limited (VSNL) on international telecommunications has to end; the institutional set-up comprising the Department of Telecommunications (DOT), the Telecom Regulatory Authority of India (TRAI), Mahanagar Telephone Nigam Limited (MTNL) and VSNL needs to be reformed to introduce competition into this inefficient and inward-orientated industry dominated by a labour force which belongs to militant unions. In March 2005 the

government was able to raise the limit of foreign investment in the telecommunications sector to 74 per cent.

Power sector reforms

2. The task of rationalizing electricity prices and of eliminating subsidies to farmers and domestic consumers began slowly during the first phase of the reform but it must be completed soon to prevent the present power system breaking down.

Higher education and intellectual property rights

3. The reform of the education sector is under way, but progress has been slow. Considerable expansion of India's elite institutions of science and technology and drastic rationalization of generalist undergraduate degree-offering institutions and of education systems are needed. The government has initiated a move to allow foreign educational institutions to establish educational institutions within the country. The government has also initiated a move to develop a system of intellectual property rights to provide adequate safeguards to intellectual property and to open up the possibility of large rewards for innovators.

Amendment of the Industrial Relations Act

4. To enable Indian companies to compete with global transnational corporations (TNCs), it is necessary to amend the draconian Industrial Relations Act – a creation of the Nehru regime to make firms' entry into and exit from industries flexible by providing them with adequate power to hire and retrench workers when needed. Virtually no progress has been made in this matter.

Legal reforms

5. To make the legal system accountable to the public and to the state for its activities and to enable it to protect property rights and enforce contracts, reforms of the system of administration of judiciary and of outdated legislations are necessary. Very little progress has been made in this area.

Agricultural sector

6. The government has achieved a partial reduction in subsidies on agricultural input prices. But a comprehensive reform is needed to free farmers from all domestic restrictions on storage, transport and sale of agricultural products. Since the present policy of maintaining low output prices and subsidized input prices results in the imposition of a net tax on farmers, it is necessary to introduce in the domestic market, the world price for both agricultural inputs and outputs (Parikh and Shah 1999). However, in the Indian Constitution agriculture was placed in the exclusive provincial jurisdiction of provinces and not in the concurrent list. Hence it is difficult to make progress in implementing reform measures in the agricultural sector as provincial governments

and the political parties in power treat their provinces as their own independent kingdoms.

Public finance reform

7. Greater emphasis has to be placed on reforming public finance, particularly in the area of tax revenue, fiscal deficit and aggregate expenditure in second generation reforms. It is only by introducing reforms in these areas that the government can secure necessary funds to expand social services and avoid financial sector distortions (Parikh and Shah 1999).

It will be very difficult to implement reform measures in most of the areas discussed under the second generation reform. Budget deficit cannot be reduced substantially without reducing the interest and subsidy components in the budget. Reduction in both items will be possible only if the government can drastically curtail its involvement in economic activities. In India's federal state no government without an absolute majority of its representatives in federal parliament and in the majority of provincial legislature can implement reform measures adequately. The perception of governments at provincial level perhaps seems to be that money is plentiful and, like a pampered child, if they cry for more money from the centre, they will get it. The comments of Rao (2004) that the provinces incur about 55 per cent of total expenditure of the Indian state but raise only 37 per cent of total revenue support that opinion of provincial governments. But still they want more money!

Note the following comments of Bajpai and Sachs (1997, p. 155):

India continues to be trapped by preconceptions of the 1950s, and especially by the vested interests fostered by State Led Industrialisation (SLI) rather than by global economic realities of the 1990s. Key political parties continue to resist foreign direct investment along nationalist lines, despite the fact that greater foreign investment is critical for India's rapid growth . . . Similarly, trade unions which provide campaign contributions to the major political parties, continue to exercise a veto power over important reforms of labour law and exit policy. Many new regional and caste-based political movements support populistic platforms calling for large increases in government expenditures on behalf of the poor. Given that India's government spending as a proportion of GDP is already high and that the government deficit is already large, programmes based on increased overall spending are likely to be highly destabilising.

On the issues of privatization of PSEs and retrenchment of workers, Little (1996) notes that it is the fear of redundancy that is the major factor inhibiting public sector reform. This fear has been created by political parties and the party affiliated trade unions whose members swell the number of unproductive staff in PSEs. India's private sector enterprises have long been harassed by restrictive regulations. Current company laws, labour laws and urban land laws have contributed to the growth of sick industries. Current labour legislation which favours only a tiny minority of the workforce needs to be looked at askance. Little also comments that the scope for appeal to the law needs to be reduced.

We have already referred to the need for reforms in the legal system during the second generation reform period. Finally we have to agree with Bardhan's (2004) analysis of the reasons as to why it would be extremely difficult for the India polity to implement all reform measures adequately. Note the following remarks of Bardhan (2004, p. 52):

> Any process of sustained economic reform and investment requires a framework of long term policy to which the government can credibly commit itself. But the political process in India seems to be moving in the opposite direction. While becoming more democratic and inclusive in terms of incorporating newer and hitherto subordinate groups, it is eroding most of the structures of institutional isolation of long term economic management decisions against the wheeling and dealing of day-to-day politics. There are very few assurances that commitments made by a government (or a leader) will be kept by successive ones, or even by itself under pressure.
>
> With the extensive deregulation of the past decade, it was expected that corruption associated with the system of permits and licenses would decrease. There are no hard estimates, but by most anecdotal accounts, corruption has, if anything, gone up in recent years.

On the issue of fiscal consolidation and subsidy reduction, Bardhan's remarks are in line with the present authors' views that adequate fiscal consolidation and subsidy reduction are not possible when the central government has to depend for its survival on the support of regional sectarian parties. The current Manmohan Singh government relies for its survival on the support of communists and other left-orientated political parties which are not very happy about the centre implementing sensible reforms which will cut subsidies, privatize PSEs and reduce the level of an unproductive unionized labour force employed in PSEs. Unfortunately, as Bardhan says, while the political power of regional governments is increasing, their fiscal dependence on the centre is also rising as, from the mid-1950s to the mid-1990s, the fraction of state's current expenditures financed by their own revenue sources declined from around 70 per cent to around 55 per cent (Bandhan 2004).

This is a ludicrous situation and our view is that the more money that is transferred from the centre to the provinces, the less responsible provinces will become. Overall, given India's political institutional set-up it is doubtful that the present government will be able to make much headway in regard to the second generation reforms.

Approach

China

Chinese reforms differ from those of other transitional economies in two aspects. First, China adopted the populist approach towards reforms. Most reforms in China were initiated not from above but from below. The central authority simply accepted what had happened at the local level. For instance, in rural reforms, the household responsibility (HRS) was first introduced in Anhui province. It spread later throughout China without official sanction (Chai 1997, p. 76). Similarly, in urban reforms, the enterprise autonomy reform was first introduced in Sichuan province and later spread to other provinces, again without official sanction (Sung and Chan 1987, p. 12). In both cases, the central authority endorsed the reforms long after they had been adopted at the local level.

Second, China adopted a gradual instead of a big bang approach to reforms. Reforms were first introduced in sectors where the resistance was weakest and then extended to other sectors where reforms were more controversial and less popular. Thus, in contrast to its Eastern European and Russian counterparts, economic reforms were introduced first while political reforms were postponed. Rural reform preceded urban reform. In the urban reform, enterprise autonomy and incentive change were allowed to take precedence over ownership and other market institution reforms. Reforms were introduced only after extensive experimentation, and most reform measures were not introduced at once but slowly over a period of several years. The government adopted a very flexible approach to the implementation of the reforms. Reforms were halted or even reversed whenever they encountered serious problems. However, as soon as the problems were solved a new wave of reform, more radical than the previous one, was then initiated. There has been much debate about the pros and cons of the gradual approach and the 'big bang' approach to reforms (see Lal 1995; OECD 1991; Siebert 1999, pp. 175–9). The issue of which approach is more appropriate cannot be settled in theory as it depends to a large extent on each country's initial condition.

China adopted the gradual approach for several reasons. To begin with, the Chinese leaders did not have an overall reform blueprint from the outset, and thus had to proceed with the reforms in a very cautious manner. Second, reform cannot be rushed before the necessary conditions for its successful implementation have been met. Take privatization for example; the successful implementation of privatization requires that several preconditions have to be met. These include: the establishment of a social safety net to protect the victims of privatization; the establishment of a functioning capital market and a competitive product market to avoid the problems of state asset-stripping; privatization of assets and socialization of liabilities, and so on (Chai 2003, pp. 258–9). Since the provision of these preconditions is time-consuming, full privatization of SOEs in China has not yet been implemented. Finally, implementation of the reforms required a stable political and social environment. The gradual approach helps to maintain political and social stability as it softens the opposition of hardline communist and interest groups that benefit from the inefficiency of the old system. It also prevents a large fall in output and employment associated with the 'big bang' approach at the initial stage of the reforms (see Siebert 1999, p. 175).

India

In India it is unlikely that the Nara Sinha Rao government would have embraced economic reform out of a genuine desire to lift the performance of the Indian economy if the macroeconomic crisis of 1990–91 had not pushed the country to the stage of near bankruptcy. This forced the Rao government to accept International Monetary Fund (IMF) and World Bank help on the condition it agreed to implement economic reforms. Like China's leaders, Indian leaders also did not adopt the 'big bang' approach to implementing reforms. The reform package itself with the two-stage implementation process, (a) stabilization policy and (b) structural reform, emphasized the need to implement measures to stabilize the economy first and then address structural reform.

In India as in China, the adoption of the 'big bang' approach in implementing reforms could have destabilized the political and social environment in the country. The institutional parameter in India was and is far less conducive to implementing reform compared with that in China. In India's federal multiparty democratic state the government could have lost its majority and power even before the next election was due, as the adoption of the 'big bang' approach could have given the opposition parties and organized labour unions enough ammunition to shed crocodile tears for the poor and destabilize the country's political and social environment. Furthermore, since the party in power at the federal level did not have power in the majority of provinces, it would have been difficult to implement drastic measures at the provincial level. China's leaders did not have to face such problems.

Although the capital market in India was more developed in the early 1990s than in China in 1980, considerable restrictions existed on capital inflow and outflow, and the rupee was not convertible on both trade and capital accounts prior to 1990–91. Hence, in India the gradualist approach was necessary for implementing reforms.

Progress of the Reforms

China

Chinese reforms have been going on for almost a quarter of a century. The ultimate objective of the Chinese reforms is to establish a fully fledged market economy. To what extent has China achieved this objective? The transformation of a planned economy into a market economy normally involves several steps: (a) the liberalization of the economy from bureaucratic control; (b) the establishment of market institutions, in particular the product and factor markets; (c) privatization and (d) control of macro-instability. In what follows we review the progress of Chinese reform in these four areas.

Liberalization   Liberalization of a socialist economy involves (a) deregulation of enterprise activities, (b) liberalization of prices and (c) liberalization of foreign trade and investment. Since the progress of (c) will be discussed in Chapter 5, the following discussion will focus only on (a) and (b).

Deregulation of enterprise activity involves the elimination of mandatory planning and direct administrative control over enterprise activities. China so far has made significant progress in the elimination of mandatory planning. As of 2002, mandatory planning has been completely eliminated in both the industrial and the non-industrial sectors. However, progress in the eradication of administrative control over enterprise behaviour is still limited. In the agricultural sector, the commune has been dismantled, the government's compulsory procurement scheme and the central rationing of basic agricultural inputs have been scrapped, and farm households have become autonomous producers. Nonetheless, farming is not entirely free of government regulation as the government continues to control the production, pricing and marketing of food grain, which accounts for more than two-thirds of Chinese agricultural land (OECD 2002, pp. 63–4). In the non-agricultural sector, SOEs gained more autonomy with respect to output, input, marketing and investment decisions. Nonetheless, because the appointment and promotion of enterprise managers are still very much in the hands of the state bureaucracy and some key inputs such as certain industrial materials, energy and bank loans and foreign exchanges remain rationed by the authorities, the authorities have much opportunity to influence enterprise behaviour. China has made considerable headway in the liberalization of its price system. Currently, nearly 90 per cent of retail prices are completely market determined, and only some energy and utility prices are still regulated by the government (OECD 2002, p. 14).

Product and factor markets   China's overall progress in the development of market institutions is mixed. On the one hand, the country has taken substantial strides in the development of product markets. Right now most of the products are available for sale and purchase through the markets. The factor market, on the other hand, is not well developed.

1. *Labour market.* In the rural area an active labour market has now formed. This is evidenced from the increasing rate of rural labour migration not only between the agricultural and non-agricultural sector, but also within villages, between villages as well as between villages and cities and towns during 1980–99 (Rozelle et al. 1999). Nonetheless, the development of the rural labour market is still very much constrained by certain administrative and institutional barriers. Rural–urban migration is still restricted by the household registration system which stipulates that rural households need residential permits to stay in the cities. In 2001, the household registration policy was relaxed in small cities and towns, but it still applies to large cities (OECD 2002, p. 552). In recent years, the enforcement of this regulation is not strict in the large cities and, as a result, many rural residents moved to the cities illegally and have become the floating population. Nonetheless, they do not have the same rights as other urban residents with respect to housing, education and social insurance, even if they find a job in the urban area, since they are not regarded as an urban resident. Regional migration within the rural area is also highly restricted by the local protection policy. A rural enterprise cannot recruit labour from other localities unless it can convince the local authority that local labour cannot meet the demand, qualitatively or in terms of skill (OECD 2002, p. 552).

    In the urban area, the labour market in the informal sector is very active, but that of the formal sector, especially the SOE sector, remains rather restricted. This is evidenced from the low rate of labour mobility in this sector. The rate of labour turnover at enterprise level can be measured in terms of separation and hiring rate, both of which are very low in China. The separation rate was 11 per cent in 1999 as compared to 25 per cent in Russia and between 10 and 40 per cent in OECD countries; the hiring rate in Chinese SOEs was only 10 per cent in 1999 (OECD 2002, pp. 550–51). The low rate of labour turnover at SOE level, is attributable to several factors. First, SOEs' right to hire workers is still very restricted. A sample survey carried out in some coastal cities in 1999 found that most SOE workers continued to be hired as a result of assignment by the government and 'job inheritance' as in the old system (Chai 1997, p. 55; OECD 2002, p. 551). Second, an enterprise's right to fire workers remains very restricted. The proportion of tenured workers which the enterprise cannot fire is still rather high. It still amounted to 50 per cent of the total SOE workforce in 1997 (OECD 2002, p. 564). Moreover, the firing of workers needs official sanction and the enterprise also needs to provide a guarantee that the laid-off workers get special support. Finally, the social welfare system in the urban area is still enterprise based. Workers relied on the SOEs for the supply of pensions, unemployment benefits, medical care and other welfare. This makes workers reluctant to quit their jobs and enterprises reluctant to dismiss their workers. By the late 1990s, the state-sponsored social insurance system has been established, but the financial constraint of fully implementing this system is enormous. It remains to be seen whether it will be a perfect substitute for the enterprise-based system.

2. *Capital market*. The capital market is heavily regulated by the government. Savings are now mostly held by decentralized units such as households and the enterprises, and invested mainly in two forms of financial assets, that is, bank deposits and securities. The government mobilizes and controls the allocation of these savings through a state-controlled banking system and security market.

    The Chinese banking system is dominated by the state banks. The big four state banks (the Industrial and Commercial Bank of China, the Agricultural Bank, the Bank of China and the Construction Bank) are responsible for three-quarters of loans made in China. Despite the ongoing banking reform (see Lardy 1998; Laurenceson and Chai 2003), commercialization of the state banks has made very little progress. Loans are offered not according to commercial principle but to government policy objectives. Hence, policy loans continue to dominate the loan portfolio of the state banks. As a result, the bulk of savings deposited at the banking system is used to finance SOEs and government investment projects. As SOE profitability deteriorated, the non-performing loans (NPLs) of the state banks soared. Recent estimates reported by the People's Bank of China indicate that 27 per cent of the state banks' total loans in mid-2001 were NPLs (OECD 2002, p. 238).

    The Chinese security market is narrowly based as it is dominated by government bonds, which accounted for 97 per cent of total securities issued at the end of 2001 (*ZGTJNJ 2002*, p. 665). Enterprise shares made up 1 per cent of total securities issued. The issue, transfer and pricing of enterprises share are strictly controlled by the government. Share price on the stock market is not allowed to fluctuate more than 10 per cent (OECD 2002, pp. 514–18). Enterprises allowed to issue shares are mainly confined to the SOEs. Hence, almost all capital raised in the security market has been obtained by the SOEs, whereas most non-state enterprises (NSEs) are more or less excluded from the formal capital market. A high proportion (about 65 per cent) of shares of listed companies are a state or legal person shares which are non-tradeable in order to maintain the state majority ownership of the companies.

3.   *Land market.* In rural areas, land was *de facto* privatized under the HRS, as farmers received the right to use the land for 30 years, which right can be transferred. But so far few transactions of land use right have occurred. In 1995, it was estimated that less than 3 per cent of agricultural land was exchanged through the rental market (Brandt et al., in press). The slow development of the agricultural land market is mainly attributable to the lack of supply. Though an increased number of farmers found more profitable employment off the farm, they are reluctant to part with their contracted land. They prefer to keep it for social security reasons as land entitlement constitutes the principal element of social security in a rural area. Since their property right over the use of land is not secure, as ownership still remains with the village authority which periodically carries out administration allocation of land in response to demographic change in the village even within the specified contract period of 30 years (Krusekopf 2002), farmers are afraid that they might lose the right to use land if they rent it out.

In urban areas, the government retain ownership of all land, but use rights can be transferred to the users for 70 years for residential land and 50 years for commercial land. These use rights can be mortgaged and sold. The land use rights in an urban area is assigned to land users either by market, in the form of auction, or by administrative means. However, so far, with the exception of Guangdong province, most of the land use rights in Chinese major cities are allocated administratively (Li 2003, p. 211).

Privatization   China has made significant progress in the development of its private sector. From 1998, China's privatization ratio, that is, the output share of the private sector, reached 72 per cent if all NSEs are considered as private enterprises. This ratio compared favourably with those achieved in other transitional economies (Siebert 1999, p. 177). Unlike other transitional economies, privatization in China is not achieved through the outright sale of state and collective properties. In the agricultural sector, the method of privatization is contracting out. The collective-owned land, together with farm animals and tools, were contracted out to the farmers under the HRS. Farmers promised to meet a certain grain delivery quota and tax obligations. After meeting these obligations, farmers have the exclusive use rights over the allocated land. The method of land allocation is based mainly on the egalitarian principle, that is, the number of persons per household. The objective was to ensure that an individual household could grow enough grain to satisfy their needs. Nonetheless, the farmers' property right over the allocated land is still very much restricted. To begin with, the ownership title of the land belongs to the village not the farmers. Second, as mentioned before, the village government has the right to periodically reallocate the land among households in response to demographic change in the village. Third, farmers are allowed to keep the land for only a limited period of time, which currently is set at 30 years. Finally, land assigned to the farmers cannot be sold but its right can be transferred.

In the non-agricultural sector, the development of the private sector is achieved through the promotion of NSEs. Chinese traditional NSEs consist of collective enterprises, township and village enterprises (TVEs) and private enterprises. Of late, NSEs also include foreign-funded enterprises and non-sole state-funded joint stock companies. Among these various types of NSEs, TVEs and private enterprises are most important as they provide most of China's non-agricultural employment and, most important of all, they are the main contributors to China's rapid growth in recent years. Chinese TVEs include both rural collectives and rural private enterprises. In the late 1990s, the private component of TVEs dominated Chinese TVEs as it accounted for well over half the total output and employment of TVEs (Lin and Yao 2001, p. 145). In fact, the distinction between collective TVEs and private TVEs is blurred as many collective TVEs are simply disguised private enterprises in order to avoid political persecution and gains from tax concessions accorded to the collective. Hence, the actual share of the private component in TVEs is much higher than the above figure.

Initially, the development of NSEs was promoted by the government to soak up the surplus labour generated by the increased productivity as a result of the introduction of the HRS in the countryside. Later it was promoted as a source of competition to the SOEs. After almost a quarter century of development, NSEs have replaced SOEs as a dominant force in the non-agricultural sector. In 2001, NSEs accounted for more than two-thirds of the output of the Chinese industry, retail trade and construction activity (see Table 2.1).

In the non-agricultural state sector, privatization in the form of divestiture of the existing SOEs is also carried out in China, but this is mainly confined to small SOEs in small and medium-sized cities. By 2002, 80 per cent of small SOEs below county level had been privatized (*JJYJ* 7/2003, p. 4). In regard to the large and medium-scale state-owned enterprises (LMSOEs), only partial privatization in the form of a management contract system has been carried out during 1980–94. Under this system, management of the enterprise was contracted out to the insiders of the SOE, either manager and/or workers, and the contractee promised to meet a certain profit delivery quota and perform certain planned tasks as stipulated by the government. In return, the contractee was allowed to retain all excess profits which could be used to finance bonus payment and housing construction and so on for the benefits of the staff and workers (Chai 2003, p. 247).

Since 1994, partial privatization of LMSOEs takes the form of corporatization. The objective of corporatization is to strenghten the enterprise budget constraint without implementing full privatization. Under this scheme, LMSOEs are converted into joint stock companies with the state still controlling a dominant share of the company and the rest of the shares owned by other institutions, individuals or foreigners. The state is expected to exercise its ownership function through state holding companies. The management of the company is supposed to be separated from its ownership. The board of directors, as in a Western corporation, assumes full independent decision-making power and serves as an agent of the shareholders. It has the power to appoint a manager. Managerial performance is monitored by the annual shareholders' meeting and the prices in the stock market. By the end of 1999, more than half of Chinese industrial LMSOEs had been converted into joint stock companies (OECD 2002, p. 434).

State ownership in the newly incorporated companies can be sole, majority or minority ownership, depending on the significance and competitiveness of the industry. For strategic industries and industries of natural monopoly, sole or majority ownership is retained, whereas for competitive industries, only minority state ownership is required. Hence, corporatization leads to the diluting of state ownership, which is confirmed by a survey which found that, although the state retained majority ownership in most incorporated LMSOEs in 1998, its share had been reduced from 100 per cent to just over 50 per cent (Lin and Zhu 2001). Consequently, the role of the state in LMSOEs is reducing. While in 1994 state ownership accounted for more than two-thirds of the enterprises and total assets of LMSOEs, by 1999 the state share of both enterprises and assets had declined to just half (Jefferson et al. 2003).

Though corporatization has diluted the state share of Chinese LMSOEs, it has done very little to improve their corporate governance (OECD 2002, ch. 13). As the OECD study shows, the power of the Chinese board of directors is very limited. Theoretically, the board is supposed to appoint the manager; in practice, the manager is usually appointed directly either by the local authorities or by the SOE's holding companies that control the listed companies. Few boards have independent directors as very often local authorities and the party, which are in control of the holding companies, nominate most directors. Moreover, the disclosure and transparency of financial management of Chinese companies is still very limited as the quality of Chinese accounting and auditing are not yet up to the international standard. The stock market has so far failed to perform the monitoring function of Chinese companies. As two-thirds of the shares are non-tradeable, share prices do not reflect corporate results. Chinese shares are found to be even more expensive than those of Japan. The price to earnings (P/E) ratio of Shanghai and Shenzhen A shares reached 69 and 67 by the end of 2000, as compared to a P/E ratio of 15 prevailing in OECD markets (OECD 2002, p. 578).

Aside from the limited impact of corporatization on the corporate governance of Chinese SOEs, it also led to the problems of insider control of the SOEs which manifest itself in the form of asset-stripping, decapitalization, wage manipulation, privatization of assets, socialization of liabilities, and so on (Chai 2003, p. 255).

Macro-stability One of the most difficult problems facing any transition economy is to maintain macro-stability, especially inflation, without using the old method of direct administrative monetary control. A transitional economy is prone to inflation. As the enterprise reform is incomplete and enterprise budget constraints remain weak, economic liberalization tends to be accompanied by an explosion in investment and wage expenditure, causing a periodic outburst of inflation. This inflation can be controlled only by administrative means, that is, a credit quota, since an effective indirect monetary control mechanism has yet to be developed. However, the reassertion of administrative control of money supply quickly leads back to state intervention in enterprise behaviour and stops liberalization in its tracks (Perkins 1994, p. 41). Thus, once inflation is under control, the government is forced to loosen the administrative control over money supply to restart the reform process until the next wave of inflation emerges. Thus, a cyclical pattern in macro-stability and an alternate period of stop and go growth in output and prices are generated.

China has experimented with indirect monetary control since the mid-1980s by regulating the amount of credit supplied to the banks by varying the reserve ratio and the discount rate it charges on its loan to the banks. However, the effectiveness of these indirect monetary control instruments proved to be limited for two reasons. The first is the pressure exerted by local government on local branches of the People's Bank to provide credit to the big four state banks to enable them to meet the region's need. The other is the weak budget constraint faced by the specialized banks, which do not bear the risk of their loan decision. Hence, the government is forced to continue to rely on the credit quota to control inflation. As a result, a cyclical pattern in China's macro-stability and an alternate

period of stop and go growth in output and price has again been generated. Altogether, four such cycles can be detected during the 1980s and
1990s (see Table 2.2).

However, in recent years, especially during 1998–2003, there are indica-
tions that China has finally mastered the technique of controlling inflation
without using direct monetary control. Since 1998, the People's Bank has
scrapped the credit quota system. As evidenced from Table 2.2 the stop and
go growth of Chinese output and prices has disappeared during 1998–2003.
Chinese GDP growth has been stabilized during this period at 7 to 8 per
cent a year, the rate of fluctuation has been reduced to 0.9 per cent and the
rate of inflation is practically nil. The improved performance of China's

*Table 2.2   Rate of growth of China's GDP and consumer price index,
1979–2003*

Year	GDP	Price
1979	7.6	2.0
1980	7.8	6.0
1981	5.2	2.4
1982	9.3	1.9
1983	11.1	1.5
1984	15.3	2.8
1985	13.2	8.8
1986	8.5	6.0
1987	11.5	7.3
1988	11.3	18.5
1989	4.2	17.8
1990	4.2	2.1
1991	9.1	2.9
1992	14.1	5.4
1993	13.1	13.2
1994	12.6	21.7
1995	9.0	14.8
1996	9.8	6.1
1997	8.5	0.8
1998	7.8	−0.6
1999	7.2	0.7
2000	8.4	0.4
2001	7.0	0.7
2002	8.3	−0.8
2003	9.3	1.2

Sources: *ZGTJNJ* 1999, pp. 57 and 293; *ZGTJNJ* 2004, pp. 55 and 323.

macro management has much to do with the increased harshness of the budget constraint of the state banks and enterprises following the Asian crisis. In the aftermath of the crisis, in order to prevent a collapse of its banking system, the Chinese government made a serious attempt to address the non-performance loans of the state banking system. Currently the ratio of non-performing loans to total loans is 22 per cent and the government intends to reduce this to 15 per cent. To achieve this goal the government introduced drastic measures which include criminal prosecution of bank managers who are found to be responsible for non-performing loans. The tightening up of the lending policy by the banks led to a credit crunch, which in turn contributed to the increased harshness of SOE's budget constraint (*JJYJ* 7/2003, p. 3).

India

Enterprise autonomy   The Industrial Licencing Department which issued licences to industries prior to the 1991 reform, and which was the major pillar of India's infamous Quantitative Restriction (QR) regime, was abolished in 1991. In the case of establishment of most industries, the licence is no longer required. But there is still very little operational autonomy in practice for the top managerial staff in PSEs, which continue to suffer from day-to-day formal and informal intervention by the government. The top management positions in PSEs continue to remain vacant for a long time and many enterprises continue to incur large deficits, thereby placing considerable strain on national and provincial budgets. Political considerations of the party in power continue to be the guiding force behind investment and production decisions in PSEs, which continue to provide a relatively autonomous mechanism for the exercise of political patronage and power (Jalan 1996).

The reforms have sought to address mainly the problems of private sector industries. Regulatory bodies have been established to oversee the activities of some private sector industries but the relevant ministries and even the nation's High Courts on occasions override the decisions of these bodies.

While the success of the reform is contingent upon the capacity of the PSEs to improve their operational efficiency as the governments are unwilling to finance their deficits through the budget, the PSEs cannot achieve this efficiency as long as they continue to require ministerial and bureaucratic clearance for their commercial decisions. Improving efficiency requires the top-level managers to have autonomy in regard to hiring and firing of labour, and designing and implementing the wage and salary structure for the PSEs' employees. But without substantial amendment of labour laws, particularly that of the Industrial Disputes Act, unproductive industrial labour cannot be retrenched.

The PSEs are now encouraged to raise new equity for expanding their activities directly from the market rather than from the government but their capacity to expand depends on their ability to attract capital from the market. This can only be possible if PSEs' activities are based on the sound economic principle of covering cost (economic and environmental) and earning a reasonable return on the investment through an appropriate price policy (Joskow 1999).

Input and output prices   However, even after the reform measures began to be implemented, the enterprises' managers did not have the autonomy to determine the prices of their outputs. For example, the continuation of the practice of underpricing electricity and subsidizing nitrogeneous fertilizers, and the inequitable allocation of canal water, meant that the excessive use of power, fertilizer and water in agriculture continued unabated. None of the input subsidies is effectively targeted at the poor. Despite considerable liberalization in agricultural trade in the early part of the reform period (up to 1995), about 80 per cent of India's agricultural imports are still covered by non-tariff barriers and exports of most agricultural products are still subject to quantitative restrictions. Such restrictions, combined with the government's policy of keeping the domestic prices of some staple products, for example, rice and wheat, lower than and in other products higher than their international prices, continue to maintain asymmetry between domestic and international prices thereby preventing the markets in India's agricultural sector from being integrated with the global market (Srinivasan 2000).

Although the government delicenced the domestic agricultural trade sector in 1991–92, it continued the practice, which began in 1970, of providing minimum support prices (MSP) to farmers for a large number of food and non-food crops, for procurement through the Food Corporation of India (FCI) of food for maintaining a buffer stock as well as for distribution of food from the stock, through the PDS to the population below poverty line (BPL) and above poverty line (APL) at issue prices which were below the MSP or procurement price of the FCI. Since the procurement cost of the FCI, which also includes the cost of storage and wastage, is higher than the procurement price, which reflects MSP, the gap between the rise in the procurement cost of the FCI consequent on the rise in MSP and other costs, and the fall since the late 1990s in the issue price for BPL people, has widened the pre-existing deficit of the FCI, thereby forcing a significant rise in government subsidy to the FCI. While the MSP and the issue prices provide the benchmark for the market prices of food grain, the rise in the FCI's economic cost (procurement price and cost) above the open market price and the fall in the open market price resulting from excess supply due to a rise in MSP and a bumper crop as a consequence of timely monsoon, has been widening the gap between the FCI's procurement price and the open market price (GOI 1999a). Hence, even during the reform period, domestic open market prices of agricultural crops have failed to become free market equilibrium prices. Since the sale of agricultural crops to the FCI is voluntary and the FCI also cannot take up all excess supply, and sometimes even refuses to procure certain crops, the decline in the open market price and the rise in the cost of cultivation due to rises in cost of labour, fertilizer, seeds and so on have reduced the surplus generated from agriculture in years of large excess supply.

Labour markets The labour markets in the agricultural sector and in the informal sector in urban areas are not regulated. But in several Indian provinces, the respective governments introduced an informal wage rate (cash and kind) and, through the village Paridayats (village governments), tried to make this rate effective by informally forcing land holder families to hire only labourers from their own villages.

Even during the reform period in the urban organized sector, both in public and private sector enterprises, the labour market is under the control of trade unions, some of which are the most militant in the world. Public sector enterprises are overstaffed. Even the labour force in each PSE providing essential services such as postal services, telecommunications and power is controlled by unions. Overstaffing of PSEs by unproductive unskilled and semi-skilled labour due to pressure from political leaders and militant unions is one of the prime reasons for huge losses being suffered by many PSEs. Even in private sector enterprises, powerful trade unions join with managers to ensure that within firms labour is not efficiently allocated (Srinivasan 2000). In some educational institutions (colleges) funded by the public sector it was revealed[1] that the total number of non-teaching staff (administrators and cleaners) was higher than that of the teaching staff.

In one of India's premier universities, it was revealed that the wage bill of the non-teaching staff was higher than that of academic staff. These academic and non-teaching staff are also a unionized labour force. Labour in India's organized industrial sector can be compared with Hinduism's 'sacred cows'. Employees of PSEs are by and large a semi-productive labour aristocracy which enjoys relatively high wages, status of employment, pension and health benefits, housing allowance, paid vacation, leave travel concessions and other prerequisites of which the vast majority of India's labour force is deprived (Srinivasan 2000). Such handsome pay and perks are still being enforced and maintained by India's draconian labour laws, corrupt political leaders and trade union pressure. This is why the vast majority of the labour force in PSEs has still retained their jobs and perks under economic reform.

Note the following comments of Mahalanobis (1969, p. 442):

> Certain welfare measures tend to be implemented in India ahead of economic growth, for example, in labour laws which are the most highly protective of labour interests in the narrowest sense, in the whole world. There is practically no link between output and remuneration; hiring and firing are highly restricted. It is extremely difficult to maintain an economic level of productivity or improve productivity . . . the present form of protection of organisational labour, which constitutes, including their families, about 5 or 6 per cent of the whole population would operate as an obstacle to economic growth and would also increase inequalities.

Unfortunately what Mahalanobis said in 1969 about India's industrial labour force still holds during the reform period. The blame for this situation can, to a great extent, be placed on India's first Prime Minister, the socialist Nehru and his Labour Minister, V.V. Giri.

Privatization of PSEs   Microeconomic theory suggests that infrastructure service providers such as telecommunications, water and electricity suppliers, are natural monopolies as their long-run average cost curves continue to decline to a level of output which can satisfy the entire market demand. If these operate as private monopolies, their activities should be brought under public regulation to ensure that they produce on a large scale and supply their output to the consumers at a low price based on their average cost per unit of production. However, in India these service providers are public monopolies and the level of exploitation of consumers in terms of high prices charged and low level of output produced is quite high. Hence, one commentator (Srinivasan 2000) suggests that the efficiency gains would have been higher if these were privatized and operated as privately owned monopolies because they would have a greater incentive to reduce costs. The privatization process in India has taken the form of disinvestment through the sale to private investors of equity in public enterprises. But the rationale to be used for determining the percentage of equity in an enterprise to be sold to private investors has not been made clear. Also the investment commission established by the previous government to oversee the disinvestment process could not function properly, as its powers to monitor the disinvestment process were curtailed and its credibility was considerably dented because of its inability to act on its recommendations.

The major hindrance to privatization of PSEs is opposition to disinvestment of powerful rent-seeking vested interests – political leaders, party officials, bureaucrats and trade unions. If a part of an unproductive labour force cannot be retrenched, then the privatization process cannot make progress.

The government's concern with respect to privatization of PSEs relates to its apprehension that the interests of employees might suffer after the transfer of management into private hands. Hence, the government inserts a clause in the shareholder agreement that there is no retrenchment of employees for a period of at least one year after privatization and that even after one year, retrenchment will be possible only under the Voluntary Retirement Scheme (VRS) (GOI, *Economic Survey*, 2003/04). Hence the reduction in employment in PSEs after disinvestment, during the ten-year period from 1991–92 to 2000–01, constituted only a meagre 20 per cent of total employment (GOI, *Economic Survey*, 2003/04). Interestingly, the retrenchment of employment after disinvestment was marginal.

Over a period of 12 years, from 1991–92 to 2000–03, the value of PSE assets privatized as a proportion of total value of assets of all PSEs is only 1.34 per cent (GOI, *Economic Survey*, 2003/04). In terms of US$ the total asset value of all PSEs at the current rate of exchange stands at roughly $489 billion and the value of assets privatized is about $66 billion. Hence very little progress has been made in regard to privatization. What has been achieved can be termed privatization by stealth. However, non-performing assets constitute a sizeable proportion of total public sector enterprises. At the end of the financial year 2001–02, the value of gross non-performing assets of public sector banks stood at Rs 565 billion accounting for 11.1 per cent of gross bank advances and 4.9 per cent of banks total assets (GOI, *Economic Survey*, 2003). At the 2001 rate of exchange, the value of these assets stood at roughly US$11.9 billion. At the end of the 2002–03 financial year, 167 574 small-scale industrial units with an outstanding bank credit of Rs 41 billion were declared non-viable. Also at the end of the 2003–04 financial year, out of the 227 central public sector units operating in the country, 68 units (30 per cent of the total) remained non-viable and were registered with the Board of Industrial and Financial Reconstruction (BIFR) for their revival. Apart from the central public sector units, many provincial public sector units remained non-viable.

It is difficult to privatize public sector industrial units with substantial non-performing assets and employing a highly unionized and unproductive labour force which continues to receive wages and other perks through subsidies from the government. On the other hand, while it is easier to at least partly privatize the profit-making public enterprises, the communists and other left-orientated political parties, on whose support the survival of the central government depends, oppose such a move.

Therefore, the new government of Dr Manmohan Singh is unlikely to achieve much progress as Sonia Gandhi's Congress Party does not hold the majority of seats in the federal parliament and as it professes to be more socialist than the previous government. Thus the entrenched rent-seeking groups in PSEs can become even more powerful.

Macroeconomic stability   India, in general, has tried to maintain macroeconomic stability by ensuring price stability, with occasional lapses, over a reasonably long period of time under planned development. However, in the 1980s, the government's political compulsions such as providing subsidies on food, fertilizers and to loss-making PSEs, including nationalized banks, raised the level of expenditure, whereas the lacklustre performance of the economy under the dirigiste regime failed to raise sufficiently the level of GDP, and consequently the level of revenue for the government, to cover its rising expenditure. Hence large fiscal deficits had to be financed by loans from the financial market and via deficit financing, which in turn adversely affected the rate of inflation. In India, experience shows that the money supply growth which contributes to credit growth is strongly influenced by the behaviour of the budget deficit as well as the behaviour of foreign exchange reserves. The rate of growth in broad money supply (M3) reached a high level of 19.4 per cent during 1989–90 and its impact was felt on inflation in 1990–91. In 1990–91, the year in which India's economic reform programme began to be implemented, the annual inflation rate based on wholesale prices rose to 12.1 per cent from 9.1 per cent in 1989–90 (GOI, *Economic Survey*, 1991/92).

During the immediate pre-reform and early reform period, the aim of achieving growth with reasonable price stability was sought by implementing a policy of aggregate demand management, which aimed at monitoring expenditure, limiting the size of the fiscal deficit and reducing the growth of money supply.

However, since inflation in India, at least in the short term, is also influenced by supply-side shocks, monetary management policies were combined with measures to contain the adverse effects of supply shocks through adequate buffer stocks of food grain and other sensitive stocks (Singh 1982). In the reform period since 1990–91, the twin objectives of monetary policy continued to be (a) the pursuit of price stability and (b) ensuring the availability of sufficient credit for the productive sectors of the economy. The high interest rate and administered interest rate regime of the pre-reform period was modified during the reform period and the Reserve Bank's discount rate was lowered gradually to allow the commercial banks to lower their lending rates. Throughout the 1990s, the monetary policy stance of maintaining a 'soft' interest rate regime, which allows greater flexibility for the interest rate structure, and of keeping a close eye on the movement of prices was pursued by redirecting the thrust of the monetary policy from direct to indirect instruments. Thus changes in the bank rate and cash reserve ratio (CRR), combined with the liquidity adjustment facility (LAF) and open market operations (OMO), have emerged as the major tools of liquidity management in the country in the late 1990s and early 2000s. Along with these, the regulatory reforms introduced into the financial system, which include a move towards full disclosure, transparency and effective supervision of the banking operations in line with international best practices (GOI, *Economic Survey*, 2000/01), have enabled the Reserve Bank of India to promptly respond to emerging situations relating to price level changes, liquidity needs of the economy, short-term supply shocks, and so on – without any major shift in the policy.

Table 2.3 illustrates the growth in the wholesale price index (WPI) and the consumer price index (CPI) since 1989–90. In India, as food items alone are accorded close to 60 per cent of total weight in the calculation of the CPI, the CPI becomes very sensitive to even a moderate level of food shortages, and it relates only to industrial workers, whereas in the WPI the coverage of commodity groups is considerably broader and the weight given to food items is also not so high. The WPI is regarded as a better indicator of inflation rate than the CPI. Table 2.3 presents the growth in WPI and CPI. The sharp acceleration in the growth in CPI in 1998–99 was primarily due

Table 2.3   Inflation in India

Year	WPI based	CPI based
1988/89	7.5	8.7
1989/90	7.5	6.1
1990/91	10.3	11.6
1991/92	13.7	13.5
1992/93	10.1	9.6
1993/94	8.4	7.5
1994/95	10.9	10.1
1995/96	7.7	10.2
1996/97	6.4	9.3
1997/98	4.8	7.0
1998/99	5.9	13.1
1999/2000	3.1	3.4
2000/01	7.2	3.7
2001/02		4.3
2002/03	5.1[1]	4.0
2003/04		3.9

Note: 1. 2001/02 to 2003/04.

Sources: GOI, *Economic Survey*, various issues.

to a 25.6 per cent rise in retail prices of essential commodities during the year. Initially the higher rate of growth in 2000–01 was caused by a sharp rise in fuel prices. Otherwise the growth rates in both WPI and CPI have decelerated since 1991–92. In 2002–03, the inflation rate based on WPI declined to 2.6 per cent (GOI, *Economic Survey*, 2003/04).

However, consistent reduction in fiscal deficit to bring it down to 5 per cent or below 5 per cent of GDP, which was a major item in the reform agenda to reign in on domestic demand and on the widening external deficit, has not been achieved mainly due to, among other things, the realities of the Indian political system which have been discussed earlier. While the fiscal deficit of the central government remained around 6.6 per cent of GDP in 2001–02 after a consistent decline to 4.1 per cent in 1996–97 from 7 per cent in 1990–91, the combined fiscal deficit of the central and state governments, which declined from 9.4 per cent of GDP in 1991 to 7.3 per cent in 1997–98, continued to increase after that to stand at 10 per cent of GDP in 2001–02 (GOI, *Economic Survey*, 2002/03; 2003/04). But India's official GDP figures are also considerably underestimated as the vast underground economy generates 50 per cent of India's official GDP according to one commentator (Kamath 1993b). If this income can be unearthed and the activities brought under the purview of India's tax department, India's budget deficit will turn into a large surplus and the GDP will increase greatly. No serious attempt has been made to address this issue.

SUMMARY AND CONCLUSIONS

China's long march to becoming a fully fledged market economy is not yet complete. The size of the state sector is still very large and the role of the state in economic activity is still overwhelming and, most important of all, the factor markets have yet to be fully developed and the budget constraints of the state enterprises remain weak. But there is no doubt that China has travelled a considerable distance between plan and market. As at 2002, China has covered more than half, and perhaps two-thirds, of the journey.

It is unlikely that India's political system and the institutional rigidities in the labour market will allow India to be totally transformed into a total market economy. It is virtually impossible to reform India's political system and labour market to make these institutions pro-reform and pro-growth. The size of the state sector has virtually remained intact and Manmohan Singh's new United Progressive Alliance government has abolished the Disinvestment Ministry which the previous Bharatiya Janata Party (BJP)-led National Democratic Alliance government created. Under the Common

Minimum Programme (*The Telegraph* 2004) worked out by the Alliance Partners, the government cannot privatize the so called '*Nava ratnas*' ('new gems') but can privatize loss-making PSEs with the proviso that the labour force, the so-called 'sacred cows' of India's organized industrial sector, cannot be easily downsized without the agreement of trade unions and without protecting the welfare of labourers. Subsidies and other transfers on most items will have to be continued. Within these constraints, India's progress towards a fully fledged market economy is likely to be considerably slower than that of China.

NOTE

1. Revealed to K.C. Roy in private conversation with academic staff employed in these institutions.

3. Agricultural development

Agriculture plays a crucial role in the early stages of modern economic growth. According to Kuznets (1966), agriculture contributes to growth through the provisions of (1) foodstuffs, (2) industrial materials, (3) labour force, (4) funds for financing industrialization, (5) markets for industrial products and (6) materials for exports. Accordingly, the experiences of industrial countries reveal that modern economic growth would not have been possible without an accompanying rapid agricultural growth (the concurrent hypothesis) or without having been preceded by rapid agricultural growth (the prerequisite theory). Empirical studies confirm this, as the case of Japan confirms the concurrent hypothesis and the case of the UK the latter (Minami 1994a, pp. 20–21; 1994b, pp. 64–5).

In view of the importance of agriculture for economic development the agricultural policies are an integral part of a country's development policies. The objective of a country's agricultural development strategy is to maximize the contribution of agriculture to economic growth, therefore it includes the following elements:

1. to increase agricultural output, and in particular, food production;
2. to increase farmers' welfare by raising their income level; and
3. to extract agricultural surplus to finance industrial development.

Obviously, there are some trade-offs between the objective of increasing the income level of farmers and that of the extraction of surplus from agriculture. The purpose of this chapter is to evaluate the performance of the Chinese and Indian agricultural development policies during the post-war years in terms of the above criteria.

The gross value of agricultural output grew at a rate of 3 per cent a year in China during the pre-reform period from 1952 to 1978 (Table 3.1). From a historical perspective this growth rate is quite impressive since the agricultural growth rate in China from the end of the 14th century to the middle of the 20th century was relatively low and averaged only 0.5 per cent a year (Perkins and Yusuf 1984, pp. 34–5). However, China's pre-reform growth rate is more or less similar to that of India.

The real difference between China and India comes about in the post-reform period, when China's rate jumps to a high 6 per cent, whereas India's

Table 3.1   Agricultural growth rates[1] of China and India (% per year)

	Pre-reform	Post-reform	Entire post-war period
China	2.9[2]	6.2[4]	4.3[6]
India	3.0[3]	3.9[5]	3.2[7]

Notes:
1. Growth rates refer to gross value of agricultural input (GVAO) which includes farming, forestry, animal husbandry and fishery. Chinese growth rates are derived from GVAO in 1980 prices:
2. 1952–1978.
3. 1950/51–1990/91.
4. 1979–2003.
5. 1992/93–2002/03.
6. 1950/51–2002/03.
7. 1952–2003.

Sources: *ZGTJNJ* 2004, pp. 27 and 476; GOI, *Economic Survey*, various issues.

agricultural growth rate only shows a modest rise of 3.9 per cent. The accelerated growth rate of China's agriculture which is sustained through the post-reform period has significantly contributed to the overall growth rate of China's economy of the entire post-war years during which Chinese agriculture grew at 4.3 per cent, whereas India's agriculture grew at a rate of only 3 per cent a year. Thus, the Chinese agricultural growth rate has outperformed that of India during the post-war years by about 60 per cent.

CROP VERSUS NON-CROP PRODUCTION

The structure of agriculture in both countries is similar, with crop production making up an overwhelming proportion of agricultural output. However, the share of crops in total agricultural output in China has declined sharply from 83 per cent in 1952 to a mere 56 per cent in 2000. A similar trend is also observable in India. Moreover, in both countries the livestock industry has become increasingly important in the course of development. In China its share in total agricultural output shot up from 12 per cent in 1952 to 31 per cent in 2002; and similarly for India. In the *Economic Survey* (2000/01) the GOI confirms that over the years, the contribution of the livestock sector to agricultural GDP has increased from 17 to 29 per cent. The growth rate of crop output in both countries is similar to the trend of total agricultural output. In China, crop output grew at a rate of 2.5 per cent a year between 1952 and 1978 (during the pre-reform period). In contrast, this growth rate shot up in the post-reform period, for example, in the years between 1979 and 2000, to 4.5 per cent. For the entire post-war period (1952–2000) crop output in China grew by 3.5 per cent a year. In India, crop output grew at merely 2.5 per cent between 1970–71 and 1999–2000. Thus China outperformed India in crop output during the post-war years by about 40 per cent.

GRAIN VERSUS CASH CROPS

A relatively high growth of crop output can be achieved by concentrating on cash crops with a high value of output per hectare instead of grain crops, as the experience of some of the East Asian countries has shown (Perkins and Yusuf 1984, p. 36). In both China and India this strategy to achieve a high growth rate of crop output is constrained by the objective of both governments to achieve food self-sufficiency.

Compared to Indian farmers, the Chinese farmers in the pre-reform period of collectivized agriculture had very little freedom to choose cropping patterns. Hence, as Table 3.2 shows, from 1957 to 1978 the areas sown with grain and cash crops remained virtually the same and their growth pattern experienced very little change. In contrast, Indian farmers operated under the mixed economic system and had more choice about cropping patterns. Thus, in India, the growth rate of areas sown with cash crops show a definite growth during the pre-reform period.

However, the cropping pattern in post-reform agriculture in India changed very little, since the trend away from low-value grain crops to high-value cash crops simply continued in the post-reform period. In China the

Table 3.2   Annual average growth rate of sown acreage of grain and cash crops (%)

	Pre-reform		Post-reform	
	Grain	Cash crop	Grain	Cash crop
China	−0.1[1]	Negligible[1]	1.4[2]	2.5[2]
India	0.1[3]	1.3[3]	−0.04[4]	1.1[4]

Notes:
1. 1957–1978.
2. 1979–2003.
3. 1970/71–1990/91.
4. 1990/91–2002/03.

Sources: GOI, *Economic Survey*, various issues; SSB 1989a, pp. 133 and 140; *ZGTJNJ* 1981, p. 139; 2004, p. 486.

picture is quite different, for the cropping patterns changed drastically after the reforms. When the household responsibility system was introduced, Chinese farmers used their newly gained freedom in cropping decisions to increase the acreage of areas sown with cash crops. Thus the higher growth performance in Chinese agriculture during the reform period can, to some extent, be attributed to the partial abandonment of Mao's policy of 'taking grain as the key link' for a policy which allowed farmers to diversify their crops into high-value cash crops.

SOURCES OF GROWTH

The opportunity to diversify crop patterns during the reform period explains, however, only a small proportion of the relatively high growth rate of China's agricultural output compared with India. There were other factors behind the relatively high and sustained performance of China's agriculture in the reform period and these need to be considered in some detail. Analytically, agricultural output (O) is determined by the amount of sown area (Ls), and its yield O/Ls. The sown area in turn depends on the amount of cultivated area (Ld) and the multiple cropping index (MCI), that is, the ratio of sown area to cultivated area. Hence,

$$O = Ld\ MCI\ O/Ls \tag{3.1}$$

Hence, agricultural growth can be achieved by increasing the area of cultivated land, multiple cropping index and/or the level of land productivity or yield. Hence,

$$G(O) = G(Ld) + G(MCI) + Els\,G(O/Ls) \tag{3.2}$$

where G represents the growth rate and Els the output elasticity of sown area.

For the entire post-war period $G(Ld)$ is negative according to the official data. But the official data in China is known to underestimate the actual arable land by 30 to 40 per cent. But as long as the under reporting of land quantity is constant the measure of the land growth index would not be affected (Fan and Zhang 2002, p. 80). As elegantly put by Perkins and Yusuf (1984, pp. 48–9), 'the Chinese spent six centuries for new land to be developed and by 1980 there was not much unoccupied left'.

Since early 1956, the population growth, combined with industrialization and most recently urbanization, has exerted a lot of pressure on the land and has taken its toll on the total cultivated area, which was estimated at

107.9 million hectares in 1952. After having risen to 111.8 million hectares in 1957 (Perkins and Yusuf 1984, p. 54) it started to decline. By 1965 the total area cultivated had decreased by about 7 per cent and amounted to 103.6 million acres and it shrunk to 99 million hectares in 1978. However, if the official data is to be believed, by 1995 the decline had halted and the total area cultivated remained the same as it had been in 1978 (*ZGTJNJ* 1996, p. 355). Thus, for the entire post-war period from 1952 to 1995 $G(Ld)$ in China is -0.3.

Instead of an increase in the cultivated area, China's agriculture relied on the more intensive use of existing land to boost agricultural output. The intensity of land use is made possible by raising the multiple cropping index (*MCI*). The *MCI* can be raised by finding ways and means to shortening the planting and harvesting cycle so that a given piece of land can be used for more than one crop a year. China's *MCI* in the early 1950s was already relatively high as it reached 1.309 in 1952 (Chen and Galenson 1969, pp. 106–7). However, it increased to 1.500 in 1966 and by 1995 it reached 1.578 (*ZGTJNJ* 1999, pp. 381–91). Thus the rate of growth of *MCI* between 1952 and 1995 is about 0.4 per cent a year. Thus it was large enough to more or less offset the decline in the total cultivated area and to stabilize the sown area for Chinese crops during the post-war years. Thus for the entire post-war period the growth of Chinese agricultural output in the crop sector is mainly due to an increased yield per hectare sown. According to equation (3.1), the agricultural yield must have increased by about 3.5 per cent a year to produce the amount of growth that China's agriculture experienced.

In contrast, $G(Ld)$ in India is positive and the total area cultivated, according to the Food and Agriculture Organization (FAO) statistics, increased from 160 million hectares in 1971 to 166 million hectares in 1993 and declined thereafter to 161.8 million hectares in 2000. Unfortunately, no data on the *MCI* is available, but as established by Chen and Galenson (1969, pp. 106–7) it was 1.03 in the mid-1950s – significantly lower than that of China. A relatively low basis means a relatively high potential for an increase of the *MCI*. Thus the case for an increase in *MCI* is a strong likelihood. Using equation (3.2), since India's $G(O)$ is lower than 2.5 per cent, $G(O/Ls)$ obtained by subtracting $G(Ld)$ and $G(MCI)$ from $G(O)$ must have been significantly lower than 2.5 per cent. Thus the lower crop output growth of India is mainly due to its relatively slower growth in crop yield as compared to China.

This hypothesis can be confirmed by comparing Chinese yield with that of India, focusing exclusively on the most important crop for both countries, namely, the grain crop. In India, the annual average rate of growth of grain output for the entire post-war period from 1960–61 to 1999–2000, for

Table 3.3   Grain yields of China and India (kg/hectare)

	1960/61	2003
China	1209	4873
India	710	1562

Sources: China: SSB 1989a, p. 146; *ZGTJNJ* 2003, p. 7; 2004, p. 490. India: GOI, *Economic Survey*, various issues.

which data is available, is 2.4 per cent (GOI, *Economic Survey*, 2000/01, p. S16). In contrast, the corresponding rate of growth in China for the same period is 3.0 per cent (*ZGNCTJDQ* 1989, pp. 146–7; *ZGTJNJ*, various issues). As Table 3.3 shows, the relatively higher growth rate of grain output in China is mainly due to its higher growth rate of grain yield.

China's grain yield in the early 1960s was already 70 per cent higher than that of India despite it having experienced the worst weather conditions in the post-war years. By 2003, China's grain yield had risen by an average of 2.8 per cent a year. In contrast, the grain yield grew considerably slower in India, by only 1.9 per cent a year. As a result, the grain yield in China in 2003 was almost three times that of India.

FACTORS BEHIND THE YIELD DIFFERENCES

Assuming a production function of $[O = F(L_d, TI, MI, t)]$, the growth of yield can be expressed as follows:

$$G(O/L_d) = E_{t_i} G\left(\frac{TI}{Ld}\right) + E_{mi} G\left(\frac{MI}{Ld}\right) + \lambda \qquad (3.3)$$

where *TI* and *MI* stand for traditional inputs, such as water, organic fertilizers, and labour with shovels and hoes, and modern inputs, such as chemical fertilizers and powered machinery, and E_{ti}, and E_{mi} represents the output elasticities of traditional and modern inputs, and $E_{ti} G(TI/Ld)$ and $E_{mi} G$ (*MI/Ld*) are the increase in land productivity due to increases in the application of traditional and modern inputs per unit of land. Thus they represent the growth contribution of increased inputs. λ stands for shifts in the production function due to technological progress. λ is a residual derived by subtracting the growth contribution of inputs from $G(O/Ld)$. λ represents the growth of total factor productivity due to technological change.

Based on the above analytical framework, the differences between India's and China's yield growth can be traced back to the differences in $G(TI/Ld)$ and $G(MI/ld)$ and λ. In the following discussion, to keep the analysis manageable, we will focus on crop output only. Also, due to data constraints, we will limit the analysis to the period between 1970 and 2000.

The increased application of traditional inputs in a given piece of land in the form of deeper ploughing, closer planting as well as other methods of labour-intensive cultivation techniques, such as a more intensive use of labour, are unlikely to have any significant impacts on output growth. What it means is that E_{ti} is likely to be limited in labour surplus economies like those of China and India. The main reason is that they have for centuries employed labour-intensive cultivation techniques and pushed these to the very limit, simply because of population pressure on the land, scarcity of land and a plentiful supply of rural labour. This is borne out by the fact that attempts to mobilize surplus labour, to engage in closer planting and deeper ploughing and so on through the collectivization and communization of China's agriculture by Mao Tse-tung in the late 1950s ended in failure because farm output fell substantially (Perkins and Yusuf 1984, p. 50). Thus the different application of labour per unit of land is unlikely to contribute much to the divergent yield in both countries. However, since large areas of land in both China and India are dry, due to different and varying environmental and rainfall conditions, the increased application of some of the traditional inputs, such as water, through irrigation, does make a considerable difference in increasing the output. An increased application of water per unit of land can be proxied by the rate of irrigation, that is, the share of irrigated land in the total cultivated area. The irrigated portion of land in China is much higher than that in India. In 1970, the rate of irrigation was 36 per cent in China (Perkins and Yusuf 1984, p. 52) and by 2001 it had increased to 42.7 per cent. In contrast, in 1970 only 19 per cent of the cultivated area was irrigated in India. This was increased to 33 per cent by 2000 (FAO, *Production Yearbook*, 2002) but the gap between India and China in terms of the share of irrigated land in total cultivated acreage remains wide, with the Indian 2000 level still remaining below the 1970 level in China. Thus irrigation is one of the major factors in explaining the differences in the growth of grain crop yields between the two countries.

Another important factor behind the difference in crop yield between China and India is their different application of modern inputs. Among the various types of modern inputs, the use of chemical fertilizers is the most important one, as this, combined with improved plant varieties, timely supplies of water, pesticides and so on, directly contributes to the increase in land productivity.

Table 3.4   Utilization of chemical fertilizers (nutrients) (in kg per hectare)

Year	China	Year	India
1952	0.80		
1957	3.21	1960/61	2
1965	12.84		
1970	24.7	1970/71	14
1978	58.98	1980/81	35
1990	174.6	1990/91	75
1995	239.8	1995/96	87
2000	265.5	1998/99	100
2003	287.6	2002/03	85

Sources: China: 1952–65, Chen and Galenson 1969, p. 114; 1970–95, SSB 1989a, pp. 340–41; *ZGTJNJ* 2004, p. 475. India: GOI, *Economic Survey*, various issues.

Table 3.4 compares the consumption of chemical fertilizers of Chinese and Indian farmers in the post-war period.

In the post-war period both countries have increased their rate of application of chemical fertilizers, but that of China grew much more rapidly than that of India. In the former it grew at an annual rate of 12 per cent between 1952 and 2003, whereas in India, from 1960/61 to 2002/03, it grew by 9 per cent. In absolute terms, the gap between India and China in the use of chemical fertilizer per hectare grew even wider from a difference of 1.8 to 1 in 1970 to a level of almost 3.4 to 1 in 2003.

The general argument that the increased use of machinery, another modern input, increases productivity has to be considered carefully in such countries as China and India. Its effects tend to be ambiguous as machinery tends to replace labour and hence it increases labour productivity rather than land productivity. Of course, both countries have experienced an increase in the rate of mechanization over the years. The rate of mechanization is conventionally measured in terms of the number of tractors per cultivated area. However, this measure does not seem a suitable indicator for two reasons. First, it focuses only on a single item, namely, tractors, to the exclusion of other power tools used in agriculture, such as power pumps, grain milling machines, milking machines and so on. Second, it is well known that tractors in China, for example, are less frequently used for agriculture and more often for transport. Hence, a more reliable measure of agricultural mechanization is the consumption of rural electrical power per hectare, as most power is used to run machines rather than to light the

Table 3.5   Rural consumption of electric power (kilowatt hours per hectare)

Year	China	Year	India
1952	0.45	1950/51	NA
1962	15.80	1960/61	NA
1970	94.50	1970/71	38.20
1980	322.60	1980/81	130.20
1990	882.50	1990/91	454.90
1995	1 742.80	1994/95	724.50
2003	22 525.60	1999/2000	1 015.6

Sources: China: 1952–80, Perkins and Yusuf 1984, p. 89; 1990 and after, *ZGTJNJ* 2004, p. 479. India: GOI, *Economic Survey*, various issues.

farmers' homes. Table 3.5 shows the rate of growth of rural electricity consumption.

As Table 3.5 shows, India's rural consumption of power per hectare in the early 1970s was only 40 per cent that of China's. Over the period from 1970 to 1995, for which a comparison can be drawn due to availability of data from both countries, the rate of electric consumption increased rapidly, at an annual rate of growth of 12 per cent in both countries. However, by 1995 India's rural power consumption per hectare was still only 42 per cent of the comparable rate in China.

Apart from the increased application of both traditional and modern inputs, the yield can also be increased by technological change which leads to the growth in total factor productivity, TFP or λ. Unfortunately, the data for TFP estimates for India's agriculture are hard to come by. Estimates are available only for the period from 1970 to 1993. Table 3.6 presents the TFP estimates for India's agriculture from 1970 to 1993 and those of China's agriculture for the same period.

The rate of TFP growth in India's agriculture increased from 1.45 per cent per year from 1973 to 1980, to 2.33 per cent in the 1980s. However, from 1989 to 1993 it slowed down to only 1.21 per cent per annum. Thus for the entire period under discussion the annual average growth rate amounted to only 1.66 per cent. Given that the crop yield in India in that period was 1.9 per cent (GOI, *Economic Survey*, 2000/01, p. 15), the growth of TFP accounted for more than 85 per cent of the overall growth of crop yield in India in that period.

In contrast, the TFP in Chinese agriculture remained stagnant from 1970 to 1977. However, under the reforms between 1978 and 1993 Chinese agricultural TFP growth leaped to 4 per cent a year. For the entire period the

Table 3.6 Estimates of TFP for China's and India's agriculture, 1970 to 1993

Year	China	India	Year	China	India
1970	95	100	1984	141	125
1973	96	99	1985	147	128
1974	100	96	1986	146	124
1975	101	109	1987	152	126
1976	99	104	1988	150	148
1977	98	113	1989	154	140
1978	102	115	1990	163	139
1979	106	99	1991	167	139
1980	108	112	1992	174	144
1981	115	118	1993	185	146
1982	123	116	AVGR* 1970–93	2.94	1.66
1983	130	129			

Note: * Annual average growth rate.

Sources: China: Fan and Zhang 2002, p. 833. India: Mukherjee and Kuroda 2003, table 1.

growth in TFP was 2.94 per cent, which is almost double that of India's agriculture. According to estimates by Wen (1993, table 7) the growth of crop yield of Chinese agriculture in the years from 1970 to 1989 amounted to 3.5 per cent. Hence the growth of TFP accounted for about 84 per cent of the increase of Chinese crop yield during this period. Thus it can be said that in both China and India roughly three-quarters of the increase in crop yield in agriculture can be explained by the growth of TFP.

The source of growth of TFP differs between the two countries. In Indian agriculture the growth of TFP since the early 1970s was mainly the result of the introduction of Green Revolution technology (Mukherjee and Kuroda 2003, p. 4). In China, the growth of TFP is the result of a combination of factors, for example, the introduction of Green Revolution technology, the reforms of the Chinese agrarian institutions and the improved price incentives for Chinese farmers. China had actually adopted Green Revolution technology much earlier than India, namely, in the late 1960s. However, under the inefficient commune system this technology did not have the chance to demonstrate its worth, and hence the TFP remained stagnant until late 1978. However after 1978, TFP increased rapidly due to the following three factors (see Chai 1991). First, there was a continuing increase of diffusion of high yielding varieties (HYV) of rice, wheat, corn and sorghum. Second, since the late 1970s the agricultural purchase prices had been raised significantly which had boosted the price incentives for

Chinese farmers to increase their productivity. Third, the commune system was dismantled and the household responsibility system (HRS) was introduced. The move from the collective to the family farm had greatly increased the work incentives for the Chinese farmer.

FOOD GRAIN PRODUCTION AND SELF-SUFFICIENCY

Table 3.7 presents data on China's and India's self-sufficiency ratio in food grains in the post-war years. Both countries experienced difficulties in feeding their large population in the 1950s and 1960s owing to a policy of preferential development of industry at the expense of agriculture adopted by both governments. Thus the food self-sufficiency ratio for India in that period slipped from 93.7 per cent in 1952 to 86 per cent in 1966, as Table 3.7 shows. The widening gap between domestic output and demand for food grains was met by increased imports.

In China, the policy mistake of the Great Leap Forward, coupled with poor weather conditions, led to a substantial fall in food grain production

Table 3.7   Food grain self-sufficiency ratio in China and India, 1952–2003

Year	China	India
1952	100.9	93.7
1957	101.0	95.7
1960	101.9	94.8
1966	98.4	86.1
1970	98.6	97.3
1975	99.7	97.9
1980	96.5	94.7
1985	100.0	102.5
1990	96.0	103.4
1995	96.2	100.5
2000	NA	105.6
2001	98.8	109.7
2002	102.7	98.3
2003	99.9	89.2

Note: Indian figures refer to net production as a percentage of net availability; Chinese figures refer to production as a percentage of apparent consumption.

Sources: China: SSB 1989a, pp. 146, 520 and 534; *ZGTJNJ* 2004, pp. 491, 723 and 726. India: GOI, *Economic Survey*, various issues.

and resulted in one of the largest famines in world history. Between 1959 and 1961 the famine-induced mortality rate is estimated to have been between 16.5 and 43 million people. While the failure of India's policy of prioritizing industrial development at the expense of the agricultural sector was less spectacular and costly than that of the Great Leap Forward in China, both countries eventually reversed their policies, China in the mid-1960s and India in the early 1970s. Because significant amounts of resources were channelled back into grain-producing agriculture, both countries subsequently experienced a higher growth of grain output and sustained it, as Table 3.8 shows.

For the entire period from 1951 to 2003 China's grain output grew at an annual average rate of 2.1 per cent, whereas that of India amounted to 2.4 per cent. In the same period, China's population grew at an average annual rate of 1.7 per cent, whereas that of India grew at an annual rate of 2.1 per cent. Thus in both countries the growth rate of food production was greater than that of the population, a result which these two countries, in contrast to other less developed counties (LDCs), achieved without relying on higher imports of food grains.

Within the overall grain output, for India the main items are cereals and pulses. For the overwhelming majority of Indians, the three main items of staple diets are two cereals – rice and wheat – and some pulses. While cereals provide the human body with energy, pulses with their high vitamin content provide nourishment to human bodies. But since the adoption of Green Revolution technology in Indian agriculture in the late 1960s, efforts have been primarily directed to expanding the area of cultivation and increasing the yield for rice and wheat production to achieve self-sufficiency in cereal production. However, the same attention was not paid to expanding the area of production of pulses.

Table 3.8   Food grain production in China and India (million tons)

Year	China	India
1951	143.7	50.8 (1950/51)
1961	147.5	82.0 (1960/61)
1966	214.0	72.3 (1965/66)
1971	250.1	108.4 (1970/71)
1981	325.0	129.6 (1980/81)
1991	435.2	176.4 (1990/91)
2002	457.1	212.9 (2001/02)
2003	430.7	174.2 (2002/03)

Sources: China: as for Table 3.7. India: GOI, *Economic Survey*, various issues.

Our research shows that during a 30-year period, the area under cereal cultivation declined marginally by 1.2 per cent from about 101.8 million hectares in 1970–71 to 100.7 million hectares in 2000–01, and under pulse cultivation by 3.2 per cent from 22.6 million hectares in 1970–71 to 21.8 million hectares in 2000–01. On the other hand, during the same period as for cereals, the area under wheat and rice production increased by 45.1 and 18.9 per cent respectively. As far as the yield per hectare is concerned, during the same period, the yield per hectare of total food grains, cereals, pulses, rice and wheat increased from 872, 949, 524, 1123 and 1307 kilograms per hectare respectively to 1732, 1974, 615, 2077 and 2761 kilograms per hectare (GOI, *Economic Survey*, 2003/04), thereby recording rises of 98.6, 108.0, 17.4, 85.0 and 111.2 per cent respectively. Therefore, among wheat, rice and pulses, wheat recorded the highest increase in yield per hectare, followed by rice, and pulses recorded only a marginal increase.

The main factors that contributed to a substantial increase in wheat yield per hectare were partial mechanization of wheat cultivation and greater expansion of irrigation facilities as compared with rice and pulses cultivation. In 1999–2000, the shares of area under irrigation in total area under cultivation were 87.2 per cent for wheat, 54 per cent for rice and only 16.1 per cent for pulses (GOI, *Economic Survey*, 2003/04). Also the rice and pulse cultivation were not as mechanized as wheat. As a result, while the per capita availability of cereals increased marginally from 417.6 grams in 1971 to only 457.3 grams in 2002, and that of pulses declined considerably from 51.2 grams in 1971 to 35.0 grams in 2002. Therefore, India had to import pulses from time to time.

Since for India the rate of growth in agricultural output exercises a strong influence on overall GDP growth and per capita GDP growth, not so impressive growth in agricultural output had implications for India's per capita GDP growth. Compared with India, however, the food grain self-sufficiency ratio in China has declined in recent years, which is mainly due to China's relatively higher growth rate of per capita income. During the period from 1985 to 1998 the Chinese GDP per capita grew at an annual rate of 8 per cent a year (*ZGTJNJ*, various issues) whereas that of India, measured as per capita net national product (NNP) at 1993/94 price grew at only 2 per cent per annum (GOI, *Economic Survey*, 2001/02, p. 1).

Since the demand for food grain is determined by

$$G(G)r = G(P) + nG(y) \tag{3.4}$$

where $G(G)r$ is the required rate of grain production, $G(P)$ and $G(y)$ are the rates of growth of the population and income per capita, and n is the income elasticity of demand for grain. Since the value of $G(y)$, and most probably also of n in China was higher than that of India, the required rate of growth of food grain in China is likely to be comparatively much higher than that of India. Hence the gap between the actual supply and demand for food grain had to be met by regular imports; thus there has been a relatively lower food self-sufficiency ratio of food grain in China in recent years, a trend which is likely to continue.

The relatively higher consumption of food grain per capita in China as compared to India can be easily observed. In 1957, China's per capita apparent consumption of food grain was 298.5 kg, and in 2001 it was 354.6 kg. The comparable figures for India were 136.9 kg for 1951 and 159 for India. Thus there is a considerable gap in per capita grain consumption between India and China, which actually widened from 2.2 to 1 in 1951 to 2.5 to 1 in 2001. This gap has also been noted by other studies (Garnaut 1996, p. 36). However, these figures have to be used with care since a large part of the Indian staple diet is not made up of grains but of pulses. Thus, the per capita grain consumption in India must not be considered in isolation.

THE SUPPLY OF FUNDS

The Chinese government has been spectacularly successful in its effort to mobilize and extract agricultural surplus to fund industrial development as compared to its Indian counterpart. In China, agricultural surplus is extracted from farmers through a system of visible and invisible taxation. In the early 1950s the major visible tax paid by Chinese peasants was an agricultural tax, which was a form of land tax. Perkins and Yusuf (1984) estimate that this amounted to a total sum of 3 billion yuan a year in 1957. As regards to indirect taxes, there were two types in the early 1950s. One was a fixed percentage mark-up above cost of all consumer goods sold in rural areas. This was estimated to net the government 5 billion yuan a year in 1957 (Perkins and Yusuf 1984). The other invisible tax was the grain tax, which consisted of the compulsory delivery to the state of a certain percentage of grain production, as that of other agricultural commodities, at a price below market prices. This was known as the compulsory procurement scheme. Since the gap between the quota price, which was actually paid to the peasants, and a free market price for the grain was considerable, this procurement can be regarded as an invisible tax. In 1957, it amounted to 3 billion yuan a year. Thus, altogether, in 1957 alone, the Chinese government collected about 11 billion yuan of visible and invisible taxes from Chinese agriculture.

However, the government's spending on the agricultural sector in 1957 amounted to only 3.5 billion yuan a year (Perkins and Yusuf 1984, p. 15), hence the net revenue contribution of China's agricultural sector to the government was 7.5 billion yuan in that year. Since the total government expenditure in the non-agricultural sector in 1957 was 31.25 billion yuan, the net government revenue from the agricultural sector accounted for 24 per cent of government expenditure in the non-agricultural sector.

The agricultural contribution to funding of economic development has declined in recent years in China. With the rapid development of industries and the service sector, there are multiplying sources of funding and a shift away from agricultural sources. According to recent OECD estimates (2002) the shift has been so drastic that by 1998 the contribution of the agricultural sector had turned negative, for example, the fiscal revenues from visible and invisible taxation on agriculture were actually smaller than the amount spent by the government on the sector. It was found that agriculture had received a net injection of funds from the fiscal system of 21.3 billion yuan each year in recent times. However, the government's invisible taxation on grain under its grain procurement scheme still netted the government revenue of 50.2 billion yuan each year. As a result, the Chinese government still received a net revenue of 28.9 billion yuan each year from agriculture through the procurement scheme, a sum which constitutes about 4.6 per cent of total government expenditure in the non-agricultural sector.

In contrast, the role of the agricultural sector in supplying funds for Indian industrialization is rather limited. Ishikawa (1986, pp. 23–5) found that in the 20-year period from 1951–52 to 1970–71 the gross capital formation of the Indian public sector was mainly financed by the government deficit spending or inflation tax, foreign savings and private voluntary savings in the non-agricultural small business sector. Unlike China, Indian agriculture operates within the free market mechanism and is based on private property rights. Thus the government has very little control over the saving activities of the farm sector and agricultural production. Neither has the government made any determined attempt to extract agricultural surplus by manipulating the terms of trade or by other fiscal transfers. In regard to food grains, the Indian government exerts very little control on either farm production or marketing activities (see Zhou 1997, ch. 4). As in China, the Indian government also provided a minimum support price for grain producers but, since Indian farmers are free to sell their products to private traders at a higher price (GOI, *Economic Survey*, 2001/02, p. 93), this measure was of little relevance in extracting agricultural surplus and functioned more to stabilize the level of income of farmers.

FARMERS' WELFARE

To compare the welfare of the farmers in China and India is a hazardous venture as there is no common set of criteria, and the given criteria are constantly shifting. The task is made more difficult by the relative paucity of consumption and income data for Indian farmers. Due to the given constraints, the following discussion focuses only on the more recent period from 1983 to the late 1990s, for which comparable data is available.

Farmers' welfare is usually measured in terms of per capita income and consumption. For various reasons, per capita consumption reflects more accurately their material well-being. Table 3.9 presents estimates of per capita real consumption expenditure of Chinese and Indian farmers for selected years between 1983 and 2000.

Table 3.9 shows that the real per capita consumption of Chinese farmers expanded at 6 per cent each year during the period from 1987 to 2000. In contrast, the comparable figure for their Indian counterparts grew at only 1.5 per cent a year. Thus, Chinese farmers increased their real per capita consumption at almost three times the level of Indian farmers in those years.

The gap between the Chinese and Indian farmers in terms of consumption standards can be corroborated by a comparison of their relative consumption patterns. According to international standards, the consumption standard is considered poor when the Engel coefficient is in the 50 to 59 percentage range, whereas it is considered as moderately comfortable with a coefficient in the 40 to 49 percentage range. The Engel coefficient for Chinese and Indian farmers was very high in the early to mid-1980s. In 1985 in China it was 58 per cent and that of India was 66 per cent. Thus, while the farmers of both countries were considered poor in terms of consumption standard, those in India were 'very poor' and relatively worse off than their Chinese counterparts. By 2000, their lot had improved as the Engel coefficient had dropped to 59.4 per cent in India and to 49 per cent for China. Thus, in the period under consideration both countries managed to lift the consumption standard of their farmers to a higher category, but the gap between Chinese and Indian farmers remains.

Individuals tend to judge their standard of material well-being in relation to the standard of living enjoyed by their neighbours. Thus, if income is distributed fairly evenly, people are less likely to feel deprived. Income

Table 3.9   Rural per capita real consumption expenditures

Year	China (yuan)	India (Rs)
1983	242.8	1347.7
1994	410.0	1576.5
2000	648.7	1732.9

Sources: China: *ZGJJNJ* 2004, pp. 327 and 380. India: figures from www.RBI.org.

Table 3.10   The incidence of rural poverty (%)

Year	China (yuan)	India (Rs)
1985	11.9	45.7 (1983)
1995	2.6	37.2 (1994)
1998	3.9	27.1 (2000)

Sources: China: OECD 2002, pp. 108–9. India: www.planningcommission.in.

Table 3.11   Relative inequality of Chinese and Indian rural households (in terms of Gini coefficient)

Year	China	Year	India
1985	0.26	1983	0.298
1995	0.33	1994	0.282
1999	0.35	2000	0.258

Note: The Chinese Gini coefficient refers to the distribution of per capita income; the Indian Gini coefficient refers to the distribution of per capita consumption expenditure.

Sources: China: OECD 2002, pp. 108–09. India: see Table 3.10.

inequality can be measured in two dimensions, that is, absolute inequality and relative inequality. The former is measured in terms of the percentage share of rural households falling below the poverty line. The definition of what constitutes poverty is problematic; however, the data in Table 3.10 can be used as a rough indicator.

Table 3.10 shows that the incidence of rural poverty in both countries has been reduced over the last 20 years. However, the incidence of rural poverty seems to be much higher in India than in China, for in the mid-1980 it was almost four times higher, affecting nearly half the rural population. Even though this had been reduced to roughly one-quarter of the rural population by the late 1990s, the gap in poverty incidence between China's and India's farmers had actually widened to a ratio of 7 to 1.

Table 3.11 compares the relative inequality of the rural Chinese and Indian households. In the mid-1980s the relative inequality among rural households in India was higher than that in China, as Table 3.11 shows. However, when the economic reforms in China, supported by the open-door policy, had taken hold, their impact was to drastically increase the relative inequality, so that by late 1990 the situation had been reversed and rural inequality in China was more than one-third higher than that in India.

SUMMARY AND CONCLUSIONS

India's agricultural resources are comparatively much richer than China's. While India's geographical area is roughly one-third of China's, the size of its cultivated area is the same as that of the USA and much larger than that of China. In China, only 10 per cent of the territory is cultivatable, whereas in India 57 per cent is cultivatable. Indian agriculture has another edge over China, which is that its agrarian system is free from the negative influences of communist ideology and constitution. Despite these advantages, Indian agriculture has not been able to outperform China during the post-war years. China's agriculture has been relatively successful as compared to its Indian counterpart in meeting the three development objectives mentioned at the beginning of this chapter.

In regard to food self-sufficiency, China and India have been equally successful but China has been able to achieve higher agricultural growth and to provide a higher living standard for its farmers than has India. Moreover, it was able to do this while simultaneously extracting agricultural surplus to support its industrialization drive. The same cannot be said about Indian agriculture.

The main reason for the success of China's agriculture lies in its increasing the yield per hectare, which has achieved a much higher level than agriculture in India. The secret behind this can be traced back to the higher application of both traditional and modern inputs per unit of land and a higher growth rate of factor productivity as compared with that of India.

4. Industrial policy

Industrial policy is defined here as a government policy aimed at particular industries to achieve the outcomes that are perceived by the government to be efficient for the economy as a whole. Industry here refers to mining, manufacturing, construction and utilities. The aim of this chapter is to compare the objectives, tools and effectiveness of industrial policies between China and India.

OBJECTIVES OF INDUSTRIAL POLICY

China

China's post-war industrial policy can be divided into two main phases, namely, the pre-reform era (1949–78) and the post-reform era (1978–present, that is, the early 2000s). One of the main features of the pre-reform Chinese industrial policy is the priority development of capital-intensive heavy industries. Heavy industries received the major share of state fixed investment during the pre-reform period. Within the heavy industrial sector, the government promoted, in particular, the metal (especially iron and steel) and machinery industries. Facing a hostile external environment, the goal of the Chinese industrial policy during this period was twofold: (1) to achieve economic independence by minimizing the imports of foreign capital, fuel and intermediate goods; and (2) to catch up with the economies of the advanced industrial counties in the shortest possible time.

To achieve both objectives under the constraint of a given hostile external environment it is rational for China to develop its capital-intensive heavy industry first, even though this appears to contradict the comparative advantages that China had. As demonstrated in the Feldman-Mahalonobis two-sector growth model (Jones 1976, pp. 110–16), under the assumption of (a) a closed economy and (b) a constant capital-output ratio in both the light and the heavy industrial sector, the allocation of investment funds to the capital-intensive heavy industrial sector instead of the labour-intensive light industries might have caused China's output and consumption to experience an initial slowdown, even though it would have quickened their growth rates in the long run because of the expanded capacity to produce capital goods. As a result, a developing country like China would be able to catch up much faster with the development of the advanced industrial nations in a much shorter period than would be possible with a policy prioritizing labour-intensive light industrial development.

Another unique feature of the Chinese industrial policy in the pre-reform phase was the emphasis on the industrialization of the Chinese countryside. In contrast to the Soviet Union, which had promulgated the development of large-scale, capital-intensive, urban industrial plants in conglomerates utilizing modern technology, China under Mao stressed the development of small-scale, labour-intensive, rural-based industrial plants utilizing intermediate technology. The objective of this rural-based industrial policy was twofold: (1) to achieve the Maoist socialist objective of eliminating, or at least alleviating the three 'big divides', for example, the stratification between town and country, industry and agriculture, mental and manual labour; and (2) to fully utilize China's large surplus rural labour and its widely dispersed mineral and energy resources to produce industrial goods much needed by agriculture.

Yet another unique feature of the Chinese industrial policy in the pre-reform period was defence-based industrialization. From the early 1950s, the Chinese government made significant efforts to correct the lopsided concentration of industry along the coastal regions by promoting industrial development of the interior. This emphasis was dramatically heightened in China's self-reliance period from 1964 to 1971. In this period China faced an increasing military threat, first from the USA and then from the USSR, and began a massive industrial investment in the remote regions of South-West and West China. This became known as the Third Front Construction (Naughton 1988). Its main objective was the creation of an alternative industrial base in these regions that would allow China to continue to produce and fight in the event of an attack on its urban centres along the East Coast. This defence-based industrial policy cost China a large amount of its investment resource and played a significant role in its stagnant industrial productivity performance in that period. The Third Front Construction only ended in 1971 following the visit of US President Nixon to China which ended China's isolation.

The focus of Chinese industrial policy has changed during the reform period. In the initial stage of the reforms from the late 1970s to the early 1980s, the industries targeted for prioritized development shifted from the heavy industries to the light ones. The rationale behind this change in emphasis is not difficult to understand. The past concentration of resources in the heavy industrial sector at the expense of the development of the agriculture and light industries had taken its toll on Chinese consumption standards.

The prediction of the Feldman-Mahalanobis model that priority on heavy industries in the long run will be accompanied by a higher rate of growth of light or consumption goods industries did not occur. Contrary to the assumption of the model, the capital-output ratio in both industries did not remain unchanged but, in fact, rose rapidly due to the various systemic factors discussed in Chapter 6 (see especially Table 6.8). Since the growth of the consumer goods sector depends on the ratio between the proportion of investment funds allocated to the heavy industrial sector, Bi and its capital-output ratio, Vi, that is, Bi/Vi (Jones 1976, p. 115), given Bi, an increase of Vi drags down the growth of the consumption good sector. Consequently, during the 1960s and 1970s consumption per capita in China grew at an average of only 1 to 2 per cent a year (Chai 1997, p. 2). Hence, to arrest the stagnant consumption standard, the Chinese government had little choice but to promote the light industrial sector in the late 1970s and early 1980s.

In the 1980s Chinese industrial policy focused on the elimination of infrastructural bottlenecks and the shortage of certain basic industrial materials (see Jiang 1996). In the past, concentration of resources in heavy industry had not only neglected the development of light industries but also that of other complementary industrial branches, a fact which resulted in increasing shortages of transport facilities, energy, as well as industrial and construction materials. By the late 1970s it was estimated that one-quarter of Chinese industrial capacity remained unutilized because of the shortage of electricity (Chai 1997, p. 4). At the same time the transport system was able to satisfy only 50 to 70 per cent of the country's transportation needs (Chai 1997, p. 5). Similarly, supplies of steel, cement and timber fell short of their respective demand by as much as 60 to 70 per cent in the late 1970s. To alleviate these shortages, Chinese industrial policy during this period targeted mainly transport, communication, energy supplies (coal, electricity and petroleum) and some important industrial raw materials such as iron, non-ferrous metals and chemicals.

By the early 1990s the Chinese economy had become increasingly open due to the ongoing liberalization of its trade and foreign trade investment (FDI) regime that had started at the onset of the reform period. In 2001, China was considered advanced enough in this respect to be finally re-admitted to the World Trade Organization (WTO) and as part of the package it committed itself to the complete liberalization of its trade and FDI regime (see Chapter 5). The increasing openness of the Chinese economy raised the threat of international competition for Chinese industries. Thus the goal of the Chinese industrial policy in this period was to create a new, more competitive industrial structure that would enable the Chinese industries to survive competition from foreign goods that would follow in the wake of China's readmission to the WTO. Thus, since the early

1990s, Chinese industrial policy has confined itself to target the so-called 'pillar industries' (see Lu 2000, pp. 17–19), which consist of the high value-added and high-tech industries, such as machinery, electronics, automobiles, aerospace products, ICT, as well as bio-tech industries. In addition, some selected basic industries, such as petroleum processing and the construction industry, also received preferential treatment.

India

The strategy chosen by India for its post-independence industrial development was very similar to that chosen by China. While China began its industrialization programme in 1949, India began its programme in 1951 with the commencement of the First Five Year Plan. India, like China, also followed the same Feldman-Mahalanobis two-sector growth model.

During the first 15 years of India's Stalinist-style, comprehensive planning regime, the bulk of investment funds went to the heavy industries sector within which capital goods industries received the major portion of allocations. The argument was that investment in capital goods industries was necessary to supply the intermediate goods necessary for building up consumer goods industries to manufacture and supply consumer goods for the consumption of the masses. Hence, if iron and steel and other capital goods are produced in the early stage of the build-up to the industrial structure, the nation's rate of savings will rise as people would not be able to consume steel (Bhagwati and Desai 1971; Roy et al. 1992).

Such emphasis on the development of heavy industries in the early stage of economic development emanated from the need to implement the policy of self-reliance of the Congress Party which had led India to independence and assumed political power in the post-independence period. Such a policy, supported by a comprehensive quantitative restriction (QR) regime, aimed to (1) significantly expand the role of the public sector at the expense of the private sector with a view to preventing the concentration of economic power in the hands of capitalists in the private sector, to (2) achieve a greater equality in the distribution of income, and (3) a perceptible reduction in the level of poverty of the masses (GOI, *Economic Survey*, 1951/52). Unlike in China, in India the government never had a vision to implement economic policies to accelerate the rate of economic growth with the aim, among other things, of catching up with the West.

However, since the vast majority of the poor in India live in rural hinterlands which accounted for more than 80 per cent of total population in the early 1950s, the reduction of inequality in income distribution and in the level of poverty required the establishment of hundreds of small-scale and light manufacturing industries in the countryside, as was done in China to eliminate 'big dividers' between industrial urban and agricultural rural areas, and in Taiwan to commence its programme of industrialization (Clark and Roy 1997).

During the first two decades of India's industrialization, the heavy industry and power and communication sector maintained a share of almost 60 per cent in total plan outlay, whereas the small-scale light manufacturing sector managed a share close to only 3 per cent for the first 15 years of planned investment outlay. This share continued to decline thereafter, reaching 0.5 per cent in 2000–01 (GOI, *Economic Survey*, 2003/04).

In India, during the early years of industrialization, industrial capacity expanded after 1951 for two decades, mainly through the creation of new capacities despite the existence of unutilized capacities in the existing units (Bhagwati and Desai 1971). The prevailing QR regime, with myriads of controls and regulations, inhibited the overall growth of the industrial sector until the mid-1980s by creating difficulties for the import of equipment and other inputs necessary for greater utilization of existing capacities and for facilitating the growth of exports of manufactured goods. The period from the mid-1960s to the mid-1980s witnessed a general stagnation in industrial activities (Ahluwalia 1985).

However, as the economy began to be slowly liberalized from the mid-1980s, the infrastructural bottlenecks began to adversely affect the performance of the industrial sector (Ahluwalia 1991a; GOI 1996). Power deficit remained at around 9 per cent during the mid-1990s. Along with the shortages in the supply of power, the supply of transport and communication facilities, and of outputs of a number of basic activities such as steel, coal, cargo handling and freight loading were unable to cope with the demand (RBI 2003).

THE TOOLS OF INDUSTRIAL POLICY

China

The tool that the government used to implement its industrial policy in the pre-reform period was the central allocation of investment funds and production materials. Industrial enterprises were issued mandatory output targets, the implementation of which was backed up by the central allocation of investment funds, fuel, production materials and foreign exchanges. In addition, the domestic market for the targeted industries was protected by high-tariff and non-tariff barriers. Price control was also used to promote the targeted industries. Prices of inputs for the heavy industries were deliberately kept low in order to subsidize their cost.

In line with the slow but steady transformation of the Chinese economic system from a planned economy to a market-orientated one, during the transition period the tools of the Chinese industrial policy also changed. For the government found it increasingly difficult to use a direct means of control, such as central planning and financing, direct financing, price control and administrative means to implement its industrial policy. Increased trade liberalization and the re-entry of China into the WTO also eliminated the leverage of the government to use the tool of trade protection as this was no longer acceptable to WTO. Consequently, the government found itself increasingly relying on the granting of financial and fiscal incentives in the form of preferential interest and tax rates and favourable finance conditions for targeted industries to implement its industrial policy (see Lu 2000, p. 5). These tools were similar to those used by the market-orientated economies of Japan and South Korea in the 1960s and 1970s to achieve their industrial policy objectives. Apart from fiscal and financial incentives, the Chinese government also uses the control of FDI to channel foreign funds, technology and other resources to the targeted industries.

In recent years (that is, the early 2000s), industrial reorganization has also become an important tool in China's industrial policy. For example, the government planned to develop some 30 to 50 large enterprises or enterprise groups through mergers and acquisitions (M&As) to compete successfully on the world market. These chosen enterprises benefited from being given a wide range of government assistance and support measures (see OECD 2002, p. 133).

India

Before India's independence in 1947, the Indian economy operated under a free market system, but, after India's independence, Nehru's socialist regime brought the economy under a centrally planned system of the Soviet type. Hence, public sector industry began to expand to take control of the main pillars of the economy and to move beyond to other areas of production. Resources to industries – finance, inputs and so on – were allocated and production targets were fixed centrally by the planning commission (Bhagwati and Desai 1971). The comprehensive QR regime ensured the survival of the industries by virtually eliminating international competition and the role of price mechanism. While such a policy had an in-built bias against efficiency, it allowed the public sector units to easily obtain all the resources, including imported inputs, and to expand without any economic rationale. But even the private sector's industrial development and investments have been directed by the state via physical controls operated primarily through an exhaustive licensing system combined with a setting of 'targets' by the planning commission in the course of the formulation of successive Five Year Plans.

The industrial policies and planning techniques during nearly the first two decades of Indian planning operated within a framework of detailed physical targets derived without reference to notions of costs and benefits in a systematic manner, supported by industrial licensing and trade policies designed to make corresponding investments profitable. Industrial licensing, which was concerned with excessive details, operated without any economic criteria to choose between alternative projects, and contributed to accentuation of the undesirable features of an unplanned expansion of industries. The excessive reliance on industrial licensing also led to a neglect of instruments for encouraging investments in priority areas.

Nevertheless, to encourage industries to export their products the industrial policy during this period also included export subsidization policies which essentially took two major forms: (1) fiscal measures, and (2) import entitlement schemes, entitling exporters to premium-carrying import licences. The fiscal measures included exemptions and refunds from indirect taxes (sales, customs and excises) available to exporters.

Through the 1980s, the rigidities of the industrial policy and centralized planning of the first two decades of India's development began to be slowly relaxed. Import policies were liberalized and tax concessions were granted to firms. Throughout almost the whole of the 1970s, under the draconian import control rules, all other imports except the consumer goods imports, which were mostly banned, and those under the 'Open General Licence' (OGL) list, which also included capital goods, had to be routed through the state trading corporation. There were also no uniform rules governing import of all intermediate goods as all types of these goods were placed under four categories – permissible, OGL, restricted and banned – requiring different regulations for processing these different kinds of intermediate goods imports. Chand and Sen's (2002) study on import liberalization reveals that since 1977–78 an increasingly large number of items of capital goods and intermediate goods which were under the 'restricted category', were continuously shifted to the OGL category, thereby allowing the domestic industries to obtain most of the imports relatively easily and at a lower cost as customs duties on items imported under the OGL category were subject to lower import duties. As a result the number of capital goods imports increased from only 79 in 1976 to 1170 in April 1988 – thereby recording an increase of 1381 per cent. Furthermore, throughout the 1980s, the import licensing rules for the capital goods imports were applied with less and less vigour (Pursell 1992) and a gradual increase in imports of capital and intermediate goods forced the domestic producers of intermediate goods to be more competitive by making their products more cost-efficient (World Bank

1989). However, it has to be noted that limited liberalization of imports that continued from 1977–78 to the end of the 1980s, was a back-door economic reform, not an openly declared reform. However, a substantial openly declared reform of India's industrial policy was undertaken in 1991 – as part of a whole package of reforms to improve the overall economic position.

NEW INDUSTRIAL POLICY 1991

In the aftermath of India's financial crisis in July 1991, the government took bold steps to free up the economy from the shackles of controls by abolishing the industrial licensing machinery and eliminating a large number of government-induced entry restrictions, licensing requirements and controls on corporate behaviour. The trade policy changes introduced made imported inputs cheaper and more accessible for industry, and exposed a large segment of India's industries to international competition. Many items of imports including intermediate goods and raw materials were brought under OGL and the peak import tariff on dutiable items came down initially from 150 per cent to 110 per cent, and continued to decline afterwards. The floor interest rate on commercial bank loans was reduced and government control over capital issues was withdrawn (GOI, *Economic Survey*, 2000/01). A number of other measures such as tax incentives to companies for industrial restructuring, tax holidays for industries in infrastructure and power transmission, incentives for attracting foreign investment and policies for gradual disinvestment in the public sector enterprises were introduced (GOI, *Economic Survey*, 2003/04).

The primary objective of these policy measures were to make the industrial sector efficient and capable of facing foreign competition by eliminating restrictions on their capabilities to grow. Nevertheless considerable restrictions remain on the autonomy and on the capacity of the industrial sector to reform. Indian tariffs still remain high by Asian and international standards, and the trade regime remains relatively restrictive. Furthermore the vastly expanding regulatory state was driven not only by the logic of regulation itself, but also by the pressures to expand state bureaucracy. This bureaucracy in turn created more regulations (Clark and Roy 1997). Hence although the licence, permit and quota Raj (Encarnation 1989; Evans 1995) have been abolished, the regulatory state has not completely disappeared (Kamath 1993b). These factors continue to adversely affect the performance of the industrial sector.

The licensing restrictions on consumer goods imports that were largely responsible for the high share of protected industries in mid-1995 had not been completely eliminated by 2002. India has been able to retain the restrictions on import of consumer goods on the ground of balance of payment deficit under Article XVIII-B of the General Agreement on Tariffs and Trade (GATT) rules governing the conduct of international trade activities by member countries. However the pressures from the USA, the European Union (EU) and the WTO are forcing the country to eliminate its restrictions on consumer goods imports. The arguments were put forward by political party leaders at the centre and at provincial levels, as well as by bureaucracy, consumer goods manufactures and leftist economists, that liberalization of imports of consumer goods by allowing the importation of a larger quantity of consumers goods will hurt the domestic import competing industries by draining India's foreign exchange reserves and the economy. However such arguments have been strongly repudiated by Little (1996) on the grounds that international competition has improved the efficiency of industries to eventually increase the size of the industry, and foreign exchange reserves have increased greatly. The principal reason, as Little suggests, is political. The vast majority of the population, including trade union leaders and political leaders, love to possess and consume better quality consumer goods, but their hypocrisy and the need to maintain their vote banks for retaining power after the next election and for regular flow of rents to them, prevent them from liberalizing import trade of consumer goods and from accelerating the pace of reform of the industrial sector. However despite the difficulties as mentioned above, the Indian government achieved considerable progress in the area of liberalization of the external trade sector in 2003–04 by reducing 'peak' customs tariffs on non-agricultural goods to 20 per cent and eliminating the special additional duty of customs (SAD) of 4 per cent (GOI, *Economic Survey*, 2003/04).

Outcome of Industrial Policy

China
In terms of the growth rate of the industrial sector Chinese industrial policy performance is impressive. Table 4.1 presents World Bank data to compare the growth rate of Chinese industry with that of its East Asian neighbours. Industry in this table comprises mining, manufacturing, construction, electricity, water and gas. In the period from 1960 to 2002 China's industrial growth averaged 12 per cent per year, which was overall the highest growth rate in the East Asian region. Only South Korea was able to approach the Chinese rate of growth during this period. It should be noted that official Chinese industrial growth data may be overestimated because Chinese industrial statistics suffer from several weaknesses (Field 1996, pp. 93–100; Maddison 1998). One of the main weaknesses is that it is based on gross value. Because there are no deductions for the cost of raw materials or

Table 4.1   The growth rate of industry[1] in selected Asian economies (%)

	1960–79	1980–90	1990–2002	1960–2000
China	10.0	11.1	12.6	11.6
Asian NICs:				
Singapore	10.5	5.2	7.3	7.9
South Korea	16.9	11.4	6.2	11.5
ASEAN 4:				
Malaysia	NA	6.8	7.5	7.7[2]
Thailand	11.1	9.8	4.9	8.7
Indonesia	8.3	7.3	4.5	6.9
Philippines	7.2	−0.9	3.5	3.2

Note: 1. Growth rate of real GDP of the industrial sector (mining, manufacturing, construction, electric power, water, gas supply).

Source: World Bank, *World Development Indicators*, 1981, pp. 136–7; 2002, pp. 204–6; 2004, table 4.1.

semi-finished inputs purchase from other enterprises or for capital depreci-ation, GVIO (gross value of industrial output) contains a substantial amount of double counting. Another main weakness is the factory report-ing method, under which the entire output of each enterprise is assigned to a single branch of industry irrespective of the nature of the goods actually produced. Despite the efforts of the State Statistical Bureau (SSB) to clean up the Chinese industrial growth data Wu (2002) found that the rate of growth of Chinese manufacturing sector was overestimated by nearly 1.6 per cent per annum during the post-reform period.

In terms of the rate of industrialization Chinese industrial policy perfor-mance is also impressive. The share of industry in China's GDP increased from 20 to 49 per cent between 1952 and 1998 (*ZGTJNJ* 1999, p. 56). By the year 2002, the Chinese rate of industrialization hit 51 per cent, which, according to World Bank data, is the highest in the East Asian region (see Table 4.2). It is well known that the rate of industrialization of a country follows an inverted u-curve pattern of development in relation to its per capita income. The share of industry in the GDP rises initially as the country's per capita income grows. The industrial share reaches its peak as a country becomes a middle-income country, and the share begins to fall as it further develops into a high-income country. China's national income per capita in the year 2000 in terms of purchasing power parity (PPP) – adjusted exchange rate was estimated to be US$3940 (World Bank, *World Development Indicators*, 2002, p. 232). Hence China can be classified as a

Table 4.2   The share of industry in GDP in 2002 (%)

China	51
Japan	31
Asian NICs:	
Hong Kong	13
Singapore	36
Taiwan	NA
South Korea	41
ASEAN 4:	
Malaysia	47
Thailand	43
Indonesia	44
Philippines	33
World	29
Low Income	30
Middle Income	34
High Income	27

Source: World Bank, *World Development Indicators*, 2004, table 4.2.

member of the group of middle-income countries. As Table 4.2 shows the Chinese rate of industrialization is not only the highest in the East Asian region, it is also more than 40 per cent higher than the average of the world's middle-income countries.

China's performance in industrial upgrading is also impressive. The structure of Chinese manufacturing is different from other developing countries. Unlike other middle-income countries in the world in which manufacturing structures are dominated by light industries, the share of heavy and chemical industries in China's manufacturing output is very high. In 2000, according to World Bank data, it was 42 per cent. This share is lower than that of the East Asian newly industrialized countries (NICs) with the exception of Hong Kong, but higher than that of most Association of South East Asian Nations (ASEAN) countries, with the exception of Malaysia (see Table 4.3).

However, in terms of productivity growth, Chinese industrial policy performance is mixed. During the pre-reform period, the productivity performance of Chinese industry was poor. Table 4.4 shows 'growth accounting' of Chinese industry. According to this, growth of the Chinese industry, $G(O)$, can be disaggregated into growth resulting from an increase in the amount of labour and capital employed, for example, $G(L)$ and $G(K)$

Table 4.3   The share of heavy and chemical industries in total manufacturing output in selected Asian countries, 2000 (%)

	Machinery and transport equipment	Chemicals	Total
China	30	12	42
Japan	39	10	49
Asian NICs:			
Hong Kong	33	4	37
Singapore	62	14	80
South Korea	45	9	55
ASEAN 4:			
Malaysia	46	11	57
Indonesia	25	11	36
Philippines	15	13	28

Source: World Bank, *World Development Indicators*, 2004, table 4.3.

respectively, and the rate of growth of total factor productivity or techno-logical progress expressed as a residual, t (see Mankiw 2003, p. 232):

$$G(O) = Ek\ G(K) + El\ G(L) + t \qquad (4.1)$$

where Ek and El are output elasticities of capital and labour.

During the pre-reform period (1952–79), $G(O)$ was 11.8 per cent and $G(K)$ and $G(L)$ were 12.4 and 8.3 per cent respectively. Hence the value of t for this period is only 1.8 per cent (see Table 4.4). Given the relatively low rate of growth of total factor productivity, most of the industrial growth in China in the pre-reform period can be explained by the relative increase in input of labour and capital. In other words, China's rapid industrialization in the past was achieved at very high cost because it was achieved through the huge sacrifice of leisure and consumption by the population.

The question arises as to why the rate of growth of total factor productivity was so low in the pre-reform era when the rate of industrialization was so high. This is due to a number of factors. One of the major reasons is undoubtedly the relative overdevelopment of capital-intensive heavy industries at the expense of the relatively labour-intensive light industries. Since this policy neglected the principle of comparative advantage, it had a deleterious consequence on the allocative efficiency of Chinese industry.

Another major factor is the defence-related industrialization strategy in the form of the 'third front construction' at the height of China's self-reliance

Table 4.4   Sources of growth in China's industry (%)

	1952–79	1980–98
G(O)	11.8	9.5
G(L)	8.3	1.8
G(K)	12.4	1.1
El G(L)	5.0	1.1
Ek G(K)	5.0	2.8
t	1.8	5.2

Notes:

G: annual average rate of growth.

O: real GDP of industry in 1990 prices obtained by inflating the nominal GDP of industry by industrial ex-factory price index.

L: number of persons employed in industrial production. Obtained by subtracting from the total number of persons employed in industry from the number of persons not involved in industrial production. The share of persons not engaged in industrial production is estimated at 16 per cent by Jefferson et al. (1996). This share is used to calculate L.

K: real fixed assets in industry used in industrial production in 1990 prices obtained by multiplying the total real assets in industry by the share of real fixed assets used for industrial production. The latter is estimated by Jefferson et al. (1996) at 82 per cent.

The total real fixed assets in industry is calculated according to the perpetual inventory formula, for example:

$$Kt = Ko - d\,Ko + It$$

where Kt is the current year's real fixed assets, d is the rate of depreciation which is assumed to be 4.4 per cent (see Jefferson et al. 1996). It is the real increment of fixed assets in the current year due to fixed asset investment. The real increment of fixed assets is obtained by deflating the nominal increase in fixed assets by the industrial ex-factory price index for the period prior to 1980 and by the fixed asset investment price index for the period after 1980.

El and Ek: output elasticity of labour and capital assumed to be 0.6 and 0.4 respectively (see Perkins 2001, p. 282).

t: growth rate of total factor productivity.

Sources: *ZGTJNJ*, various issues; *ZGGJTJZL*, various issues; *ZGGDZCTZIJZL*, various issues.

period between 1964 and 1971. As Naughton (1988) shows, most of the massive industrial investments in the remote regions of South West China were wasted because of the relative lack in that region not only of infrastructural facilities but also of fuels and other raw materials. In addition, the region hardly had any marketing outlets. Moreover, workers relocated to the area had to live and work in inhospitable conditions.

Yet another factor that explains the relatively low rate of growth of overall factor productivity during this period of industrialization was the inefficiency of China's industrial organization. The majority of China's industrial enterprises were state owned in the pre-reform period. Thus they were operating under a centralized planning system with a soft budget constraint and were facing hardly any competitive pressure. Thus enterprises did not aim at profit maximization but at fulfilment of the output targets to the neglect of quality and cost. In order to fulfil their output targets, enterprises would constantly search for slack and hoarding of inputs, and engaged in excessive vertical integration (see Rawski 1975, p. 7). Enterprises also had a very little incentive to innovate as successful innovation would invite the planning authorities to ratchet up their output target in the following period.

Finally, the self-reliance strategy practised by China in its international economic relations during this period cut off China's contact with new technologies developed in the Western world and contributed to widening the technological gap between China and the industrialized countries.

However, the productivity performance of China's industry improved significantly in the post-reform period. As indicated in Table 4.4, between 1980 and 2000 $G(O)$ is 9.5 per cent, $G(K)$ 7 per cent, and $G(L)$ only 1.8 per cent. Hence t climbed up to 5.2 per cent. Thus the growth of TFP or technological progress accounted for almost 60 per cent of China's industrial growth in this period.

What caused the accelerated productivity growth of China's industries during the reform? First, the organizational overhaul of China's industrial system itself undoubtedly played a significant role. While the process of reform in the Eastern European economies after the collapse of communism is similar to that of China, the reform of the industrial system in China followed a much slower and gradual approach. There was no wholesale privatization of China's state-owned industrial enterprises. As mentioned earlier, China instead adopted a two-pronged strategy to reform its industrial SOEs. First, small SOEs were sold to private entrepreneurs; whereas the state retained the ownership title of large-scale and medium-sized SOEs but their managerial rights were contracted out. Several studies (see Chai and Tisdell 1999; Jefferson and Rawski 1994) confirm that the contracting-out of the managerial rights of large and medium-sized SOEs contributed positively to the growth in their efficiency. According to these studies, the SOEs under contract gained increased autonomy in their input, output, finance and investment decisions. Moreover, their profit incentive was significantly enhanced as they were allowed to retain an increased proportion of their profits. This increased autonomy and profit retention induced managers to strengthen incentives for workers. And this, coupled with increasing competitive pressures from a growing non-state sector, resulted in a considerable increase in their productive efficiency.

Second, the government promoted the development of small and medium-sized non-state enterprises (NSEs). These newly developed NSEs have proved to be more efficient and productive than the partially privatized

SOEs (see Jefferson and Rawski 1994, p. 56). Furthermore the presence of NSEs has exerted a strong competitive pressure on SOEs to improve their efficiency.

Third, the shift from an unbalanced industrial development strategy to a more balanced one in the reform period, with due emphasis on both the heavy and light industries, also contributed significantly to the surge of productivity in recent years (that is, the early 2000s) as this has helped Chinese industry to enhance its allocative efficiency.

Last but not least, the abandonment of the old policy of self-reliance and its substitution by an open-door policy gave a strong boost to Chinese industrial productivity. The open-door policy, and especially the establishment of Special Economic Zones (SEZs) helped to attract a massive inflow of foreign direct investment in the industrial sector. The impact of FDI on China's industrial development in the reform period can be seen from the growing share of FDI in China's gross domestic capital formation, from less than 1 per cent in 1983 to 11 per cent in 1999 (OECD 2002, p. 325). The growing share of FDI accelerated the transfer of Western technology and managerial know-how into Chinese industries.

The open-door policy also caused an increased share of exports in Chinese industrial output. The evidence from several cross-country studies indicates that the growth in industrial exports has a strong positive correlation with the productivity growth of domestic industries. This is because the competition in world markets exerts a strong pressure on domestic industries to adopt the best practices in manufacturing and to improve production efficiency. Furthermore, a growth in exports also increases foreign exchange earnings which enable domestic industries to finance the imports of advanced technology.

The objective of China's industrial policy in recent years (that is, the early 2000s) is to strengthen the international competitiveness of its domestic manufacturing industries. To what extent has this objective been achieved so far?

A number of studies on the competitiveness of Chinese manufacturing have been conducted recently because of China's entry into the WTO. Some of them found that the Chinese manufacturing industries are uncompetitive, especially in comparison with those of the Organisation for Economic Co-operation and Development (OECD) countries (OECD 2002, ch. 4; Yu and Zheng 2000). Others, such as Lall (2001), however, found that in comparison with other developing countries China's manufacturing industries are very competitive.

The lack of consensus on the competitiveness of China's industries is largely due to the absence of a set of common criteria in the measurement of competitiveness. The most frequently used criterion is the given level of labour productivity. However, this criterion is fraught with technical measurement problems. Moreover, the level of productivity depends heavily on the labour-capital ratio and the level of technology adopted by a country's industries, both of which are conditioned by the country's stage of development. Hence it is not meaningful to compare a developing country like China's level of productivity with that of more advanced countries like those of the OECD. Finally, a relatively low level of labour productivity does not necessarily prevent a country's industry out-competing the industries of developed countries, as the disadvantage of low labour productivity can be more than offset by the advantage of a relatively low wage level. In the case of South Korea, for example, the McKinsey Global Institute found that its industrial labour productivity in the years 1975, 1987 and 1997 was almost 30 per cent lower than that of its US counterparts, and yet this did not prevent Korea from competing successfully in the international market as its share of world manufacturing exports increased markedly from nil in 1963 to 3 per cent in 1995.

Another popular measure of competitiveness is the 'competitiveness index' used for example in the *World Competitiveness Report* by the World Economic Forum. This index is based on a large number of variables and should, therefore, provide a more balanced assessment. However, many of these variables, according to Lall (2001, p. 10), are fairly subjective and impressionistic, and are drawn exclusively from comments of business executives. This index normally ranks countries in terms of their investment environment for international investors and thus is not a good instrument by which to measure a country's real economic efficiency.

Yet another measurement of competitiveness is the innovation capability (see Yusuf and Evenett 2002). However, innovation by itself does not guarantee commercial success. This is evidenced, for example, by the case of Japan which has been very successful in innovation over the last ten years as it has had a record number of patents filed and acquired every year over the last decade (see Posen 2001, p. 30); yet it still suffers from ten years of lost growth and even experienced a declining share in world manufacturing exports (see Porter et al. 2000, p. 9).

In view of the ambiguity in the existing indexes of competitiveness, Lall (2001) proposes the adoption of the relative manufactured export performance as the better indicator of a country's industrial competitiveness. This indicator is not only more manageable, it is also less ambiguous as export data are more accurate and more easily available. Lall (2001) measures the manufactured export performance of a country in terms of both quantity and quality. A country is first ranked according to its share of world manufactured exports and then in terms of its quality. The latter is measured in terms of a country's ability to upgrade its export structure from low-technology, low-skill and largely labour-intensive products to high-technology, high-skill and capital-intensive products.

Table 4.5 presents the findings of his study. These indicate that the Chinese achievements, measured in terms of both criteria, are very impressive in recent years (that is, the early 2000s). In terms of quantity, the total manufactured exports for China in 1985 ranked tenth in the developing world and its share in total developing world manufactured exports was even lower than that of India. But by 1998 China had replaced Taiwan as the top performer of manufactured exports in Third World countries. In the same year, China also started to lead the developing countries in resource-based and low-tech manufactured exports. Though Chinese manufactured exports were still dominated by low-tech products which accounted for more than 50 per cent of its total manufactured exports in 1998 (Lall 2001, p. 126), it has doubled its share of the medium-tech manufactured exports from 12 to 20 per cent between 1985 and 1998 and that of high-tech products from 5 to 20 per cent between 1985 and 1998 (see Lall 2001, p. 126). Consequently, China's position in the developing world in terms of medium-tech manufactured exports has jumped from tenth to third position, and in terms of high-tech exports from eighth to fourth position. By 1998, China's share in exports of high-tech products in the developing world was equal to Malaysia's and not far behind that of Singapore, which was the leader of the group in high-tech exports of the developing countries.

However, the use of export performance to measure a country's industrial competitiveness needs to be qualified by taking into consideration the following factors: (a) the technological depth of high-tech exports and (b) the role of multinational companies (MNCs) in high-tech activities. High-tech exports do not necessarily indicate a country's advancement in terms of technological capabilities if it simply comprises of simple labour-intensive processes such as the assembly of high-tech products originated in foreign countries. Similarly, the role of MNCs in high-tech exports is equally important in the measurement of domestic technological production capability for high-tech exports. In both aspects, Chinese high-tech exports compare favourably with those of Singapore and Malaysia. Though Singapore is ranked first in high-tech exports in the developing world group, most of its goods are simply driven by MNCs. In 1994, for example, MNCs accounted for 90 per cent of its manufactured exports (Ramstetter 1994). The situation is only slightly better for Malaysia, where MNC activity accounted for 70 per cent of its manufactured exports (Ramstetter 1994). Moreover, Malaysia's high-tech exports are mainly driven by electronics and electrical assembly activity in export processing zones, which have a low-level linkage and content to the domestic industry. In contrast, the share of MNCs in China's total manufactured exports in

Table 4.5a Manufacturing exports of the top 13 countries in the developing world, 1985

Total manufactures		Resource based manufactures		Low-tech manufactures		Medium-tech manufactures		High-tech manufactures	
Country	% share	Country	% share	Country	% share	Country	% share	Country	% share
1. Taiwan	13.9	1. Singapore	10.3	1. Taiwan	24.1	1. S. Korea	24.9	1. Taiwan	20.4
2. S. Korea	13.8	2. Brazil	9.7	2. S. Korea	18.8	2. Taiwan	14.1	2. Singapore	20.2
3. Singapore	9.0	3. Venezuela	7.3	3. Hong Kong	15.8	3. Brazil	12.1	3. S. Korea	16.1
4. Brazil	8.4	4. Malaysia	5.8	4. Brazil	5.9	4. Singapore	10.3	4. Hong Kong	10.3
5. Hong Kong	7.6	5. Algeria	5.0	5. Turkey	4.8	5. Mexico	8.3	5. Malaysia	10.1
6. Malaysia	4.1	6. Kuwait	4.7	6. India	4.4	6. Hong Kong	7.0	6. Mexico	8.1
7. Mexico	4.0	7. S. Arabia	4.6	7. China	4.1	7. Turkey	3.1	7. Brazil	3.8
8. Venezuela	3.4	8. Indonesia	3.6	8. Singapore	2.6	8. Malaysia	2.3	8. China	1.4
9. India	3.0	9. Taiwan	3.5	9. Pakistan	2.3	9. Thailand	1.9	9. Philippines	1.2
10. China	2.9	10. India	3.2	10. Thailand	2.0	10. China	1.7	10. India	1.1
11. Turkey	2.8	11. S. Korea	3.1	11. Mexico	1.7	11. Argentina	1.6	11. Niger	0.8
12. S. Arabia	2.0	12. China	2.9	12. Macau	1.2	12. India	1.4	12. Thailand	0.7
13. Algeria	1.9	13. Argentinia	2.8	13. Malaysia	1.1	13. Venezuela	1.3	13. Argentina	0.6

Source: Lall 2001, p. 124.

Table 4.5b   Manufacturing exports of the top 13 countries in the developing world, 1998

Total manufactures		Resource based manufactures		Low-tech manufactures		Medium-tech manufactures		High-tech manufactures	
Country	% share	Country	% share	Country	% share	Country	% share	Country	% share
1. China	16.8	1. China	9.5	1. China	30.2	1. S. Korea	18.3	1. Singapore	21.5
2. S. Korea	12.1	2. Brazil	8.8	2. Taiwan	11.6	2. Mexico	17.9	2. Taiwan	13.3
3. Taiwan	10.6	3. Singapore	8.3	3. S. Korea	9.1	3. China	13.3	3. S. Korea	12.4
4. Mexico	10.4	4. S. Korea	7.4	4. Mexico	7.2	4. Taiwan	11.4	4. Malaysia	11.8
5. Singapore	10.3	5. Malaysia	6.3	5. Turkey	4.8	5. Singapore	7.6	5. China	11.5
6. Malaysia	6.6	6. S. Arabia	6.1	6. Hong Kong	4.7	6. Brazil	5.7	6. Mexico	10.8
7. Thailand	4.5	7. Indonesia	6.0	7. India	4.5	7. Malaysia	5.3	7. Philippines	6.5
8. Brazil	3.9	8. Thailand	4.9	8. Thailand	4.1	8. Thailand	3.6	8. Thailand	5.4
9. Philippines	2.8	9. India	4.5	9. Indonesia	3.2	9. Argentina	2.1	9. Hong Kong	2.1
10. Indonesia	2.7	10. Mexico	4.0	10. Singapore	2.6	10. Indonesia	2.0	10. Brazil	1.1
11. India	2.6	11. Argentina	3.5	11. Malaysia	2.5	11. Turkey	1.9	11. Indonesia	0.9
12. Hong Kong	2.3	12. S. Africa	3.3	12. Pakistan	2.3	12. S. Africa	1.6	12. India	0.6
13. Turkey	2.2	13. Taiwan	3.2	13. Brazil	2.1	13. India	1.5	13. Turkey	0.5

Source: Lall 2001, p. 124.

the mid-1990s was just above 55 per cent (Lardy 1995) and therefore relatively lower than that of Malaysia and Singapore. Furthermore, the local content of Chinese high-tech exports is much higher. For example, the local content in the manufacture of colour televisions in Malaysia is around 30 per cent (Lall 2001, p. 323), while in China it is more than 95 per cent (Gao 2003, p. 252).

India

India's industrial performance has lagged far behind that of China. In Table 4.6, we compare the growth rate of China's industry with that of India's industry.

As Table 4.6 shows, since 1970, the rate of growth recorded by China's industrial sector was consistently higher than that recorded by India's industrial sector. In the 1970s and the 1990s the growth rate of China's industries was more than double the rate recorded by India's industries. In Table 4.7 we present a comparative picture of the share of industry in GDP of China and India since 1965.

As Table 4.7 shows, even in 1965, when the Chinese economy was under Stalinist-type planning and total state control of industrial production, the contribution of industry to GDP was 39 per cent compared with 22 per cent for India. In 1980, when China's transition to a market economy had just begun, the share of industry in its GDP reached 40 per cent compared with only 26 per cent for India, and by 2000 this share for China was more than 50 per cent – more than double the contribution of India's industrial sector to its GDP.

In terms of industrial upgrading, India's achievement was impressive too. In 1990, the share of heavy and chemical and other manufacturing in total manufacturing reached 77 per cent, but in 2000 it declined to 73 per cent mainly because of the decline in the share of chemical industries to 7 per cent in 2000 from 12 per cent in 1990 (World Bank, *World Development Indicators*, 2003).

Table 4.6   Growth rate of industry in China and India

Year	China	India
1970–80	9.6	4.6
1980–90	11.1	7.1
1990–2002	12.6	6.0

Sources: GOI, *Economic Survey*, various issues; RBI 2003; *World Development Indicators*, various issues; *World Development Report*, various issues.

Table 4.7   Share of industry in GDP: China and India (%)

Year	China	India
1965	39.0	22.0
1970	NA	22.0
1980	40.0	26.0
1990	41.6	29.3
1995	48.0	29.0
2000	51.0	25.0
2002	51.0	27.0

Source: as for Table 4.6.

In terms of productivity growth, India's record also has been mixed. During the reform period, 1990–2001, India managed an annual growth rate in industrial output of only 6.1 per cent compared with 7.1 per cent growth rate in the pre-reform decade of 1980–90. In comparison, the industrial growth in China between 1990 and 2001 averaged 13.1 per cent compared with 11.1 per cent in the pre-reform period. Hence, it is rather surprising to note that the industrial output grew at a lower rate during the reform period than during the decade preceding the reform period in India.

Making comments on the total factor productivity of the industrial economy is not an easy task. The parameter in Solow's model (1957) is meant to capture the effects of things other than the capital stock and labour supply that might influence growth, such as government policies, institutions and the level of technology (Perkins et al., 2001). For example, efficiency can be improved by changing policies such as removing price subsidies that distort resource allocation, strengthening institutions such as judiciary and law enforcement agencies, political institutions, enterprise governance, or by introducing new technologies (including improvements in productive techniques and the introduction of products with improved quality and so on). The TFP represents a combination of all these influences that the TFP analysis cannot entirely disentangle.

So the question that one has to ask is whether the improvement in TFP can be attributed to a single variable such as better trade and exchange rate policies, or improvements in enterprise governance or effective enforcement of property rights or introduction of better technologies. Within the limited growth accounting framework these questions cannot be answered without adding many more variables for which data do not exist. Hence the parameter 'A' rather than truly being TFP growth, is simply that part of measured growth that cannot be explained by data or the traditional factors of production such as labour and capital.

The contribution of labour and capital to productivity growth depends greatly on the institutional environment within which labour and capital are employed to generate wealth. The presence of infrastructural bottlenecks, which is frequently cited by the government of India as the reason for low growth in industrial productivity, is untenable because the same bottlenecks also exist in China but the industries there achieve higher growth in productivity.

In India, all institutions have been systematically used by the state (government) at the federal and at provincial levels to satisfy the greed of political leaders, party hierarchy and the bureaucrats, and to support the directly unproductive profit-seeking activities since Indira Gandhi assumed power in New Delhi (Bhagwati 1982; 1993; Roy and Tisdell 1998; *The Statesmen Weekly* 1996). The neoclassical theory of total factor productivity is based on the implicit assumption that the state will be able to formulate the rules and regulations which will set the parameters within which wealth-generating economic activities will be carried out, and an independent and neutral judiciary and law enforcement agency (police force) will enforce these rules. But this neoclassical assumption of separation of power between the executive and judiciary and law enforcement agencies is no longer valid in India and South Asia today (that is, in 2004). Hence, even if the state can formulate these rules and regulations, the judiciary is unable to enforce them.

On the other hand, the state in China has been able to provide the appropriate institutional environment for directly productive profit-making (DPP) activities to grow to a far greater extent than in India. According to one study (Collins and Bosworth 1996), the total factor productivity in the whole of South Asia during the periods 1973–84 and 1984–94 were 1.2 and 1.5 compared with 2.2 and 4.6 for China during the same periods. Since the total factor productivity in South Asia is overwhelmingly influenced by that in India, the estimate can be accepted as a good approximation to factor productivity for India. A recent study on total factor productivity in the manufacturing industries in India between 1974–75 and 1993–94 has shown that the highest average annual growth rate in TFP of 2.7 per cent was recorded by food products. Transport equipment, non-metallic products and electrical machinery recorded 2.2, 2.04 and 1.9 per cent respectively. However, Chand and Sen (2002), in their study on productivity growth in Indian manufacturing after trade liberalization in the early 1970s, have brought into the open the total factor productivity debate in the Indian industrial sector by pointing out in these studies deficiencies such as: (1) lack of attention to a theoretical mechanism through which policy is supposed to impact on productivity growth (Rodrick 1995), and (2) lack of reliable measures of trade policy changes (Edwards 1993). The use of dummy variable by Ahluwalia (1991b) and Harrison (1994) to differentiate the post-reform period from the pre-reform period, for measuring trade policy changes has been considered by Chand and Sen as inadequate, as trade reform in India was a gradual process and not introduced in one attempt. In their analysis of the impact of trade policy change on TFP growth, Chand and Sen tried to examine the effect of import liberalization on worker's work effort, that is, whether the workers increased their working hours and productivity due to the competition faced by their products from import substitutes and to their increasing access to more sophisticated capital and intermediate goods. While their study of TFP growth in Indian manufacturing covered 30 industries over a period of 15 years from 1973 to 1988, these industries were mostly in the intermediate and capital goods category as consumer goods imports were highly restrictive.

However, in response to this criticism the authors argued that these 30 industries accounted for 53 per cent of gross value added and 45 per cent of total employment in the Indian manufacturing sector, and included consumer goods industries during the period under study. The results of their study show that that TFP growth in all three industry groups resulting from import liberalization was quite robust during 1984–88, with capital goods, intermediate goods and consumer goods recording TFP growth of 4.9, 4.6 and 3.9 per cent respectively. This result reflects the relative levels of decline in tariffs in the three groups of industries and compares very favourably with the TPF growth of −2.2, 0.7 and 0.04 per cent for the same groups of industries during the period of 1974–78 when the reduction in tariffs on imports of capital, intermediate and consumer goods was very marginal.

However, although this study of Chand and Sen was more procedurally accurate than the earlier studies, it would have provided us with a better picture of TFP growth in India's manufacturing industries if there was an indication in the analysis of the relative growth in factor productivity in public sector enterprises (PSEs) and non-PSEs among the 30 industries used for their study. Nevertheless the conclusion that emerges from all these studies is that the liberalization of import of intermediate and capital goods contributed positively to a reasonable growth in total factor productivity in India's manufacturing sector.

Table 4.5a illustrates that, as an indicator of industrial competitiveness, India's share in the manufactured export in the developing world was marginally higher than that of China in 1985, but by 1998, while India's share declined by 0.4 per cent to 2.6 per cent China's share increased by 13.9 per cent to 16.8 per cent.

India's share in high-tech exports of the developing world, as shown in Table 4.5b, was negligible and the second lowest among the top 13 exporting countries. However India's share in the world export of manufacturers and high-technology goods declined to less than 1 per cent. In 2003 India's share of manufactured exports and high-tech exports in its total merchandise export stood at 75 per cent and 5 per cent respectively, while for China the respective shares were 90 per cent and 23 per cent. But in the same year while India's manufactured exports and high-technology goods exports accounted for only 0.7 and 0.2 per cent of the world export of manufactured goods and high-technology goods, China's manufactured exports and high-technology goods exports accounted for 6.8 and 6.4 of the world export in these categories.[1] Also for the same year the share of merchandise export of China and India in the total world merchandise export stood at 5.9 per cent and 0.7 per cent respectively (World Bank, *World Development Indicators*, 2004). But local content in India's high-tech exports has generally been maintained and the role of MNCs in India's high-tech manufacturing exports has not been significant.

In conclusion, therefore, it can be said that by all accounts China's industrial policy has overwhelmingly been superior to that of India's. It has been commensurate with the needs of a highly activist East Asian developmental state which is aspiring to replace the USA as the world's economic superpower in 50 years' time. In contrast, India's policy has been that of a semi-predatory and semi-developmental state without any apparent aim of reaching such a high goal.

NOTE

1. The 2002 shares of manufactured and high-technology goods exports of India and China in their total merchandise exports have been used to derive the relative values of manufactured exports and high-technology exports of these two countries in their total value of merchandise exports in 2003.

5. Foreign trade and investment

Chinese and Indian experience with foreign trade and investment provides valuable lessons for other large developing countries. Both countries in the past have achieved modern economic growth without large-scale trade participation and foreign direct investment. Their changing foreign trade and investment strategies in recent years have had a profound impact on their economy. The purpose of this chapter is to trace the evolution of Chinese and Indian foreign trade and investment policies during the past 50 years, analyse the factors behind the changing pattern of foreign trade of both countries and assess the role of foreign trade and investment in both countries' economic growth.

CHINA'S TRADE REGIME

China had adopted an ultra-import substitution strategy in the form of autarky or self-reliance during 1949–78. Under this strategy, trade was regarded as a necessary evil. Imports were used to end imports, and exports were merely carried out to pay for imports. Hence, trade was limited as much as possible.

The self-reliance policy adopted during this period was conditioned by several factors. One of the factors was military-strategic consideration. The possession of a comprehensive and independent industrial capacity was considered vital for the survival of Chinese socialism as this enabled China to defend its own territory and, at the same time, to project the superiority of the socialist system to its population (Riskin 1987, p. 205). The general hostile international environment facing China in the early 1950s and 1960s also prompted a self-reliance policy.

The trade system adopted during this period was the command state trading system. Foreign trade was centrally planned and conducted by 12 centralized national foreign trade corporations (FTCs). All foreign exchange earned had to be surrendered to the central authority at the artificially low official exchange rate, and the use of foreign exchange for imports had to be authorized by the government. Chinese domestic prices were divorced from the foreign prices through an arbitrary internal pricing system. On the export side, the FTCs procured commodities from domestic producers at internal prices set by the government. The FTCs sold the export commodities at foreign prices on the world market. Any discrepancy between converted foreign prices at the official exchange rate and internal prices constituted profits or loss for FTCs which were then absorbed by the state budget under the 'Preisausgleich' practice as either profit delivery or subsidies. On the import side, FTCs procured commodities at foreign prices and sold them to domestic end-users at internal prices of domestically produced equivalents. Again, any profits or losses made by FTCs owing to the discrepancy between converted foreign prices at the official exchange rate and internal prices were absorbed by the state budget as either profit delivery or subsidy. As the RMB was overvalued during most of the period most domestic prices for traded goods were above world market levels and, consequently, most FTCs made profits on imports, which were used to cover losses on exports (World Bank 1988a, p. 97).

From late 1978, China cast off its self-reliance policy and adopted the open-door policy. Under the new policy, foreign trade and investment were seen as augmenting domestic resources and providing an additional source for rapid economic growth through the realization of their static and dynamic gains. Hence trade and investment were to be maximized whenever possible.

The kind of trade strategy adopted by China under the open-door policy is a dual strategy. While the import substitution strategy was still relied on, a nation-wide export orientation strategy was applied to special areas and enterprises (Naughton 1996). The special areas included the five Special Economic Zones (SEZs) (Shenzhen, Zuhai, Shantou, Xiamen and Hainan Island), the numerous Technical and Economic Development Zones and 14 bonded zones set up in the open coastal cities. The special enterprises included the Sino-foreign joint venture export enterprises, Chinese enterprises specializing in export-processing trade and those located in export production bases. Anti-export biases were removed in these special areas and enterprises through import liberalization and compensatory financial incentives for exports. Firms operating in these areas and specializing in exports were offered numerous incentives which included duty-free imports of raw materials, intermediate products, and capital goods, tax-free domestic inputs for exports, access to working capital and investment financing, accelerated depreciation schedule, and lower income taxes (World Bank 1988a, p. 183).

Under the open-door policy, China's trade system also changed. Initial changes carried out in the 1980s were modest. They aimed to transform the centralized command state trading system into a loose state trading system. To loosen up the old command state trading system, first the scope of foreign trade planning was reduced. On the eve of the reform in 1978, on the export side, the foreign trade plan covered some 3000 commodities. By the late 1980s only 112 commodities were still subject to centralized planning and the share of the planned commodities in China's total exports had shrunk to 45 per cent (Lardy 1992, p. 702). On the import side, the number of commodities under the foreign trade plan was cut down to only 17 items and their share in total imports was down to 40 per cent (Lardy 1992, p. 702).

Second, the foreign trade monopoly by the 12 national FTCs had been broken up through the decentralization of trading rights. The number of enterprises with trading rights increased sharply to 4000 in 1990 (Chai and Sun 1993, p. 3).

Third, domestic prices were increasingly linked to the foreign prices through the introduction of the agency system in 1984. Under this system FTCs acted as agents in importing and exporting commodities on behalf of domestic enterprises on commission. Hence, domestic end-users were charged at, and domestic producers received, the foreign price equivalent. On the eve of the reforms only 20 per cent of all importable and exportable commodities had their domestic prices based on world market prices. By the early 1990s, the percentage share of import and export commodities, which had their domestic prices, based on the foreign prices had risen to between 80 and 90 per cent respectively (*CP* 1992, p. 19).

Last but not least, the rigid centralized foreign exchange control system was loosened through the introduction of the foreign exchange retention system and parallel foreign exchange markets. Under the foreign exchange retention system, domestic enterprises contributing to foreign exchange earnings were allocated a foreign exchange use quota in proportion to the foreign exchange earned. In order to use the quota, enterprises had to use RMB to buy back the foreign exchange from the state bank at the official exchange rate. The foreign exchange purchases, subject to the approval of the higher authorities, could then be used to import goods or could be sold for domestic currency at the parallel foreign exchange market. As the parallel market rate was higher than the official rate, enterprises provided with a foreign exchange use quota were able to receive a certain amount of quota rent. Initially only 25 per cent of foreign exchange earned was allowed to be retained. By 1991, the foreign exchange retention quota was raised to 80 per cent (HKTDC 1991, p. 17).

Formal parallel foreign exchange markets or swap centres existed as early as 1985. In these centres enterprises could sell the surplus of its retained foreign exchange to another enterprise at the market rate. By 1992, more than 100 swap centres had been established in all of China's major cities and more than 70 per cent of foreign exchange used by Chinese firms was already traded and priced at the market rate (Chai and Sun 1993, p. 7).

With the increased decentralization of trading rights and foreign exchange use rights, the mode of the state control over import and export decision had changed from that of plan control to that of direct and indirect trade controls. Direct trade controls consisting of an import and export licensing system were introduced in 1980 to control the growth of outside-plan imports and exports.

The indirect trade controls consisted of import and export tax. The average (unweighted) tariff rate for imports was 38.4 per cent in 1986 (World Bank 1988a, p. 149). Since the tariff structure was cascading with duties of finished products significantly higher than those of raw materials and intermediate products, the effective rate of protection was much higher and was between 53 and 68 per cent in 1986 (World Bank 1988a, p. 154).

From the early 1990s, China's trade strategy entered a new phase of development. In an attempt to regain its membership of GATT, China had stepped up the pace of its import liberalization. In 1991, the tariff was reduced for 45 import commodities (*CM*, no. 6 1992, p. 10). In 1992, tariffs on another 225 import commodities were cut and, as a result, the average import tariff was reduced by 7.3 per cent (*CM*, no. 6 1992, p. 10). At the same time, China has also stepped up its effort to achieve a realistic exchange rate for the RMB and its convertibility. In 1994 the RMB was sharply devalued and the restriction on swap rate was abolished in an attempt to achieve a unified exchange rate. In 1996, the RMB became convertible on the current account.

After a long and protracted negotiation, which lasted for almost 15 years, China's long march to membership of the WTO came to an end with the signing of US–China bilateral WTO accord in 1999, and in 2001 China was formally admitted into the WTO.

Admission into the WTO commits China to significantly reduce its tariff barriers (TBs) in both industrial and agricultural commodities. The average tariff for agricultural commodities is scheduled to be reduced from an average of 19 per cent in 2001 to 15 per cent in 2005. As for industrial goods, the average tariff is due to be cut from 15 to 9 per cent during the same period (OECD 2002, table A.1.1).

Admission to the WTO also commits China to significantly reduce its non-tariff barriers (NTBs) on both agricultural and industrial goods. Finally, admission also means that the scope of its state trading will be drastically reduced. Three years after admission, all enterprises, regardless of whether they are private, state owned or foreign owned, will have the right to sell goods throughout China. However, state trading will continue for a small range of basic agricultural and other key commodities (OECD 2002, table A.1.2). Nonetheless, China has committed itself to all state-owned enterprises making their trading decisions solely on commercial consideration and that the government will not interfere directly or indirectly with their decisions.

THE INDIAN TRADE REGIME

India's trade and investment regime was similar to that of China for almost 40 years since the Soviet-style planned development programme began with the commencement of the First Five Year Plan in 1951. Nehru, an avowed socialist, was bent on imposing on India, a state controlled and directed self-reliant development, with the primary objective of alleviating the poverty of the masses by bringing the highly capital-intensive 'basic and key' industries of the economy and economic power under control while, at the same time, preventing concentration of the same economic power in the private sector, thereby virtually eliminating any chance of growth in the competitive industrial sector (Bhagwati and Desai 1971; Clark and Roy 1997; Roy 1986; Roy et al. 1992; 1995).

This state control of the highly capital-intensive 'basic and key' industries of the economy under Stalinist centralized planning combined with comprehensive and pervasive economic and social controls on the private sector, stunted economic growth. Confiscatory tax rates with escalating controls in the 1960s produced one of the world's largest and most thriving underground economies, accounting for around 50 per cent of economic activity. This statist development policy led to systematic neglect and suppression of voluntary exchange and market activity, although the law of the land upholds private property rights individual and firm (Kamath 1993b).

Controls under Nehru's socialist planning included strict controls on individual licensing; restrictions on capacity expansion; controls on monopoly and restrictive practices covering even normal non-monopoly trade practices; price and distribution controls; and comprehensive external sector controls, including an elaborate import licensing system, prohibitive tariffs and direct controls over allocation and utilization of foreign exchange.

The import and exchange control policy regime, in the immediate aftermath of the foreign exchange crisis of 1957, aimed at comprehensive, direct control over foreign exchange utilization. For the overwhelming bulk of imports, the government did not explicitly aim at using tariffs to siphon off the resulting import premia. While the allocation of permissible imports was effected broadly by two administrative categories – private sector and public sector – there was further operational distinction between imports of raw materials, spares and components, as against imports of capital goods and equipment. Allocation of these different permissible imports by these categories among industries, and further still by firms and plants, was carried out by an elaborate administrative machinery which evolved through the period from the mid-1950s to the end of the 1960s. After leaving aside the amount required to meet the first charge, the available foreign exchange was allocated among different user units, all of which had to process import applications through three licence-issuing authorities which disposed of the overwhelming bulk of licences under two main categories – Established Importers (EI) and Actual Users (AU) – which again were broken down into a number of categories.

The tasks of granting import licences and allocating foreign exchange among alternative claimants and uses in a direct control system should be carried out with reference to a well-defined set of principles and criteria based on a system of priorities. However, in India, there had been few such criteria which had been followed in practice. In the absence of any clear economic criteria for determining import allocations, the most likely *modus operandi* had been to go by single administrative rule, history and 'pragmatism' at the decision level (Bhagwati and Desai 1971). In the case of consumer goods, although their direct import was severely restricted, this was offset by the growth in domestic production of the same and other manufacturers. The import allocation system which operated right up to the mid-1980s, by and large, had eliminated the possibility of domestic competition as well as foreign competition. The latter was ruled out by the use of the principle of indigenous availability under which every item of indigenous production, even if its cost of production exceeded the landed price ex-duty of the imported item, was automatically shielded from competition through imports, the onus being placed on the buyer to show conclusively that he/she could not buy the product from indigenous producers.

Furthermore, any producer willing to declare his/her unit's production capacity and actual production known to the relevant authority in charge of indigenous clearance could anticipate automatic protection of the unit regardless of its costs, efficiency and comparative advantage. Hence, such an import policy served to divorce market-determined investment decisions from any guidelines that international opportunity costs might otherwise have provided.

Since, during the period of extensive import control of the 1960s, the import premia (difference between the market price and landed cost gross of duty) as a percentage of cost, insurance and freight (cif) price was quite large for almost all commodities, the use of an explicit tariff had been virtually discontinued. However, implicit nominal tariff rates did rise by 300–400 per cent in some cases and the effective tariff rates rose even further. Since the business and industry groups, politicians and bureaucrats benefited enormously from this stringent import control regime, which provided them with a protected domestic market, they actively lobbied for the continuation of this regime (Bhagwati and Desai 1971). Considerable restrictions were also placed on India's export trade during the first two decades of India's development.

The domestic policies of the government through export controls and quotas, export duties and inflationary pressures aimed at promoting domestic consumption were responsible for inhibiting the expansion of export earnings. While there was a sluggishness in world exports of many items of India's traditional exports, India, due to the policies implemented, failed to maintain her competitiveness in foreign markets and hence to make the best use of whatever trade possibilities were available. The government's policies on imposing lower excise duties for domestic consumption than export levies and promotional activities undertaken for domestic consumption for some key export products, such as tea and coffee, undermined the export performance of these products. A large number of products were affected by such controls, the most prominent among them being jute manufacturers, tea, cotton textiles, vegetable oilseeds and oil, raw wool, raw cotton, coffee, manganese ore and hides and skins.

Around the mid-1960s, the government's efforts to improve the performance of the export sector by implementing a scheme of export subsidy consisting of (1) fiscal measures such as tax concessions and direct subsidy, and (2) import entitlement schemes permitting exporters to obtain premium carrying import licences, did not achieve much success as it was implementing the policy in a selective manner without any economic rationale.

The policy of export promotion ultimately became one of indiscriminate export promotion which created a pervasive bias towards fixing the subsidy inversely to the competitive strength of the economy. The production and trade in India, during the first two decades of planned development appeared to have been governed by the two principles that India should produce whatever it can and should export whatever it produces (Bhagwati and Desai 1971).

Physical controls were also extended to controls on prices and distribution of many manufactured products, although not all of them were subject to the same type of control at the same time. The controls were apparently motivated by desires to achieve different goals, but no real benefit accrued to the final consumers of the products using the inputs under price and distribution controls. Overall controls over price and distribution exercised by the government were advised, and formed part of the policy of direct intervention without a careful consideration of direct efficiency and alternative ways of achieving the goals.

In the 1970s, it began to dawn on some policy-makers that without liberalization of trade and investment policies, the performance of the economy would not improve. However, implementation of extensive liberalization measures proved extremely difficult in the face of opposition of business groups not willing to improve efficiency in production and face competition in the market, and of ministers, preventing import of anything that can be produced at home. Nevertheless, some measures of liberalization such as currency devaluation, greater reliance on tariffs and the simplification of tariff implementation procedures, removal of some controls on prices and so on did occur. During Rajiv Gandhi's Prime Ministership in the 1980s, greater success was achieved in liberalizing trade and investment policies. However, the economy still operated under considerable restrictions.

However, the slightly improved performance of the economy in the 1980s was not enough to offset the damage to the economy caused by the repressive trade and investment regime of the previous three decades. As a result the real per capita GDP grew by only 1.9 per cent during 1960–90.

The 1990s' reforms forced on India by a foreign exchange crisis included liberalizing trade and foreign investment flows, floating the currency and virtually dismantling the industrial licensing system except for 18 critical industries. Quantitative controls on imports of non-consumer goods have virtually disappeared, although controls on imports of consumer goods still remain. Foreign investment rules have been relaxed. The maximum nominal tariff rates for many products came down from around 400 per cent in 1990–91 to below 50 per cent in 2000–01. However, in 1999, India's average tariff rate was about 34 per cent compared with about 18 per cent for China, and it is still higher than the nominal tariff rate in all East Asian countries and in Australia. If the government meets its WTO obligations it will be forced to reduce its average tariff rate significantly. It aims to reach an average tariff level of 20 per cent by March 2005 (DFAT 2001). In compliance with the WTO regulations, India has bound about 67 per cent of its tariff lines. For non-agricultural products, with a few exceptions, the ceilings of 40 per cent *ad valorem* in finished products and 25 per cent in intermediate goods, machinery and equipment have been agreed. The phased reduction of these duties will be completed in 2010. However, on agricultural goods, the bound rate ranges from 100 to 300 per cent. India is also required to phase out all quantitative restrictions by 2003. The number of tariff lines on which quantitative restrictions were maintained has declined from 2714 in 1997 to 1429 in 2000 (GOI, *Economic Survey 1994/05; Economic Survey 2000/01*).

CHINA'S TRADE VOLUME AND PARTICIPATION RATIO

Chinese import and export volumes fluctuated a great deal in the post-war years (Table 5.1). The movement of imports dominated these fluctuations.

Table 5.1   *Average annual growth rates of China's exports and imports,*
               1952–2003

	Exports	Imports
1952–57	14.3	6.0
1957–62	−1.4	−4.9
1962–65	14.4	20.0
1965–70	0.3	2.9
1970–75	26.3	26.3
1975–78	10.3	13.3
1978–80	36.3	35.6
1980–85	8.8	16.1
1985–90	17.8	4.8
1990–95	19.0	19.9
1995–2000	10.9	11.3
2000–03	20.7	22.4

Source: *ZGTJNJ*, various issues.

China has experienced eight big waves of imports since 1952. The first wave of imports occurred during the First Five Year Plan (FFYP) period and was mainly due to the imports of Russian technology in forms of complete plants for the FFYP. The second wave of imports occurred in 1958 and was mainly triggered by increased demand for capital goods to support the Great Leap Forward (GLF) programme. With the failure of the GLF programme, Chinese imports declined during the crisis years (1960–62). It recovered in 1963 and rose by 25 per cent in 1965. Imports slowed down once again during the Cultural Revolution (CR) period. However, it rose sharply in 1972 and 1973 with the recovery of the economy from the disruption caused by the CR and the end of China's isolation from the West following the successful 'ping-pong diplomacy'. The fifth wave of imports occurred in 1978 when it rose by 37 per cent. This was triggered by the launching of another GLF programme by Chairman Hua using Western equipment and technology. The sixth wave of imports occurred in 1985. This time, it was mainly due to the loss of control over imports amid the decentralization of trading rights and foreign exchange use rights (see Zhang 1988, p. 411). The seventh and eighth import surge occurred in 1988 and 1993. Both import surges were preceded by a government policy of accelerated reform and liberalization. Since exports were meant to finance imports, the export trend in China followed closely that of imports.

The relative importance of foreign trade in the Chinese economy can be

Table 5.2   China's trade participation ratios, 1952–2003 (%)

Year	Percentage
1952	9.5
1955	12.1
1957	9.8
1962	7.0
1965	6.9
1970	5.0
1975	9.7
1978	9.8
1980	12.6
1985	23.1
1990	30.0
1995	40.2
1997	36.2
2001	44.0
2003	60.0

Source: ZGTJNJ 2004, pp. 53 and 713.

measured by the ratio of foreign trade (total exports and imports) to GDP or trade participation ratio (TPR). As shown in Table 5.2, TPR increased initially between 1952 and 1955 due to large-scale imports of industrial plants to build up China's industrial production capacity and large-scale exports to finance these imports.

The TPR declined after the successful completion of the FFYP and it stabilized at about the 10 per cent level in 1957. It subsequently dropped to 5 per cent at the height of the self-reliance period in 1970 during the CR. Following the restoration of diplomatic relations with the USA and other Western countries, China's TRP rose once again in the early 1970s but soon reverted to its old stagnant trend until the late 1970s.

After the initiation of the open-door policy, TPR rose from 10 in 1978 to 60 per cent in 2003. However, it is worth noting that part of the increase in TPR during this period was due to the sharp devaluation of the RMB. The yuan/dollar exchange rate stood at 1.7 in 1981 but fell to 8.9 by 2003. This means that the RMB had depreciated by almost 80 per cent during this period. Since the trade volume is recorded in US$ in Chinese statistics, it has to be converted into yuan using the official exchange rate in order to compare with Chinese GDP. The sharp appreciation of the US dollar against the yuan thus artificially inflated the trade volume and hence TPR. Furthermore, a significant proportion of China's trade is generated by importing materi- ' als and parts for further processing and assembly. The processed and assembled products were then re-exported. This also inflated China's real trade participation ratio.

INDIA'S TRADE VOLUME AND PARTICIPATION RATIO

As in China, India's import and export trade also fluctuated throughout the period of planned development. After the mid-1950s, considerable shortage in food grain production resulting from untimely rainfall, and the consequent rise in food prices and in the inflation rate, caused a severe shortage in the availability of foreign exchange. At the same time, while most of India's export items were natural-resource based and labour-intensive manufactures, the government's trade policy also was not geared to export promotion. Hence considerable restriction was placed on import trade. This trend continued up to the early 1970s. Both imports and exports recorded negative growth from time to time. Gradually, as the foreign trade regime slowly began to be liberalized, from the mid-1970s both import and export trade began to grow. From the late 1980s, the growth rate in real gross domestic product began to improve considerably and the import and export trade also grew accordingly.

A country's trade participation ratio depends significantly on the extent of outward orientation of its trade regime. India's highly restrictive trade regime was built by Mahalanobis on the assumption that India, as a major primary goods exporting country, had little chance of increasing its export earnings because of inelasticity of foreign demand for India's exports. Hence the manufacturing sector had to be developed through the deployment of the import substitution policy. Thus Mahalanobis failed to understand that a developing country such as India could create its comparative advantage through an open trade regime (Bhagwati and Desai 1971). Naturally, India's trade participation ratio has remained quite low reaching just 25 per cent in 2003/04. Up to 1980, the year when China began seriously to restructure its economy, India's trade participation ratio was higher than that of China. But after 1980 China's ratio surpassed that of India and continued to accelerate, reaching 60 per cent in 2003. The growth in India's import and export trade and India's trade participation ratio are illustrated in Tables 5.3 and 5.4.

Table 5.3   Growth in India's export and import trade, 1956–2003 (%)

Year	Export	Import	Year	Export	Import
1956	−0.51	22.46	1979	16.27	23.96
1957	9.80	20.72	1980	6.41	46.29
1958	−11.86	−18.03	1981	6.31	14.22
1959	8.77	21.09	1982	23.17	4.73
1960	0.65	15.73	1983	4.50	1.66
1961	4.10	−0.76	1984	16.26	21.67
1962	1.22	3.34	1985	9.30	13.87
1963	15.84	4.87	1986	4.11	−1.15
1964	4.87	16.08	1987	23.53	11.12
1965	−1.05	−1.29	1988	35.95	23.09
1966	45.84	15.73	1989	39.67	25.45
1967	3.26	2.07	1990	22.30	24.24
1968	9.19	−7.32	1991	27.50	10.66
1969	4.19	−13.92	1992	26.93	33.11
1970	10.42	−3.95	1993	29.07	13.58
1971	0.38	13.94	1994	19.48	21.32
1972	21.70	−7.22	1995	26.75	62.39
1973	21.66	47.88	1996	17.78	19.25
1974	40.70	67.09	1997	8.53	11.97
1975	14.55	28.34	1998	8.49	17.74
1976	36.50	−4.96	1999	11.38	14.22
1977	12.13	14.18	2000	24.15	13.93
1978	−2.09	11.10	2001	7.90	0.70
			2001/02	−1.60	1.70
			2003/03	20.30	19.40

Source: IMF (2002); GOI, *Economic Survey*, various issues.

CHINA'S IMPORT AND EXPORT STRUCTURE

Chinese imports in the post-war years consisted mainly of manufactured goods (Table 5.5). Manufactured goods' share of imports averaged around 80 per cent throughout the entire period. Within the manufactured goods sector, a large share of imports was accounted for by machinery and equipment. The share of machinery and equipment in total imports has fluctuated largely owing to the fluctuation of domestic fixed investment. However, their share, on average, made up 40 per cent of China's total imports. The share of primary goods imports had been maintained at about the 20 per cent level. Within the primary goods import sector, foodstuffs

Table 5.4   India's trade participation ratio, 1950–2003 (%)

Year	Ratio
1950	12.17
1955	12.14
1957	13.43
1960	11.51
1962	10.47
1963	9.93
1965	8.93
1970	7.72
1975	10.91
1980	13.61
1985	10.58
1990	12.80
1995	17.86
1997	18.23
1999	18.44
2000	20.17
2001/02	21.70
2002/03	24.60

Source: as for Table 5.3.

Table 5.5   Composition of Chinese imports, 1965–2003 (selected years, %)

Year	Primary products				Manufactured products		
	Food	Fuels	Others	Total	Machinery and equipment	Others	Total
1965	7	1	10	18	39	43	82
1970	7	1	9	17	39	43	82
1985	7	1	5	13	31	56	87
1990	8	2	9	19	41	39	80
1993	3	6	7	16	42	43	85
1996	6	5	12	23	40	39	79
1998	5	5	9	19	41	40	81
2001	5	3	2	10	36	54	90
2003	1	7	10	18	47	52	99

Source: World Bank, *World Development Indicators*, various issues; *ZGTJNJ* 2004, p. 716.

Table 5.6   Composition of Chinese exports, 1953–2003 (selected years, %)

Year	Primary products		Manufactured products
	Minerals	Total	
1953	0.8	79.4	20.6
1957	1.1	63.6	36.4
1965	3.1	51.2	48.8
1970	2.8	53.5	46.0
1978	13.8	53.5	46.5
1980	23.6	50.3	49.7
1985	26.0	50.5	49.5
1990	8.4	25.6	74.4
1995	3.5	14.4	85.6
2001	3.2	10.0	90.0
2003	2.5	8.0	92.0

Source: Zhang 1988, p. 419; *ZGTJNJ* 2004, p. 715.

accounted for the major share in the early years. But in recent years, their share declined. The share of fuel was negligible during the pre-reform period but has risen rapidly since the reforms in 1979.

Similar to Japan, prior to the start of industrialization, China exported primarily primary products and imported mainly manufactured goods. Once industrialization started, the share of primary exports declined while that of the manufactured increased. However, unlike Japan, primary exports' share decreased slowly and remained China's major export throughout the pre-reform period (Table 5.6). One of the main reasons for this was the rise of mineral fuel exports as a result of the discoveries of oil in China in the early 1960s and the sharp increase of oil world market prices in the 1970s. The rise of mineral fuel exports somewhat offset the fall of agricultural exports and hence slowed down the decreasing share of primary exports. Manufactured exports increased slowly during the pre-reform period but experienced a rapid growth during the reform period. By the 1990s they replaced primary exports as China's main exports. Within the manufactured exports, light industrial products accounted for the major share of Chinese exports throughout the pre-reform period. Since the reforms, its share has stagnated while that of heavy industrial products increased. During 1980–98, the share of machinery and transport equipment in China's total manufactured exports surged from 9 to 31 per cent (*ZGTJNJ* 1999, p. 579).

China's changing export specialization is consistent with the dynamic theory of comparative advantage (Garnaut and Anderson 1980, pp. 375–80). According to this theory, at the onset of economic development when both human and physical capital are relatively scarce in relation to natural resources, a country tends to specialize in the exports of natural-resource based (NRB) goods. The type of NRB goods can either be agricultural products or minerals, depending on the country's relative abundance of both types of natural resources. Economic growth tends to weaken export specialization in NRB goods, both through a supply and demand effect. On the supply side, economic growth is accompanied by capital accumulation, which increases the relative scarcity of natural resources in relation to capital. On the demand side, economic growth is accompanied by rising income and manufacturing output which increases domestic demand for NRB goods. Thus, a country will gradually shift from NRB export to manufactured export specialization. Within the manufactured sector, export specialization is determined by a country's relative labour and capital endowment. Initially, with a relatively abundant supply of labour to capital, a country tends to specialize in the exports of labour-intensive manufactures. With increased capital accumulation and the increased scarcity of labour, a country's specialization tends to shift to capital-intensive manufactures.

INDIA'S IMPORT AND EXPORT STRUCTURE

In Table 5.7, we present India's import trade structure. Total imports have been grouped under five categories: (a) pure primary, (b) semi-processed primary, raw materials and manufactures excluding fuel, (c) fuel, (d) capital goods and heavy manufactures and (e) others. In 1960–61, semi-processed primary and raw materials and manufactures accounted for 38 per cent and capital goods and heavy manufactures accounted for 31.7 per cent of total imports. Pure primary products and fuel accounted for 19 per cent and 8.3 per cent of total imports while all other items accounted for 2.2 per cent. However the situation changed considerably in 2000–01 due to four decades of economic development. As India achieved self-sufficiency in food grain supply in the 1970s, the share of pure primary goods in total imports declined to only 4.6 per cent. But, heightened economic activities in the 1990s raised the share of fuel imports in total imports to slightly over 31 per cent. Also the shares of processed primary, raw materials, manufactures and of capital goods slightly declined to 30.7 per cent and 12.1 per cent while the share of all other items increased to 23 per cent.

Table 5.8 illustrates the structure of India's export trade. In 1960–61, exports of agriculture and allied products, and of manufactured foods, together accounted for nearly 90 per cent of total exports, whereas the

Table 5.7 *India's principal imports (selected years, % of total imports)*

Year	1. Pure primary (food and allied products)	2. Semi-processed primary raw materials manufacturers (excl. fuel)	3. Fuel	4. Total (1 + 2 + 3)	5. Capital goods and heavy manufacturers	6. Other	7. Total (4 + 5 + 6)
1960/61	19.07	37.96	9.00	66.03	31.72	2.22	100
1970/71	14.31	46.08	8.32	68.71	24.72	6.05	100
1980/81	3.02	35.82	41.94	80.78	15.22	3.97	100
1985/86	4.36	45.87	25.37	75.60	21.79	2.81	100
1997/98	4.50	36.20	22.60	63.30	18.20	18.50	100
1998/99	6.10	39.30	17.60	63.00	16.60	20.40	100
2000/01	3.70	30.70	33.20	67.60	12.40	20.00	100
2001/02	4.50	32.50	29.50	66.50	11.40	22.10	100
2002/03	4.60	29.90	30.70	65.20	12.10	22.70	100

Source: GOI, *Economic Survey*, various issues.

Table 5.8 Composition of India's exports, 1960–61 to 2002–03 (selected years, %)

Year	Agriculture and allied products	Ores and minerals	Manufactured goods	Mineral fuels	Others	Total
1960/61	44.2	8.1	45.3	1.1	1.2	100
1970/71	31.7	10.7	50.2	0.8	6.5	100
1980/81	30.0	6.1	55.0	2.3	6.9	100
1990/91	19.4	4.5	72.9	2.9	0.1	100
1995/96	19.8	2.8	75.4	1.7	0.2	100
1998/99	18.0	2.0	78.0	0.3	1.7	100
2000/01	13.5	2.6	78.0	4.2	1.7	100
2002/03	12.8	3.8	76.6	4.9	1.9	100

Source: GOI, Economic Survey, various issues.

shares of ores and minerals, mineral fuels and of all other miscellaneous items stood at 8.09, 1.09 and 1.2 per cent respectively. However, in 2002–03, the share of agriculture and allied products declined to 12.8 per cent from 44.2 per cent in 1960–61, but that of manufactured goods increased to 77 per cent from 45.3 per cent in 1960–61. The share of ores and minerals declined to 3.8 per cent, while that of mineral fuels increased to 4.9 per cent and that of all others declined marginally to 2 per cent. Hence manufactured goods accounted for the bulk of the share of exports, and manufactured goods and agriculture and allied products together accounted for 89.4 per cent of total exports in 2000–01. This shift in India's export structure is in line with what one would expect to see from a growing economy. However India's overall performance in export trade, although improved since late 1987, has been adversely affected by several factors in recent years.

Exports from India are currently subject to 40 anti-dumping and 13 counter-veiling measures, mainly for agricultural products, textiles and clothing products, and chemical and related products (GOI, *Economic Survey*, 2003/04). Also, changes in product regulation and standards and other non-tariff barriers have adversely affected market access of Indian products. The USA imposed tariff duties in excess of 10 per cent on the top 20 product categories exported by India to the USA compared with a simple average tariff of less than 5 per cent on merchandise imports from India. A number of domestic impediments to export growth, such as infrastructure constraints, high transaction costs, high labour costs, inflexibility in labour laws, militancy of trade unions particularly those affiliated to the Maoist Political Party (CMP), untimely rainfall and pests, and a significant rise in domestic demand for tea and other beverages as well as constraints in attracting foreign investment in the export sector, have continued to adversely affect the supply response of exports.

TRADE AND GROWTH

The Chinese Experience

Most of the cross-country studies find that increased trade participation leads to higher economic growth. Frankel and Roemer (1999), for example, find that increased share of trade in income is robustly related to long-term growth. The case of China is no exception. As evidenced from Table 5.2, China's trade participation during the pre-reform period was less than 10 per cent on average, whereas during the post-reform period (1978–2001) the ratio almost tripled to 30 per cent. The spike in trade participation ratio has been accompanied by higher economic growth. The annual average rate of growth of China's GDP, according to China's official statistics, surged from about 6 per cent during the pre-reform period to 10 per cent during the post-reform period.

Though the evidence for positive linkage between trade and growth is clear in most literature, the mechanism through which trade contributes to grow is less clear. There is considerable debate in the literature on whether growth driven by increased trade is export led or import led. The export-led growth hypothesis highlights the contribution of exports to the main factors of economic growth, namely, labour, capital and total factor productivity. Increased exports increase the opportunity for labour employment. Since the export industry is highly profitable, higher exports usually lead to higher profits and a higher rate of saving, which, in turn, finance a higher rate of investment leading to a higher rate of capital accumulation. In addition, increased exports also provide increased foreign exchanges to finance the imports of capital goods, without which a higher rate of capital formation would not have been possible. Increased exports also stimulate growth of total factor productivity through the following channels. First, it enables domestic firms to produce for the world market and hence reap economies of scale. Second, it subjects domestic firms to intense competition in the world market, which tends to enhance firms' X-efficiency. Third, it enables domestic firms to gain access to the latest technology in the world. Last but not least, the latest technology adopted by the export sector is likely to spill over to the non-export sector.

However, recent research based on firm-level data casts doubt on the export-productivity growth nexus. There is a lack of robust econometric evidence to suggest that export growth causes productivity growth. In fact, the causality generally runs in the other direction, that is, high productivity in certain industries leads to exports.

The import-led growth hypothesis emphasizes the role of imports in stimulating productivity growth. According to this theory, imports affects firms' productivity in various ways (see Lawrence and Weinstein 2001). First, increased imports increased competitive pressure for domestic firms. As a result, low-productivity firms are forced to exit whereas the remaining firms are made more efficient. Second, increased imports enable domestic firms to gain access to the fruits of research and development (R&D) of foreign countries embodied in imported machinery and equipment and new products. Thus, the policy implication of the import-led growth hypothesis is that developing countries should liberalize imports instead of promoting exports.

However, the view of the import-led growth hypothesis appears to be too simplistic. It is inconceivable that import growth could be sustained without export growth in the long run because of foreign exchange constraint. It is difficult to find a country in the world which achieved high growth through only high import growth without corresponding high export growth. Thus, the causality between import and export and productivity growth resembles the problem of the chicken and the egg. It is difficult to pinpoint which is more important for productivity growth. Thus, it appears that the truth of the matter lies somewhat in the middle. Export growth increases foreign exchange earnings, which finance more imports, which, in turn, intensify competition and widening firms' choice of technology and intermediate products, which, in turn, enhance firms' productivity leading to more export growth. Hence, both export and import growths are essential for productivity growth.

The Chinese experience confirms the equal importance of export and import growth for economic growth. Table 5.9 compares China's regional export- and import-income ratio and economic growth during 1992–2001. The reason why only this ten-year period is considered in this study is because trade data for China's regions are not available prior to 1992. It is well known that China's open-door and economic reform policies in recent years have produced not only high economic growth but also increased regional income inequality. As can be seen from Table 5.9, growth has been most rapid in the coastal provinces, followed by provinces in the central region, and least rapid in the Western region. There are many factors contributing to the divergence of regional growth rates. One of the factors has been the difference in their trade performance. As can be seen from Table 5.9, the export-income ratio of high- growth coastal regions is much higher than that of the low-growth interior provinces. The coastal provinces, owing to their geographical location, better transportation and communication infrastructure and government preferential development policy, experienced high export growth and hence had a higher export-income ratio than the interior provinces.

Table 5.9 also shows that the high-growth coastal provinces have not only high export-income ratios but also high import-income ratios. In other words, the regional export and import share in income are highly positively correlated. Hence, it is not possible to determine which share is more important for economic growth. The interdependence of export and import share in the case of China can be explained by the fact that, as mentioned earlier, a significant proportion of Chinese exports is the processing and assembly trade, which involve processing and assembling imported intermediate products for exports. In 1998, for instance, this kind of trade still made up 53 per cent of China's total foreign trade (General Administration of Customs of the People's Republic of China 1998, p. 12).

Table 5.9   China's regional trade and growth, 1992 and 2001

	Growth rate of GDP	Export share in GDP (%)		Import share in GDP (%)	
	1992–2001	1992	2001	1992	2001
Eastern provinces:					
Beijing	11.1	16	23	34	57
Tianjin	12.2	32	40	37	42
Hebei	12.8	1	5	4	3
Liaoning	9.7	16	18	13	17
Shanghai	12.5	36	45	40	57
Zhejiang	14.3	16	30	9	16
Jiangsu	14.5	12	26	12	22
Fujian	15.6	29	29	27	19
Shandong	13.1	11	16	8	12
Guangdong	14.0	82	75	84	65
Guanxi	11.6	8	5	6	3
Hainan	12.3	13	10	26	15
Central provinces:					
Shanxi	9.8	9	12	3	3
Inner Mongolia	10.0	7	5	6	7
Jilin	10.8	4	6	11	8
Heilongjiang	8.7	26	5	9	5
Anhui	13.3	4	6	8	4
Jiangxi	11.9	6	4	4	3
Henan	11.8	4	3	3	2
Hubei	12.2	6	3	6	4
Hunan	10.6	6	4	6	3
Western provinces:					
Sichuan	10.1	4	3	4	3
Guizhou	8.6	1	4	3	3
Yunan	9.3	5	5	4	4
Tibet	11.6	3	5	16	1
Shaanxi	9.5	6	6	6	6
Gansu	9.7	5	4	3	3
Qinghai	8.9	5	5	4	2
Ningxia	9.9	7	11	3	7
Xinjiang	9.1	7	4	6	10

Sources: ZGTJNJ 1995; 1996; 2000; 2001.

The Indian Experience

In India's case, contribution of trade to GDP has been very low. As mentioned earlier, the economic and political institutions created under Nehru's regime continued to weaken the capacity of the economy to grow even after the economic reform measures were undertaken. Since the Indian trade regime under the Mahalanobis model was built on the assumption that the scope for increasing or even maintaining India's share in world exports was very limited, as India was primarily a primary goods exporter, the regime used imports to end imports rather than to increase exports (Bhagwati and Desai 1971). Hence, even after the partial dismantling of the QR regime in 1991, bias against exports continued to persist. Restrictions on the operation of an export-orientated trade regime were not completely lifted even after 1991, as ministers, business and industry leaders and other rent seekers have benefited from the continuation of the restrictive trade regime. An estimation of the trade participation ratio which is a good indicator of the importance of trade in a country's GDP growth, shows that the highest ratio of trade participation for India was 20.2 per cent in 2000 (Table 5.4) as compared with 44 per cent for China in 2000 (Table 5.2).

The growth in net domestic products of 15 major states of India is presented in Table 5.10. Other 16 states are very small compared with these 15 states. Out of these 15 states, Bihar and Assam recorded very low (9 per cent) and Rajasthan recorded the highest (15.1 per cent) growth rate. Growth rates above 14 per cent were also recorded by Kerala, Maharashtra, Gujarat, Karnataka and Haryana. The rate of growth in NDP of other states varied between 11.8 and 12.1 per cent.

Detailed statistics on the share of export and import from these states in GDP were not available. From Eastern India, West Bengal, Bihar and Orissa contributes marginally to the total export income of the country. Although West Bengal is a major producer of tea and some manufactured products, it contributes only around 5 per cent to total export income. Hence, since most of India's manufacturing activities are located in major southern and Western states and to some extent, in northern states, the total share of exports from these states in GDP would be significantly higher than the share of exports in GDP from other states. Also, the industries such as telecommunications, electrical equipment, transport services, chemicals and food processing absorbed nearly 50 per cent of FDI inflows between August 1991 and October 2003. Most of these industries were also located in Southern and Western India. And these industries which attracted foreign direct investments were also important exporters of manufactured products and services.

Table 5.10   Net state domestic product of India at current price (average annual growth rate, %)

States	1980–81 to 2001–02
Northern	
1. Haryana	14.6
2. Panjab	13.4
3. Uttar Pradesh (UP)	12.4
Western	
4. Rajasthan	15.1
5. Gujarat	14.1
6. Maharashtra	14.1
7. Madhya Pradesh (MP)	11.8
Southern	
8. Kerala	14.8
9. Karnataka	14.6
10. Tamil Nadu	14.9
11. Andhra Pradesh	14.9
Eastern	
12. Orissa	12.1
13. Bihar	9.9
14. West Bengal	13.8
15. Assam	12.9

Source: GOI, *Economic Survey*, various issues.

Overall, while the trade policy measures undertaken during the 1980s sought to enhance the access of domestic manufacturers to imported capital goods and raw materials not available in the domestic market, domestic industries were exposed to a limited degree of competition by placing selected items of import under the Open General Licensing system. However the tariff structure was not simplified and high tariffs continued to constrain growth by raising the cost of essential growth-sensitive imports. Although the trade policy reforms of the 1990s led to considerable reduction in customs tariffs, the dismantling of other trade restrictions and attempts to align domestic trade policy to international norms, restrictions on trade and foreign investment continue to persist. Nevertheless total exports and imports as a percentage of GDP (trade participation ratio) has been rising since 1980. The average export-import ratio which is an indicator of the import financing capacity of the import has improved significantly from 64 per cent in the 1980s to nearly 85 per cent in the 1990s.

However, India's integration with the global economy is significantly less than that of China, even in 2001. In 2001, the share of trade in goods in GDP was about 20 per cent for India as compared with 44 per cent for China. In the same year the share of gross foreign direct investment in GDP was 0.6 per cent for India as compared with 4.9 per cent for China. Another indicator of the degree of integration with the global economy is the current height of tariff barriers. In 2001, the simple and weighted mean tariffs on all imports into India were 31 per cent and 28.2 per cent. These rates are quite high and need to be lowered significantly. Also on the export front, high labour costs in the manufacturing sector makes Indian manufacturers less competitive in the world market than those of China. In 2001, labour cost per worker per year, in manufacturing in India was US$1129 as compared with US$729 for China (World Bank, *World Development Indicators*, 2003).

FOREIGN INVESTMENT

The Chinese Experience

Foreign investment consists of foreign loan, foreign direct investment (FDI) and official unrequited transfers. In the 1950s, China received a substantial amount of both loan and aid from the former Soviet Union. These loans and aid filled in China's domestic saving and investment gap. They enabled China to run a trade deficit from 1950 to 1955 and were crucial to the establishment of China's core industrial projects during the FFYP period. These projects included seven iron and steel plants, 24 electric power stations and 63 machinery plants (Riskin 1987, p. 74). Eckstein estimated that without Soviet loans and aid, there would have been no capital goods imports as China was faced with trade embargoes from the West, and investment during the FFYP period would have been cut either by 15–20 per cent or by 35–50 per cent and economic growth, as mentioned previously, by more than one-half (Eckstein 1966, p. 124).

The abrupt withdrawal of Soviet aid in 1960 compounded the economic crisis generated by the failure of the GLF strategy and the bad weather affecting the farm sector in the early 1960s. This made China averse to foreign investment until the adoption of the open-door policy in the late 1970s.

Foreign investment inflow into China grew rapidly during the first half of the 1980s (Table 5.11). Entering the second half of the 1980s, growth of foreign investment in China levelled off and turned negative in the aftermath of the Tiananmen massacre but recovered in the early 1990s, after the tour of Deng Xiaoping in the Southern provinces.

Table 5.11   Volume and structure of China's realized foreign investment (US$ billion)

Year	Volume	Foreign loan	FDI	Other foreign investments
1979–84	17.1	13.0	3.1	1.0
1985	4.5	2.7	1.7	0.3
1986	7.3	5.0	1.9	0.4
1987	8.5	5.8	2.3	0.3
1988	10.2	6.5	3.2	0.6
1989	10.1	6.3	3.4	0.4
1990	10.3	6.5	3.5	0.3
1991	11.6	6.9	4.4	0.3
1992	19.2	7.9	11.0	0.3
1993	39.0	11.2	27.5	0.3
1994	43.2	9.2	33.8	0.2
1995	48.1	10.3	37.5	0.3
1996	54.8	12.7	41.7	0.4
1997	64.4	12.0	45.3	7.1
1998	58.6	11.0	45.5	2.1
1999	52.7	10.2	40.3	2.1
2000	59.4	10.0	40.7	8.6
2001	49.7		46.9	2.8
2002	55.0		52.7	2.3
2003	56.1		53.5	2.6
1979–2003	679.8	147.2	499.9	32.7

Notes:
1. Realized foreign investment is the total amount of foreign capital actually used.
2. Other foreign investment includes sale of shares, international leasing, compensation trade.

Source: ZGTJNJ 2004, p. 731.

Foreign investment in China post-1979 essentially consisted of foreign loans and FDI. Up to 1991, foreign loans accounted for the major share of China's total foreign investment. From 1992, the importance of FDI soared and by 2003 its share in total foreign investment reached 54 per cent. Most foreign loans were private and the rest were official (*ACFERT* 1984, pp. iv–183; 1990/91, p. 651). Altogether China's post-1979 foreign capital inflow was mainly non-debt creating flow as the official lending plus FDI accounted for almost 90 per cent of China's total foreign capital inflow.

After the passing of the joint venture law in 1979, FDI in China went through three distinctive phases. During the first phase (1979 to mid-1986)

FDIs were welcome but highly regulated (Chai 1986, pp. 141–50; World Bank 1988a, pp. 259–74). The second phase began in 1986 with the introduction of new FDI regulations. This policy change had been forced upon China by the sharp decline in the number of approved FDIs in 1986 because of the growing dissatisfaction of foreign investors with the Chinese investment environment. New policies introduced since 1986 have significantly reduced government intervention and have offered more incentives for foreign investors. FDI incentives in developing countries can either be product- or factor-based (Guisinger 1989). Product-based incentives aim at giving the FDI venture protection of their products on the domestic market through tariffs or non-tariff barriers. Factor-based incentives attempt to reduce the factor costs of FDI ventures through tax holidays, accelerated depreciation, subsidized infrastructure, and so on. The FDI incentives in China were mainly factor based. They usually took the form of tax holidays, investment allowance, reduction or exemption of imported raw materials and equipment from sales tax and custom duties, as well as reduced fees for land use, labour services and other public utilities. Additional incentives were provided for foreign investors in preferential treatment areas, that is, the SEZs open coastal cities and provinces (Grub and Lin 1991, pp. 45–53; OECD 2002, pp. 334–7).

Compared with the first phase, the FDI incentives offered in the second phase were significantly enhanced in many respects. The preferential treatment areas were significantly enlarged. During the first phase these had been confined to four SEZs, Guangdong and Fujian provinces, Hainan Island and the 14 open coastal cities with a total of about 117 cities and *xians* (SSB 1989b, pp. 147–9). In the second phase these were extended to cover 11 open coastal provinces, which comprised 288 cities and *xians*.

The third phase began in 1992 after the tour of Deng Xiaoping in the Southern provinces. Part of the interior regions were opened up for FDI. Consequently, another 28 cities and eight prefectures along the Yangtse River, and 13 border cities in the country's Northeastern, Southwestern and Northwestern regions were declared preferential treatment or open areas. Furthermore, two new investment categories were created, namely, the export-orientated and the technologically advanced projects, which were entitled to additional incentives regardless of their location.

China's recent admission into WTO commits China to open up its formerly closed sectors such as banking, finance, insurance, distribution and telecommunications, as well as major infrastructure facilities, to foreign investors. Furthermore, in compliance with the Agreement on Trade Related Investment Measures (TRIM), China will have to treat foreign invested enterprises (FIEs) equally as domestic enterprises and will not be allowed to impose any restriction on the activities of FIEs in the form of

Table 5.12   China's realized foreign direct investment by type of foreign ownership (%)

Year	Equity JVs	Contract JVs	Co-operative development	WOFEs	Other	Total
1979–81	8.8	47.9	43.2	0.1	0	100
1982	8.0	41.3	41.5	9.2	0	100
1985	34.9	35.3	29.0	0.8	0	100
1988	61.8	24.4	6.6	7.3	0	100
1992	55.4	19.1	2.8	22.7	0	100
1997	43.1	19.7	0.8	35.8	0.6	100
2001	33.6	13.3	1.1	50.9	1.1	100
2003	28.8	7.3	0.6	62.4	0.9	100

Source: as for Table 5.11.

such requirements as export quotas, foreign exchange balancing, local content, and so on.

As indicated in Table 5.11, the inflow of FDI spiked after 1992. Since 1997, with the outbreak of the Asian financial crisis, the growth momentum has slowed down. By the end of 2001, accumulated total amount of actual FDIs in China stood at US$393.5 billion. By the mid-1990s China became the largest recipient of FDI in the developing world, and by 2002, after the burst of the high-tech bubble in the USA, China became the world's largest recipient of FDI. However, it should be noted that Chinese official FDI statistics contain a significant amount of the so-called round-tripping FDI, which involve the re-routing of Chinese domestic capital to Hong Kong Chinese enterprises, which then invest them in mainland China in order to capture the various fiscal and financial incentives enjoyed by the FIEs (Xiao 2004). This round-tripping FDI introduces a upward bias in the level of FDI and its rate of growth.

The relative importance of various forms of FDI in China is presented in Table 5.12. The general trend is towards increased foreign ownership and control. During the first phase, foreign investors were mainly engaged in a 'lower' form of FDI. The most popular form of investment during this period was the contractual joint venture (JV) and co-operative development, both of which did not involve foreign equity capital. As evident from Table 5.12, these 'lower' forms of FDI accounted for over 80 per cent of China's actual FDI annual intake in the first phase. In the second phase, the improved investment environment and the changed attitude of the Chinese government towards foreign ownership stimulated an increase of FDI in the higher forms. Equity JVs and wholly owned foreign enterprises (WOFEs) became increasingly important. By the early 1990s, these two forms of FDI accounted for over 70 per cent of China's actual annual FDI intake. In the third phase, WOFEs became increasingly popular among foreign investors and was the predominant form of FDI in China by 2003.

In the past, most of China's FDI came from Hong Kong or Macau, followed by those from the USA and Japan. More recently, with the normalization of diplomatic relation between China, South Korea and Taiwan, the latter two countries have become major foreign investors in China. As of 2001, in terms of actual investment, the top five foreign investors in China were Hong Kong, the USA, Japan, Taiwan and South Korea.

Region-wise, over the whole period, the East Asian neighbouring countries are the main source of China's FDI. In 2001, for example, Hong Kong, Macau, Japan, Taiwan, South Korea, together with Singapore and the four main ASEAN countries, accounted for 63 per cent of China's actual annual FDI intake.

Sector-wise FDIs used to be concentrated in the service sector, especially in real estate, hotels and other tourism-related projects, which guaranteed foreign exchange earnings (Pomfret 1991, p. 102). But in the second phase there was a significant shift of FDI towards the industrial sector, due to the growing tendency of Asia's newly industrialized countries (NICs) and Japan to relocate their labour-intensive manufactured export production bases to China following the Plaza Accord in 1985. In the late 1980s FDIs in manufacturing accounted for 80 per cent of China's pledged investment inflow (OECD 2002, p. 350). In the third phase, with the opening up of the service sector to FDI, the share of real estate management and other service sectors in FDI soared once again. Nonetheless, by 2001, manufacturing still dominated Chinese FDI with a share of 65 per cent (*ZGTJNJ* 2002, p. 634).

Theoretically, FDI increases a country's rate of growth through an increase in its employment, capital formation and productivity (see, for example, World Bank 2001, pp. 87–93). In the case of China, so far there have been very few systematic studies of the growth impact of FDI (see, for example, Sun 1998). Nonetheless, there is clear evidence that FDI has contributed significantly to China's economic growth.

Table 5.13 shows China's regional distribution of actual FDI and respective growth performance. It shows that regions more exposed to FDI, such as the coastal provinces in general, experienced faster growth. This table also shows that FDI contributes to regional growth mainly through the following channels. First, it increases both the rate and quality of fixed capital formation of the region. For example, in the high-growth coastal provinces, FDI accounted for almost 13 per cent on average of their fixed capital formation, whereas in the low-growth Western provinces, FDI made up only

Table 5.13   FDI and growth in Chinese regions, 2001

	% share of FDI	Share of FDI in fixed capital investment	Share of FIES in exports
Eastern provinces:			
Beijing	3.8	9.0	40.9
Tianjin	4.6	21.9	80.1
Hebei	1.4	2.7	32.9
Liaoning	5.4	14.4	58.6
Shanghai	9.3	16.9	59.4
Zhejiang	4.8	6.9	29.3
Jiangsu	14.9	16.6	56.6
Fujian	8.5	24.6	56.0
Shandong	7.6	8.2	50.0
Guangdong	25.7	28.3	56.7
Guanxi	0.8	4.3	18.0
Hainan	1.0	18.6	47.1
Central provinces:			
Shanxi	0.5	2.7	6.0
Inner Mongolia	0.2	1.8	14.4
Jilin	0.7	4.0	28.0
Heilongjiang	0.7	2.7	11.9
Anhui	0.7	2.8	19.9
Jiangxi	0.9	4.7	10.3
Henan	1.0	2.1	17.1
Hubei	2.6	6.1	27.9
Hunan	1.8	5.4	12.2
Western provinces:			
Sichuan	1.3	3.1	14.2
Guizhou	0.1	0.4	8.6
Yunan	0.1	0.7	9.6
Tibet	0	0	2.7
Shaanxi	0.8	3.3	7.6
Gansu	0.2	1.7	11.1
Qinghai	0.1	1.5	0.9
Ningxia	Negl	0.7	15.3
Xinjiang	Negl	0.2	8.8

Source: ZGTJNJ, various issues.

1 per cent of their fixed capital formation. Second, it increases the exports of the regions. In the high-growth coastal provinces, exports in general grew faster. The reason for that apparently is due to FDI. As Table 5.13 shows, FIEs accounted on average for almost half the exports of the high-growth

Table 5.14   *Current account deficits (CAD), planned and actual (% of GDP)*

Plan	Planned CAD	Actual CAD
First plan (1951–56)	1.7	0.1
Second plan (1956–61)	1.9	2.4
Third plan (1961–66)	2.2	1.8
Fourth plan (1969–74)	0.7	0.3
Fifth plan (1974–79)	1.5	0.2
Sixth plan (1980–85)	1.4	1.6
Seventh plan (1985–90)	1.6	2.3
Eighth plan (1992–97)	1.6	1.2
Ninth plan (1997–2002)	2.1	1.0[1]

Note: 1. For 1991–2001.

Source: Reserve Bank of India (2001).

coastal regions. In contrast, FIEs accounted for less than 10 per cent of those of the low-growth Western provinces

The Indian Experience

Since the commencement of the First Five Year Plan in 1951, capital flows into India have been predominantly influenced by the policy environment. In recognition of the fact that constraints existed on increasing income from exports and of the Nehruvian objective of following the path of self-reliant development, planned dependence on foreign capital in successive plans was deliberately held at modest levels, as illustrated in Table 5.14.

It can be seem from Table 5.14 that the actual current account deficits as a percentage of GDP were lower than the planned current account deficits in all plans except the second plan (1956–61) and the seventh plan (1985–90). Even during these two plans the share of the deficit in GDP was less than 2 per cent. Economy in the recourse to foreign capital was achieved through import-substitution industrialization in the initial years of planned development. The possibility of exports replacing foreign capital was generally not explored until the 1980s. The export-led growth strategy only began to be implemented from 1991. Also a shift in the composition of capital flow, in the 1980s, in favour of commercial debt capital and, in the 1990s, in favour of non-debt flows became evident. Since India achieved lower economic growth than China, its size of current account deficit as a proportion of

GDP remained at modest levels. Therefore the size of capital inflow to India has also been considerably smaller than that to China. At the same time, since India, like China, has adopted a cautious approach to liberalization of specific capital account transactions, the size of capital inflow has not increased greatly.

It is difficult to assess the direct contribution of FDI to the economic growth process. Anecdotal evidence suggests that foreign-controlled firms often use third country exports to meet their export obligations. Information collected from annual surveys of selected foreign-controlled rupee companies on the export intensity of these firms during the 1980s and 1990s shows that these firms export only about 10 per cent of their domestic sales and their export intensity has increased modestly in the 1990s (RBI 2001). Hence it would appear that the attractiveness of the domestic market is one of the primary factors contributing to FDI flows into India.

Prior to 1991, foreign investment inflow to India had been very small. Foreign investment inflow to India has mainly been in the forms of direct investment and portfolio investment. Foreign direct investment has flowed to India mainly through joint ventures and wholly owned subsidiaries. Table 5.15 illustrates the foreign investment inflows to India since 1991–92.

As Table 5.15 shows, total FDI flow into India over an 11-year period from 1991–92 to 2002–03 was US$22.5 billion, whereas FDI flow into China in any one year since the mid-1990s was more than US$40 billion. However, in accordance with the recommendation of a committee appointed by the government of India in 2002 to devise a better way of bringing the reporting system of FDI data in India into alignment with international best practices, FDI statistics now include, besides equity capital, 'reinvested earnings', that is, retained earnings of FDI companies and other direct capital such as inter-corporate debt transactions between related entities. However, China has been including short-term and long-term loans, trade credits, bonds, grants, financial leasing, investment by foreign venture capital funds, earnings of indirectly held companies, non-cash equity acquisition, control premium and non-competition fee within FDI. Along with these, China also includes in FDI statistics, project imports which are recorded as imports in India. In India, the broader coverage system for FDI flows has resulted in upward revisions of annual FDI inflows, for the years 2000–01 and 2001–02 by US$1.7 billion and US$2.2 billion respectively (GOI, *Economic Survey*, 2003/04). However, despite the upward revision of the size of the FDI inflow to India, it remained substantially below the amount that flowed into China, although, excluding the round-tripping, the FDI inflows to China could fall considerably. For example, in 2002, the FDI flow into China was in the order of US$52.7 billion but, excluding rounding tripping, the inflow could fall to US$40

Table 5.15 India's foreign investment inflows (US$ million)

Year	A. Direct investment (FDI)	B. Portfolio investment	Total A + B	Share of FDI in total investment
1991/92	129	4	133	97.0
1992/93	315	244	559	56.4
1993/94	586	3 567	4 153	14.1
1994/95	1 314	3 824	5 138	25.6
1995/96	2 144	2 748	4 892	43.8
1996/97	2 821	3 312	6 133	46.0
1997/98	3 557	1 828	5 385	66.1
1998/99	2 462	−61	2 401	102.5
1999/2000	2 155	3 026	5 181	41.6
2000/01	2 339	2 600	4 939	47.4
2001/02	4 700	2 000	6 700	70.1
2002/03	3 600	900	4 500	80.0
Total 1991/92 to 2002/03	26 122	23 992	50 114	49.4

Source: GOI, *Economic Survey,* various issues.

billion. While macroeconomic fundamentals in India are strong, the country has a large pool of human resources and it has been liberalizing FDI policies, the government's behaviour regarding foreign investment remains unpredictable.

Whereas the manufacturing sector was the major recipient of FDI in China, public utilities, infrastructure and services, for example, energy, telecommunications, electrical equipment including computer software and electronics, transport and services sectors were the major recipient of FDI in India.

Among the top investing countries in FDI inflows to India, Mauritius heads the list. It is followed by the USA, Japan, the UK, Germany, the Netherlands, South Korea, France, Italy and Singapore (GOI, *Economic Survey*, 2003/04).

SUMMARY AND CONCLUSIONS

China's trade strategy has experienced two phases of development over the past 50 years. During 1949–78 it adopted an ultra-import substitution strategy. Since 1979 it has adopted a dual trade strategy and both import substitution and export orientation strategies are pursued. Accompanying the change of trade strategy, China's trade system shifted initially from a command-state trading system into a loose one and, later on, to a market-orientated trading system.

China's trade volume and participation ratio fluctuated in accordance with the change in its trade policy. The trade participation ratio increased sharply in the early 1950s and then dropped to its lowest level at the height of the self-reliance period. Under the open-door policy the trade participation ratio increased sharply and reached 44 per cent in 2001. However, part of this increase was inflated by the sharp devaluation of the Chinese yuan and the heavy reliance of Chinese exports on the processing and assembly trade arrangement.

The change in China's structure reflects its industrialization. On the import side, many of the imports initially were machinery and equipment but, with the increased openness and market orientation, the share in total imports of raw materials and fuels increased. On the export side, China's changing export structure is consistent with the dynamic theory of comparative advantage. Initially it specialized in exports of primary products, especially agricultural commodities. As industrialization proceeded, its comparative advantage in agricultural exports declined, whereas that of light industrial products increased. In the 1980s, however, its comparative advantage in light manufactured exports declined while that in heavy industrial products such as chemical, machinery and transport equipment improved.

There is clear evidence that increased openness to trade and FDI have partly contributed to China's high economic growth during the post-reform period. Hence, Chinese experience is consistent with the international experience that trade and FDI liberalization benefits a country's economic growth.

India's openness to trade and investment has been marginal compared to China. The economic reform measures which would have considerably enhanced India's outward orientation have only been sought to be implemented partially, due to India's political situation. It is highly unlikely that this institutional impediment can be removed in the foreseeable future. Hence, FDI inflow to India will continue to increase only at a modest rate in the foreseeable future. India never formed and followed a proactive policy on foreign investments. Prior to India's independence, the Indian National Congress in 1945 proposed elimination of even existing foreign capital from key industries (Kidron 1965). After independence, during the regime of the 'Licence Raj', foreign investment had a limited role to play in India. But even after the dismantling of the regime, politicians continue to treat foreign capital as evil to win votes in elections.

6. Saving and investment

China and India did not experience modern economic growth until the second half of the 20th century. The engine, which propelled both economies into 'take-off' and sustained growth after 1949, was the rapid increase of their rates of investment. Valuable lessons can be learned for other developing countries from their experience of investment strategy. The purpose of this chapter is (1) to examine both countries' investment strategy and their efficacy during the post-war years; (2) to explore how the rate of investment impacted upon the rate of economic growth from the demand and the supply sides in both countries and (3) to explore how such a rapid growth of investment was funded in both countries. It should be noted that the saving data of China is not strictly comparable to those of India. India is among the few developing countries where directly estimated saving data are available (Athukorala and Sen 2002), whereas in China saving data are simply derived by applying the residual method, namely, gross domestic saving is equal to gross domestic products minus total consumption.

RATE OF INVESTMENT

The Chinese Experience

The size of investment in post-war China is shown in Table 6.1. Two kinds of investment rate figures are presented in this table. The first refers to the pre-reform period. During this period, the Chinese concept of rate of investment is known as the rate of capital accumulation, which is derived as the ratio between capital accumulation and national income. The second refers to the post reform period and is known as the rate of investment. This figure is calculated according to the international standard and is equal to the sum of fixed capital formation and change in inventory divided by the GDP. Table 6.1 shows that after the communist takeover, the rate of investment had been drastically increased. During the Republican period (1931–36) the rate of investment was still very low averaging only 5 per cent (Yeh 1968, table 1). The rate of investment during the First Five Year Plan (FFYP) period (1953–57) was raised to an annual average of 24 per cent.

Table 6.1   Rate of investment in China 1952–2003 (%)

A	Rate of accumulation	%
	1953	23.1
	1957	24.9
	1959	43.8
	1962	10.4
	1971	34.1
	1976	32.3
	1977	36.5
B	Rate of capital formation	%
	1978	38.0
	1982	33.2
	1985	37.8
	1990	34.7
	1993	43.3
	1997	38.0
	2000	36.2
	2003	42.3

Sources: Rate of accumulation: *ZGTJNJ* 1992, p. 40. Rate of capital formation: *ZGTJNJ* 1999, p. 67; 2004, p. 65.

China's rate of investment experienced a second upsurge during the Great Leap Forward period (1958–62). In an attempt to overtake the UK economy within seven years and that of the USA within 15 to 20 years, the rate of investment was raised to 44 per cent in 1959.

Following the collapse of the GLF strategy, the rate of investment fell to only 10 per cent in 1962. The rate started to climb again in 1963. However, it was not until 1965 that it managed to recover to its pre-GLF level.

Chinese rate of investment experienced the third upsurge during 1970–71 at the height of the Cultural Revolution (CR) period. For fear of a Soviet invasion, the rate of growth of investment was raised 34 per cent in 1971.

Growth of investment rate slowed down since 1972 but experienced another upsurge in 1978, when the successor of Mao, Hua, launched another GLF in an attempt to modernize China as quickly as possible through large-scale imports of Western equipment and technology. Investment experienced a sharp increase and the rate of investment was pushed up to about 38 per cent in 1978. The Chinese economy underwent a readjustment during 1980–82 (Howe and Walker 1984, pp. ii–v) and investment was, once again, scaled down. However, it soon experienced another upsurge in 1985, which saw an acceleration of the market-orientated reform adopted since 1979. Local authorities and enterprises gained more financial autonomy and investment decision-making under the reforms. As their budget constraints remained soft, their investment growth remained unchecked. As a result, there had been a huge increase in their investments in 1985 and the rate of investment was pushed to a new height of 38 per cent in 1985 and 1986.

In the late 1980s, the central authority re-centralized some of the investment decision-making and financial resources in an attempt to check the excessive investment expenditure. As a result, there had been a slowdown in the growth of investment and a subsequent decline of its rate to about 35 per cent in the early 1990s.

In 1992, Deng Xiaoping used his tour of Southern Chinese provinces to reaffirm the Party's commitment to reform and the open-door policy as well as to the growth of a strong private sector in Chinese economy. As a result, the rate of investment soared to a new height of 43 per cent in 1993. The economy was soon overheated because of the investment boom. The tight credit policy adopted thereafter to control inflation saw the rate of investment slow to 36 per cent in 2000. However, the rate of investment soared again and reached 42.3 per cent in 2003.

The causes of Chinese investment fluctuation are similar to its Eastern European counterparts (Hewett 1981, pp. 504–5). During the pre-reform period the main cause stemmed from the investment drive from above. As mentioned earlier, the Chinese planners during the pre-reform era adopted the Stalinist growth strategy. Underlying the Stalinist growth strategy was the Feldman growth model. The planners' main focus under this strategy was to catch up and overtake the advanced countries in the shortest period of time through a high rate of investment. Thus, the rate of investment was constantly driven up until so many supply constraints arose that investment growth rates had to be cut. As soon as the supply constraints were loosened, the rate of investment increased once again.

Another major source of investment fluctuation came from below. During the post-reform period, decision-making power and the control of financial resources have been decentralized. Local authorities and enterprises, in order to maximize the control of financial resources, tried to push for more investment through the technique of 'hooking on the new plan' to apparently inexpensive projects whose much larger true costs were revealed to the centre only after the project was well under way. When the new projects actually began and their excess cost became apparent, the centre moved in to cut investment demand. This relieved pressure on the investment resources, but generated new pressure from below to start new projects, and eventually the cycle began again.

The Indian Experience

In China, the government adopted a deliberate policy of accelerating the rate of investment to achieve a high rate of growth to catch up with and then to surpass the West in all indicators of development. In India, the government never adopted such a policy to increase the rate of investment to reach such a high goal. The primary objective, as enshrined in the 1929 Lahore resolution of the Indian National Congress, was to ameliorate the conditions of the masses by removing gross inequalities in income through revolutionary changes in the economic and social structures of the society (Hanson 1966). But there was considerable dispute between the Gandhian ideology and Nehruvian socialism as to the nature of changes that were to be brought about in those structures. Gandhi and his followers were totally distrustful of centralized planning and big machines used for India's development. They instead preferred self-reliant village development based on agriculture and village industries, using only handmade tools.

Under Gandhian planning, production was meant to be for immediate consumption, not for distant markets, and there would be no role for middlemen and profit. Hence capital accumulation and investment were not given any importance in Gandhian planning. Gandhians basically wanted to provide people with basic food, clothing and housing, and to remove the spiritual poverty of the masses. The aim therefore was to create an economy operating at just above subsistence level (Narayan 1960; Roy 1986). Nehru also wanted to remove economic poverty of the masses but his means to achieve this objective was diametrically opposed to those proposed by Gandhians. He was in favour of Soviet-style planning and industrialization, and of expansion of state monopoly in production to achieve growth to reduce the economic poverty of the masses. This basic opposition of rival ideologies and political forces continued well into the post-independence planned development period. Hence the programmes that were to be recommended and even more, the attempts at implementing them, were to represent compromises between different ideological positions on these questions (Bhagwati and Desai 1971).

In the end, although Nehru's views won the day and India adopted the Stalinist development model, it never adopted a clear-cut investment policy. Even in the draft outline of the Second Five Year Plan (1956–61) (GOI 1956), which heralded the beginning of comprehensive planning, the first objective was to achieve a sizeable increase in national income so as to raise the level of living in the country. This did not indicate a specific rate of growth and hence a specific rate of investment that the government wanted to achieve. An increase in the rate of investment required an increase in the rate of savings. However, although the vast bulk of investment went into public sector enterprises, they made very little profit and therefore contributed very little to national savings and capital accumulation. This was due, among other things, to the explicit price control imposed by the government of India in output of public enterprises which kept the rate of profit well below what it could otherwise have been (Bhagwati and Desai 1971). Even in the late 1990s and during the last few years, attempts to push up the rate of investment to accelerate growth has met with opposition from the government's coalition partners and from congress opposition, all of whom shed crocodile tears for the poor and branded growth-orientated policies as being anti-poor. Hence, what China was able to achieve because of its political and cultural set-up could never be achieved by India due to its different political and cultural set-up.

Nevertheless, India's performance in raising her average rate of domestic saving appears to have been perhaps the most impressive aspect of her economic progress during the early days of India's planning. In 1950–51 at the beginning of the First Five Year Plan, total domestic savings and gross domestic capital formation accounted for 8.9 and 8.7 per cent of the GDP respectively. Since then rates of savings and investment continued to rise despite some fluctuating from year to year. The highest ratio of capital formation, 26.9 per cent, and that of savings, 25.1 per cent, were reached in 1995–96, but during the same period, the rate of investment in China was around 40 per cent. The rates of saving and investment in India during the period of planned development are presented in Table 6.2. Throughout the period of the 1970s and the 1980s, gross fixed capital formation hovered around 16 and 17 per cent of GDP. From 1978–79 the economy began to introduce some reform measures and hence investment began to increase slowly and steadily. The major source of investment finance in India has been household savings. But the capacity of the household sector to contribute to the total savings depends very much on the growth of the agricultural sector, and that in turn depends very much on the timely arrival of the monsoon. The contribution of private corporate sector and public sector has been dismal. This also affected the overall increase in domestic savings and hence investment.

COMPOSITION OF INVESTMENT

The Chinese Experience

Investment can be divided into fixed and inventory investment. Modern economic growth in the West as well as in Japan was accompanied by a decrease in the share of inventory investment in total investment (Kuznets 1966, pp. 252–6; Minami 1994a, p. 132). In contrast, the share of inventory

Table 6.2   Gross domestic savings and investment in India (% GDP)

Year	Gross domestic savings	Gross domestic capital formation
1950/51	8.9	8.7
1956/57	12.2	15.0
1961/62	11.7	13.6
1966/67	14.0	16.9
1969/70	14.3	14.8
1974/75	16.0	16.8
1980/81	18.9	20.3
1985/86	19.5	21.7
1990/91	23.1	26.3
1995/96	25.1	26.9
2000/01	23.7	24.4
2001/02	23.7	24.4
2002/03	24.2	23.3

Notes: 1951: First Five Year Plan; 1956: Second Five Year Plan; 1961: Third Five Year Plan; 1966: Annual Plan; 1969: Fourth Five Year Plan; 1974: Fifth Five Year Plan; 1980: Sixth Five Year Plan; 1986: Seventh Five Year Plan; 1991: Annual Plan; 1992: Eighth Five Year Plan and 2000 to 2002: Annual Plans.

Source: GOI, *Economic Survey*, various issues.

investment in China's total investment rose from about 28 per cent during the FFYP period to about 30 per cent during 1957–77 (Riskin 1987, p. 72; World Bank 1983a, vol. 1, p. 80).

The rising share of inventory investment during the pre-reform period was mainly attributable to the systemic factors. These factors included (1) the hoarding of materials by the enterprises faced with ambitious plan targets and uncertainty of supply; (2) the mismatches between demand and supply under centralized planning and (3) the lack of incentives to economize on working capital in the absence of capital charge. Finally, it was also due to the Maoist policy of self-reliance, which encouraged local authorities and enterprises to be self-sufficient in material supply.

The share of inventory investment had declined to 17 per cent during the reform period (1978–98) (*ZGTJNJ* 1999, p. 68). However, it was still significantly higher than those of other less developed countries (LDCs). For instance, the average share of inventory investment for India, Pakistan, South Korea, Malaysia, Sri Lanka, Thailand, Columbia and Mexico during 1975–78 was only 7 per cent (World Bank 1983a, vol. 1, p. 80). Since inventory investment is less productive than the fixed investment, China's inordinately high share of inventory investment inevitably adversely affects its overall investment efficiency.

Investment can also be broken down into state and non-state investment. Prior to the reform, most investments were state investment. Reforms introduced in the late 1970s saw the reprivatization of the Chinese economy. As a result, the share of the non-state investment sector (collective and private enterprises) soared from 18 per cent in 1980 to 55 per cent in 1998.

Data on the breakdown of overall investment by broad economic sectors and industrial branches are not available for the pre-reform period. They are available only for state fixed investment, which is known as state basic construction investment (see Table 6.3). During the pre-reform period, the state investment plan gave high priority to the productive sector. Within the productive sector state investment was centred mainly on industry, and on heavy industry in particular. Under the reforms, the allocation of state investment was more balanced. The share of heavy industry decreased, whereas those of the non-productive sector in general, and housing and other social overhead as well as human resources sector in particular, increased. In the 1990s, Chinese state fixed asset investment was increasingly diverted from the industrial to the service sector as a result of the increasing share of the service sector in the economy. The share of secondary industry in fixed asset investment in the state owned enterprises has declined from 59 to 29 per cent whereas that of tertiary industry increased from 40 to 69 per cent (*ZGTJNJ* 2000).

The shift in investment allocation during the reform period was mainly due to change of growth and trade strategy. As mentioned earlier, during the pre-reform era, Stalinist or Feldman growth strategy was adopted, under which the planners aimed to achieve rapid growth through a high rate of investment. As a self-reliance or autarkic trade strategy was also adopted at the same time, capital goods had to be produced at home. Hence the maximization of the rate of investment required preferential development of heavy industry (Jones 1976, p. 116).

During the reform period, both growth and trade strategy had changed. Under the new strategy, the main source of growth was no longer high rates of investment but increase of total factor productivity (TFP). Total factor productivity can be increased only if workers are well motivated and provided with sufficient consumer goods, housing and other social overhead capital. Hence there had been increased need of state investment in these areas. At the same time, with the abandonment of self-reliance policy, capital goods can be imported. Hence, preferential development of heavy industry was no longer necessary.

The Indian Experience

In Table 6.4 we present the relative shares of gross fixed capital formation and changes in inventory in total gross domestic capital formation in India

Table 6.3 Sectoral allocation of state capital construction investment in China, 1952–1992 (%)

Year	Productive	Non-productive total	Housing	Agriculture	Light industry	Heavy industry	Other
1953–57	71.7	28.3	9.1	7.8	5.9	46.5	39.8
1958–62	86.8	13.2	4.1	12.3	5.2	56.1	26.4
1963–65	83.0	17.0	6.9	18.8	3.9	49.8	27.5
1966–70	89.4	10.6	4.0	11.8	4.0	57.4	26.8
1971–75	87.0	13.4	5.7	11.3	5.4	54.8	28.5
1976–78	84.0	16.0	6.9	12.1	6.6	54.7	26.6
1979–84	60.6	39.4	20.8	7.4	7.6	40.4	44.6
1985–92	66.5	33.5	13.4	3.4	7.2	42.9	46.5

Note: Other includes transport, telecommunications, commerce, science, medical and education, and urban construction.

Sources: Ma and Sun (1981), vol. 2, p. 412; *ZGTJNJ* 1993, pp. 156 and 158.

Table 6.4　*The relative shares of gross fixed capital formation and changes in stocks in total gross domestic capital formation in India (%)*

Year	Gross fixed capital formation	Changes in stocks
1951/52	85.16	14.83
1956/57	87.24	12.34
1961/62	87.99	10.39
1966/67	87.98	10.28
1969/70	91.06	8.93
1974/75	78.53	21.46
1980/81	99.06	0.93
1985/86	87.09	12.09
1990/91	95.28	4.71
1992/93	94.35	5.64
1993/94	100.91	−0.91
1995/96	91.82	8.17
1999/2000	93.62	6.37
2000/01	98.80	1.20
2001/02	98.70	1.30
2002/03	100.60	−0.60

Source:　GOI, *Economic Survey*, various issues.

during the plan period. Each of the years in the table represents the beginning of each plan period (see notes in Table 6.2).

As Table 6.4 shows, the share of gross fixed capital in total gross domestic capital formation has been very high throughout the period of planned development. In contrast the share of inventory investment in total capital formation has been quite low. The interesting point to note here is that the share of private sector in gross fixed capital formation has been considerably higher than that of public sector although, throughout the 1960s and 1970s, the public sector industries expanded their capital base through foreign aid programmes. Despite such a high rate of fixed capital formation in Indian industries the total factor productivity of the industrial sector has remained very low. This is due to the fact that Indian workers in organized industry are not well motivated, and are highly unionized – the role of the union has never been to co-operate with the employer to maintain industrial peace and improve factor productivity but rather to disrupt production. Furthermore, since public sector enterprises could rely on large government subsidies for their survival, they did not have to be accountable to anyone for their poor performance and low factor productivity. Their poor performance pulled the overall factor productivity in India down.

Table 6.5 Allocation of planned investment to heads of development in India (% distribution)

Heads of development	Third Plan (1961–66)	Fourth Plan (1969–74)	Fifth Plan (1974–79)	Sixth Plan (1980–85)	Seventh Plan (1985–90)	Eighth Plan (1992–97)	Ninth Plan (1997–02)	Tenth Plan (2002–07)
Agriculture and allied sectors	12.7	14.7	12.3	13.9	14.4	14.7	14.0	13.3
Irrigation and flood control	7.8	8.6	9.8	10.0	7.6	7.5	6.5	6.8
Energy	14.6	18.6	18.8	28.1	28.2	26.6	25.9	26.5
Industry and minerals	20.1	18.2	22.8	15.5	13.4	10.8	7.6	5.5
Transport and communications	24.6	19.5	17.4	16.2	17.4	18.7	19.4	21.3
Science, technology and environment	0.8	0.8	NA	0.9	1.4	2.1	2.1	2.0
Social services	14.3	15.6	NA	14.5	16.0	18.2	21.3	22.8
Other services	4.8	3.0	NA	0.8	0.7	1.4	3.2	1.8
All heads	100.0	100.0	100.0	100.0	100.0	100.0	100.0	100.0

Notes:
1. Social services include education, medical and public health, family welfare, housing, urban development and other social services.
2. Other services include general economic services and general services.
3. Figures may not add up to exactly 100 per cent because of rounding.

Source: GOI, Economic Survey, various issues.

The allocation of planned investment to Heads of Development in India is presented in Table 6.5. As Table 6.5 shows, industry and minerals received a very large share of investment up to the end of the Fifth Five Year Plan, that is, up to the end of the 1970s. Along with industry, transport and communications also received a very large share of investment up to the mid-1970s. Since then, major emphasis has been placed on infrastructure development such as power and energy. In the 1980s and early 1990s energy attracted the largest share of investment. This trend is quite in keeping with India's needs. In recent years, since the economic reform began, the private sector has been playing a greater role in industry development and the state is paying greater attention to social services such as education, health and so on. Similar trends are noticeable in China as well. Overall, the share of investment going to industry has been much greater in China than in India.

IMPACT ON GROWTH: DEMAND EFFECT

The Chinese Experience

The contribution of investment to economic growth can be analysed from the demand and supply side. On the demand side, the increase in investment stimulates economic growth by creating effective demand. Total effective demand consists of consumption (C), gross domestic investment (I), and net exports (X−M). Their relative contribution to economic growth can be measured in terms of the ratio of their increases to the increase of real GNE (gross national expenditures), which are presented in Table 6.6.

Table 6.6   Relative contribution to economic growth of the components of effective demand in China, 1967–2003 (%)

Pre-reform	C	I	X−M
1967–70	53.5	49.1	−2.6
1971–75	67.1	34.8	−1.9
1976–78	53.4	58.8	−12.2
Post-reform			
1979–2003	54.0	42.8	3.2

Note: C=private and government consumption; I=investment; and X−M=net exports.

Sources: Pre-reform data: World Bank, *World Tables*, 1988–89, pp. 192–3. Post-reform data: *ZGTJNJ* 2004, pp. 65 and 323.

Table 6.6 shows that Chinese economic growth had been more dependent on consumption and investment than on exports. In both the pre-reform and reform period, domestic demand (consumption and investment) provided the main impetus for economic growth. The relative contribution of net exports had been negative during the pre-reform period. Since the reforms, it has turned positive, but still remained modest when compared with that of domestic demand. Thus the hypothesis of the increasing importance of exports in economic growth during the reform period is not confirmed.

The Indian Experience

In India, too, a similar trend is noticed. In 1960 private consumption and investment accounted for 96 per cent of GDP, and the external resource balance, -3 per cent. In 1990, the year before the economic reform programme began, the contribution of private consumption and investment to GDP declined slightly to 91 per cent but that of resource balance remained at -3 per cent. In 1998, the contribution of private consumption and investment to GDP increased to 94 per cent but that of external resource balance further worsened to -5 per cent. Hence, while in China the contribution of the external resource balance turned positive, in India it deteriorated further.

However, in China, the contribution of investment to GDP has been very high, accounting for 59 per cent of GDP during 1976–78. But in India the contribution of private investment reached a maximum of 25 per cent in 1995. These are presented in Table 6.7.

Table 6.7   Structure of effective demand in India (% of GDP)

Item	C	I	G	X−M
1960	79	17	7	−3
1970	75	17	9	−1
1980	73	21	10	−4
1990	68	23	12	−3
1995	68	25	10	−2
1998	71	23	11	−5
2002	65	23	13	−1

Notes: C=private consumption; I=investment; G=government expenditures and X−M=net exports.

Source: World Bank, *World Development Report*, various issues.

IMPACT ON GROWTH: SUPPLY EFFECT

The Chinese Experience

On the supply side, the increase of investment stimulates economic growth by creating more capital stock and expanding thereby production capacity. The contribution of investment to economic growth on the supply side depends on (a) the proportion of national income invested, I/Y, or the rate of investment and (b) the incremental output-capital ratio, $\Delta Y/I$, or the investment efficiency. Table 6.8 gives the historical values of these two variables for selected periods in post-war China for which the economic condition was relatively stable. It shows that prior to reform, the incremental output-capital ratio had dropped by almost 40 per cent between the First FYP period (1953–57) and the Fourth FYP period (1971–75). Hence, despite the higher rate of investment, the rate of economic growth fell during the latter period.

China's pre-reform investment efficiency at 0.166 during 1971–75 was one of the lowest among the developing countries in Asia (Bhatia 1988, p. 15). Several hypotheses have been advanced to explain this (Ishikawa 1983, pp. 257–8). One of the explanations is the systemic factor. These include the absence of capital charges for the use of capital by state enterprises, the availability of free loans to finance their investment and the lack of enterprise accountability for loss and profits in investment decisions. All these factors implied that enterprises were under very little pressure to economize their use of capital.

Table 6.8   *Rate of growth of GDP* ($G(Y)$), *rate of investment* (I/Y) *and incremental output-capital ratios* ($\Delta Y/I$) *in China, 1952–2003 (selected periods)*

	$G(Y)$	(I/Y)	$(\Delta Y/I)$
Pre-reform			
1953–57	8.9	24	0.371
1966–70	8.3	26	0.319
1971–75	5.5	33	0.166
Post-reform			
1978–84	9.2	35	0.263
1985–2003	9.8	39	0.251

Sources: Real national income growth data for the pre-reform period from *ZGTJNJ* 1992, p. 34; real GDP growth data for the post-reform period from *ZGTJNJ* 2004, p. 55; rate of investment data are from Table 6.1.

Another explanation for China's low investment efficiency during this period is China's lopsided investment structure. Heavy industry was given the major share of the investable resources due to the policy of preferential development of heavy industry. It is well known that the incremental output-capital ratio in the heavy industrial sector is much lower than that of the light industrial sector. Hence the heavy concentration of capital in heavy industry reduced its overall productivity.

In terms of regional allocation, the Chinese investment structure was also lopsided because it favoured interior region during this period for fear of the Soviet invasion. Whereas during the FFYP period (1953–57) the more productive coastal region received the main share of state capital construction investment (42 per cent), the interior region known as the 3rd front received merely 26 per cent of the state capital construction investment. The regional allocation of investment was reversed during the Cultural Revolution period (1964–75): the 3rd front received about half of the national total capital construction investment (Ishikawa 1983, p. 257). Because of its inaccessibility and lack of supporting infrastructure facilities and industries, about 30 per cent of the factories built in the 3rd front had remained underutilized. The morale of the labour force at the 3rd front factories was very low because of the separation of their families and lack of school facilities for their children (*DDZGGDZCTZGL* 1989, p. 93).

Last but not least, the striving of individual regional authorities for an independent industrial system regardless of cost and comparative advantage under the 'self-reliance' policy resulted in duplicate investments and lowered overall investment efficiency.

However, all the above-mentioned hypotheses remain more or less untested as the available data are not good enough to isolate the effects of these different factors and to identify their relative weights behind China's low investment efficiency.

Decentralization of investment decisions under the reforms introduced since 1979 had significantly improved the investment efficiency. As Table 6.8 shows, the incremental output-capital ratio during 1978–2003 was more than 50 per cent higher than that of 1971–75.

The Indian Experience

For India, the rate of growth of GDP, the rate of investment and output-capital ratios are presented in Table 6.9. Table 6.9 cannot be compared with Table 6.8 because figures given in Table 6.9 are for individual years, whereas for Table 6.8 they are for particular periods. Nevertheless Table 6.9 gives an indication of the trend noticed in India. Like China, investment efficiency worsened during the pre-reform period as the incremental output-capital

Table 6.9   Growth of GDP, rate of investment and incremental output-capital ratios in India

Year	GDP	Investment I/Y	Output-capital ratios $\Delta Y/I$
1960–61	7.1	14.4	0.4931
1970–71	5.0	15.4	0.3247
1980–81	7.2	20.3	0.3547
1990–91	5.4	26.3	0.2053
1995–96	7.3	26.8	0.2723
1998–99	6.8	23.0	0.2954
1999–2000	6.1	25.3	0.2411
2000–01	4.4	24.4	0.1803
2001–02	5.8	23.1	0.2511
2002–03	4.0	23.3	0.1717

Sources: as for Table 6.2.

ratio dropped from 0.4931 in the early 1960s to 0.2053 in the early 1990s. In 2002–03, it further declined to 0.1717. In India also for state enterprises, capital was heavily underpriced and there was no enterprise accountability for loss and profit of investment decisions. These led to excessive use of capital. In India also the emphasis on the policy of self-reliance and concentration of investment in a few regions may have undermined the efficiency of investment. As in China, India investment efficiency has significantly improved under the reforms.

INVESTMENT FINANCING

The Chinese Experience

Domestic investment can be financed by either domestic saving or external capital. Table 6.10 shows that Chinese domestic capital formation was mainly financed by its own saving. In fact, its domestic saving constantly outstripped its domestic investment, making China a net capital exporter rather than importer during 1960–2002.

However, external capital did play an important role during two periods of Chinese economic history. The first period was the FFYP period (1953–57). During this period, China received US\$300 million in Soviet economic loans, which accounted for 1.5 per cent of China's state capital construction investment (Ma 1961, p. 36). During this period China's trade

Table 6.10   *Financing of gross domestic investment in China, 1960–2002*
           (selected period, % of GDP)

Years	GDI	GDS	Net foreign capital inflow
1960–64	22.2	22.9	−0.7
1965–69	22.5	23.0	−0.5
1970–74	28.5	29.1	−0.6
1975–79	31.5	31.7	−0.2
1980–84	30.8	31.6	−0.8
1985–91	38.3	38.6	−0.3
1993–2000	40.0	42.0	−2.0
2002	40.0	43.0	−3.0

Notes: GDI: gross domestic investment; GDS: gross domestic saving.

Sources: 1960–69: World Bank 1988b, p. 27; 1970–2002: World Bank, *World Tables*, 1993,
pp. 184–5 and World Bank, *World Development Indicators*, 2004, table 4.9.

balance incurred a net deficit of 550 million yuan (Riskin 1987, p. 75)
which was partly financed by Soviet loans. Soviet loans, however, stopped
in 1957 and China had started to pay back the Soviet credit in 1955. In that
year, Chinese trade balance turned into surplus and became a net capital
exporter. However, the Soviet credit was not completely paid back until
1965 (Riskin 1987, p. 76).

Foreign capital assumed an increasingly important role during the
reform period. Between 1985 and 1998, the share of fixed investment
financed by external capital soared from 3.6 per cent to 9 per cent (*ZGTJNJ*
1998, p. 28). However, even during this period, China's domestic saving was
larger than its domestic investment and, hence, China was a net capital
exporter not importer.

The relative independence of China from external capital contrasts
sharply with those of Japan and other developing Asian nations. For Japan,
during its early industrialization drive, external capital contributed about
one-fifth of its investment (Minami 1994a, p. 216). Similarly, most Asian
developing countries were heavily dependent on foreign capital during the
post-war period (World Bank, *World Tables*, 1988–89; 1993).

China's unique financial position was mainly due to the rapid increase of
its rate of saving from about 21 per cent during the First FYP period to 32
per cent on the eve of the reforms. It reached 42 per cent in early 2000s. These
rates of saving were much higher than those of Japan in the pre-war period
(Minami 1994a, p. 156), which peaked at 25 per cent in 1940. They were also
much higher than those of other contemporary developing countries at

Table 6.11   Sources of saving in China, 1978–98 (selected years, %)

Sources of saving	1978	1984	1989	1996	1998
Central government budget	50.9	19.6	9.5	47.1	49.0
Enterprise and local government	34.2	34.9	39.7		
Households	14.9	45.5	50.7	52.9	51.0
Total	100.0	100.0	100.0	100.0	100.0

Note: columns may not add to 100 per cent because of rounding.

Sources: data for 1978 and 1984 are from World Bank (1988b) p. 28; the 1989, 1996 and 1998 figures are estimated from data in *ZGTJNJ* 2001, according to the World Bank's procedures and assumptions. Central government budgetary and household saving were first estimated. Enterprise and local government saving were derived as residual between gross domestic saving and the sum of central government budgetary and household saving (see World Bank 1988b, apps 2 and 3).

China's comparative stage of development. Thus, for instance, China saved 36 per cent of its GDP in 1989, whereas other low-income countries saved merely half of that (18 per cent) (World Bank, *World Development Indicators*, 1991, p. 220).

China's rate of saving during the pre-reform period was mainly attributable to the high rate of government saving. Table 6.11 shows that on the eve of the reforms in 1978, the central government was the largest saver. In fact, government (both central and local) saving accounted for about 73 per cent of domestic saving on the eve of the reform (World Bank 1985, p. 145).

Government saving is simply the difference between its current revenues and current expenditures (World Bank 1988b, apps 2 and 3). The main sources of current revenues are profit from the state enterprises, industrial and commercial taxes and agricultural taxes. The profit from state enterprises is essentially a hidden commodity tax and is usually treated in the same way as other taxes (Ma 1961, p. 42).

During the pre-reform period (1953–78), profit from state enterprises was the largest component of current revenues. Its share in total current revenues soared from 39 to 51 per cent between 1957 and 1978 (*ZGTJNJ* 1992, p. 232). The overall tax revenues (enterprise profit delivery plus other tax revenues) accounted for over 90 per cent of Chinese current revenue during the pre-reform period. The main components of government current expenditure are public consumption expenditure, which includes expenditure on education, health, defence and public administration, and expenditure in support of private household consumption. The latter includes price

Table 6.12   Average tax burden in China, 1952–1991 (%)

1952	20.4
1957	20.6
1967	24.0
1970	29.5
1978	31.1
1984	19.4
1991	16.5
1998	11.7

Sources: *ZGTJNJ* 1990, pp. 232–3; 1993, p. 219; 1999, pp. 55 and 268; and World Bank, *World Tables*, 1988–89, pp. 192–3; 1993, pp. 184–5.

subsidies and transfer payments. The relatively high level of government saving during the pre-reform period was mainly the result of the relatively high level of tax burden and the relatively low level of public current expenditure in China. Measured as the ratio between tax revenues and GDP, China's average tax burden increased from 20 per cent in 1952 to 31 per cent in 1978 (Table 6.12). It averaged 27 per cent during 1978–80. In contrast, the average tax burden was only 13 per cent for other developing countries with per capita income of less than US$300 during this period (World Bank 1988b, p. 390).

During the same period China's current expenditures were relatively low due to the relatively lower degree of urbanization. During 1952–78, according to official statistics, the percentage share of urban population in total population hardly changed. It stood at about 12 per cent in both 1952 and 1978 (World Bank 1983a, vol. 3, p. 96). In 1980, the degree of China's urbanization was only 13 per cent. In contrast, the degree of urbanization in India and other low-income countries reached 22 and 19 per cent respectively in 1980 (World Bank, *World Development Report*, 1981, p. 172). A low degree of urbanization entails low expenditure on housing and other infrastructure facilities.

Another contributing factor to low government current expenditure during this period was the relatively low central government expenditure on health and education. Health expenditure accounted for only 2 per cent of central government budgetary expenditure in 1979. This percentage had hardly changed since the early 1950s (World Bank 1983a, vol. 3, p. 51). Education accounted for only 6.6 per cent of central government budgetary expenditure in 1977, which was relatively low compared with 15 per cent for other developing countries (World Bank 1983a, vol. 3, p. 182). Despite the relatively low level of central government expenditure, China had been

Table 6.13   Farmers' tax burden (billion current yuan)

	1952	1978
Agricultural tax[1]	2.7	2.8
Monopolist profit[2]	3.4	12.0
Monopsonist profit[3]	2.5	39.6
Sub total	8.6	54.4
Total tax burden[4]	15.5	109.1
Farmer tax burden (%)	55.5	50.0

Notes and sources:
1. *ZGTJNJ* 1993, p. 220.
2. Derived as profit and taxes mark-up in industrial consumer goods prices multiplied by its retail sales in rural area. Profit and tax element of prices: figures for 1952 and 1978 are from Perkins and Yusuf (1984, p. 18).
3. The tax element of agricultural purchase is derived as the difference between free market price and average purchase price. This is multiplied by the total purchase to arrive at total monopsonist profits. The estimate for 1952 is for grain only (Perkins and Yusuf 1984, p. 21). The estimates for 1978 are for seven commodities (grain, edible oil, pig, mutton, fowl, eggs and seafoods) for which the relevant data are available. The purchase value of these products accounted for 47 per cent of total agricultural purchase in 1978. The price and purchase data are from *ZGSYWJTJZL* 1990, pp. 143–4, 267–9; *ZGGNSCTJNJ* 1991, pp. 153–5 and 346.
4. See Table 6.12.

able to maintain a relatively high standard of health and education in the past. The secret to this lay mainly with the shifting of the health and education financial burden from central government to local authorities and collectives.

The distribution of tax burden in pre-reformed China was rather unbalanced. Farmers had to bear the heaviest burden. Table 6.13 shows the various visible and invisible taxes which farmers had to pay. Agricultural tax was the most important visible tax. It is in effect a tax on land. Agricultural tax had remained relatively stable during 1952–78 at about 3 billion yuan. It had increased significantly only during the reform years.

The invisible taxes paid by the farmers include the monopolist profit and the monopsonist profits made by the state producing and trading enterprises. Prior to reform, state enterprises monopolized the supply of manufactured goods. The prices of manufactured goods were set much higher than the cost of their production. The profit mark-up plus commodity tax accounted for about 32 per cent of the manufactured prices on average during 1952–78 (Perkins and Yusuf 1984, p. 18). In the reform period it had declined to about 10 per cent (*ZGTJNJ* 1993, pp. 417 and 419). As shown in Table 6.13, the tax element of rural retail sales of manufactured consumer goods had become increasingly important during the pre-reform period due to increased sales volume in rural areas.

However, by far the most important invisible tax imposed on farmers during the pre-reform period was the monopsonist profit associated with the agricultural procurement scheme under which farmers were required to deliver to the state a certain amount of their produce at below market prices. The difference between the state purchase prices and the actual market prices constituted an element of tax or monopsonist profits made by state trading enterprises. An estimate of this tax element for eight agricultural products for which data are available is presented in Table 6.13. This shows that both the visible and invisible taxes together contributed roughly 50 per cent of China's total tax revenues during this period.

The market-orientated reforms introduced since 1979 reduced the tax elements of both agricultural purchase and rural manufactured sales. The abolishment of the state compulsory purchase scheme together with the increased sale of farm products at market outlets narrowed the market and purchase price differential. At the same time, increased competition, especially from the township and village and other non-state enterprises, eroded the monopsonist position of state industrial enterprises leading to a reduced profit mark-up of their manufactured goods sold in the rural area. Hence, overall, the farmers' share of national tax burden is expected to decline under the reforms.

Under the market-orientated reform the main source of domestic saving had been shifted to the private household saving (Table 6.11). By 1999, the share of government saving declined, whereas the share of household savings soared to 51 per cent. Thus, the continued rise of China's rate of saving since 1979 was mainly sustained by a rapid increase of its personal saving rates.

The Indian Experience

In India also a substantial part of investment expenditure was financed by domestic savings. The bulk of the domestic savings came from the household sector. Hence the bulk of the investment finance came from the household sector. Table 6.14 shows the major sources of financing of gross domestic investment and their relative contribution to total finance capital.

As Table 6.14 shows, in the early days of India's development, the contribution of the household sector to total domestic savings was around 50 per cent. The reason for such a modest contribution was that at the time of India's independence in 1947 about 88 per cent of India's total population

Table 6.14   *The sources of finance for investment expenditure in India (% of each in the total GDI)*

Year	GDS Total	Household	Private corporate sector	Public sector	GDI	Savings investment gap
	(1)	(2)	(3)	(4)	(5)	(6)
1951/52	84.33	49.91	11.64	22.77	100	15.67
1960/61	80.52	50.76	11.37	18.37	100	19.48
1970/71	94.40	65.79	9.54	19.06	100	5.60
1980/81	92.83	67.97	8.00	16.86	100	7.17
1990/91	87.83	73.49	10.14	4.19	100	12.17
1995/96	93.48	67.58	18.35	7.54	100	6.52
1999/2000	95.68	84.99	15.78	−5.10	100	4.32
2000/01	97.50	90.00	16.90	−9.50	100	2.50
2002/02	101.3	98.30	14.90	−11.90	100	−1.30

Source: GOI, *Economic Survey*, various issues.

lived in rural areas and these people relied on subsistence agriculture for their survival. Their capacity, therefore, in the early 1950s, to save was limited and a considerable part of total domestic saving came from the 12 per cent of families in urban areas. The household savings and total savings constituted only 5.04 and 8.39 per cent, respectively, of GDP in 1951–52. However, after the introduction of Green Revolution technology in Indian agriculture in the late 1960s the rate of growth of the agricultural sector and the capacity of peasant households to save more also increased. The capacity of the urban households to increase their level of savings also increased as the economy began to grow. By 2001–02, total household savings and domestic savings accounted for 98.3 per cent and 101.3, respectively, per cent of total investment.

The savings investment gap was filled mostly by foreign capital and aid inflow throughout the period and partly by deficit financing which was a token resource up to the mid-1990s.

The performance of the public sector in generating savings has been rather dismal. This is mainly due to the fact that public enterprises failed to earn a reasonable rate of return on investment, successive governments made little effort to raise revenue by reforming the tax structure, and subsidies and interest payments on loans took away a substantial part of the total revenue of the government.

India's average tax burden remained very low throughout the period of India's planned development. Even during the 1990s, when India began to

Table 6.15   Average tax burden in India, 1980–2003 (%)

Year	Tax burden
1980/81	15.2
1990/91	17.2
1998/99	14.6
1999/2000	15.6
2000/01	16.0
2001/02	17.8
2002/03	17.3

Source: GOI, *Economic Survey*, various issues.

implement economic reform programme, the average tax burden was less than 20. This is illustrated in Table 6.15.

India's agricultural sector remained sacrosanct throughout the period of development. No government, due to the fear of political backlash, ever dared to impose tax on farm income. There was also large-scale tax evasion by the business community. For three decades of planned development since 1951–52, no serious attempt was made to collect personal income tax from salaried people and wage-earners. Hence much of the tax revenue had to come from indirect taxes.

SUMMARY AND CONCLUSIONS

To summarize, China's post-war modern economic growth would have been impossible without a rapid rise of its rate of investment in the early 1950s and the sustaining of it at a relatively high level in the period thereafter. The high rate of investment led to a high rate of growth in China in two ways. First, it increased Chinese effective demand. During both the pre-reform and reform periods between one-third and one-half of the increase in GNP was due to an increase in investment. Second, it increased Chinese capital stock and hence production capacity. The rate of economic growth is the product of the rate of investment and the incremental output-capital ratio or the investment efficiency. By international comparison, the Chinese rate of investment was much higher than that of Japan and other developing countries at a comparative stage of development. Its investment efficiency, on the other hand, was much lower than those of other countries. Hence, China's modern economic growth during the post-war years was mainly accounted for by its high rate of investment. The relative low efficiency of investment was partly due to its lopsided investment structure with an overconcentration of investment in inventory, heavy industry and in 3rd front construction. It was also partly due to systemic factors. Decentralization of investment decisions under the reforms introduced since 1979 had significantly improved China's investment efficiency.

China is unique in terms of its source of investment financing. It was one of the few countries in the world which not only financed its investment through its own saving, but also exported capital during its early industrialization drive. The relative abundant supply of investment capital during the pre-reform period was mainly the result of 'forced saving' or government saving. In the past, the government was apprehensive that in the absence of forced or government saving, national saving might drop drastically. However, this proved to be wrong in recent years, during which national saving continued to rise despite the decline of government saving and most of the increased saving came from voluntary household saving.

Compared with China, India's not so impressive growth performance can be explained by the relatively modest rate of investment resulting from a modest rate of savings. However, a country's economic growth is not only dependent on the rate of investment undertaken but also very much on the conducive or growth-promoting cultural and political factors. In China, Singapore, Taiwan and Hong Kong, totalitarian and semi-totalitarian states and Confucian culture helped raise the rate of savings and investment to very high levels and enabled the government to implement investment programmes very effectively to achieve high rates of economic growth. In India political, socio-cultural institutions and ideological factors have never been very conducive to raising the level of domestic savings and investment and to implementing investment programmes effectively.

7. Population and employment

Is a high rate of population growth a blessing or a curse to a country's modern economic growth? The answer to this question is still hotly debated among economists (Clark 1967; Enke 1971; Simon 1977). The relationship between population growth and per capita income growth depends in practice on the relationship between population growth and capital accumulation, on the one hand, and between population growth and technical progress, on the other (Thirlwall 1989, p. 152). Opponents of rapid population growth argue that increased population reduces a country's rate of saving, leading to a lower rate of capital accumulation and, hence, the relationship between population growth and per capita income growth is negative. Proponents of rapid population growth, on the other hand, argue that increased population induces work and production incentives, generates economies of scale and thereby enhances the rate of technical progress. Thus, the relationship between population growth and per capita income growth is positive.

In China and India, the most populous countries in the world, there is little doubt that high population growth in the past was considered a burden rather than a blessing, for two obvious reasons. One is that high population growth is considered detrimental for per capita income growth because of its capital-diluting effect. The second reason is that high population growth means high growth of labour supply and the government faces mounting pressure to provide productive employment for all workers in order to maintain social peace and justice. Hence, both countries' governments in the past sought to control their population growth. The purpose of this chapter is to contrast the policies undertaken by both governments to counter the problem of overpopulation and unemployment during the post-war years and to assess their relative effectiveness.

THE GROWTH RATE OF POPULATION

Table 7.1 presents the results of both governments' population control policy during the post-war years. The performance of both countries during their pre-reform period in population control was very similar. Both have failed to arrest the rampant population growth. The annual growth

Table 7.1   Population growth: China and India

China (annual average rate)		India (annual average exponential rate)	
Pre-reform		Pre-reform	
1953–57	2.4	1951–61	2.0
1958–62	0.5	1961–71	2.2
1963–65	2.4	1971–81	2.3
1966–70	2.7	1981–91	2.2
1971–75	2.1	1951–91	2.2
1976–80	1.3		
1952–80	2.0		
Post-reform		Post-reform	
1980–2003	1.2	1990/91–2001/02	1.9

Sources: China: Kueh 1984, p. 449; *ZGTJNJ* 2004, p. 95. India: Krishnamurty 1984, p. 164; GOI, *Economic Survey*, various issues.

rate of population in both countries averaged about 2 per cent which is similar to the average of other low-income countries (World Bank, *World Development Report* 1989, pp. 216–17). However, the performance of both countries differs significantly during the post-reform period: while the Indian population during the post-reform period followed a similar trend in the pre-reform period and continued to grow at a relatively high rate of 2 per cent per year, China has managed to cut back its population growth rate during the post-reform period from 2 per cent to 1.3 per cent per annum. Owing to the success of Chinese population control policies during the reform period, the rate of population growth for the entire post-war years was significantly lower in China than that in India.

WHY THE CHINESE GROWTH RATE IS LOWER

To unravel the mystery of China's relatively low population growth rate as compared to that of India, we need to look at the source of population growth. The rate of growth of population is simply the difference between the average birth and death rate of a country. The average birth rate is strongly influenced by the fertility rate (that is, the average number of children a female bears in her lifetime) and the net reproduction rate (that is, the number of girls born per woman). The average death rate, on the other hand, reflects both the standard of a country's health care facilities and their accessibility to the general populace. Table 7.2 presents the determinants of

Table 7.2   Birth, death and fertility rates of the Chinese and Indian
            population

	China		India	
	1965	2003	1965	2002
Crude birth rate per 1000 population	37.9	12.4	45.0	24.0
Crude death rate per 1000 population	9.5	6.4	20.0	9.0
Total fertility rate	2.7[1]	1.8[2]	4.8[1]	3.0[2]
Average annual growth of population (%)	2.8	0.6	2.5	1.9

Notes:
1. 1979.
2. 2000–05.

Sources: China: *ZGTJNJ* 2004, p. 95. India: World Bank, *World Development Report*,
1981; 1987; GOI, *Economic Survey*, 2000/01, p. 51; World Bank, *World Development
Indicators*, 2004, table 2.1.

population growth rate in China and India for two benchmark years in both
the pre- and post-reform period.

One of the distinctive features of the Chinese and Indian population in
the pre-reform period is the high rate of births in 1965: 37.9 births per thousand population in China and in India the figure was even higher, at 45.
Another distinctive feature is that the Chinese death rate in 1965 was only
half of that of India in the same year, reflecting the excellent performance
of the Chinese health care system under Mao. The third important feature
is that during the post-reform period, both countries have succeeded in
reducing their birth rate, but China performed much better than India in
birth rate reduction. China managed to reduce its birth rate by 60 per cent
between 1965 and 1998 whereas India has reduced its birth rate by only 40
per cent. The fourth feature is that the birth rate in India remains relatively
high even after its decline during the post-reform period. In 1998 India's
birth rate at 26.5 per thousand population is 65 per cent higher than that
of China in the same year. The significantly higher birth rate of India
during the post-reform period caused its total fertility rate to remain relatively high compared to that of China. The Indian fertility rate at 2.7 in
1998 is almost 60 per cent higher than that of China. Thus, the reason why
the Chinese population growth rate is lower than India's during the post-
reform period is that the Chinese government has been more successful
than the Indian government in controlling the birth rate and fertility rate.

The current high population growth rate in India is due to the large size of the population in the reproductive age group. The estimated contribution of this reproductive age group to the high population growth rate is about 60 per cent. The persistence of the high fertility rate is due to the unmet need for contraception. This unmet need for contraception contributes 20 per cent to the high fertility rate. Furthermore, couples' desire to maintain a high fertility rate, stemming from a high child mortality rate, contributes 20 per cent to the prevalence of the high fertility rate. Accordingly, both of the above noted factors seem to have kept the couple protection rate (that is, the percentage of couples within the reproductive age group using any form of contraception) at only 48.2 per cent in 1999 (GOI, *Economic Survey*, 2004).

BIRTH CONTROL POLICY

China

The slower growth rate of the Chinese population during the post-reform period reflects the success of the Chinese birth control policy. China's population policy has evolved through different stages during the post-war years. Unlike India, the Chinese government in the early post-war years, that is, the 1950s and the 1960s, did not undertake a population control policy because of the influence of Maoist ideology. Mao's thought on population and economic growth is similar to that of Clark and Simon, who subscribe to the hypothesis that there is a positive relation between population growth and economic growth. According to Mao, 'among all matters in the world, human reserves are more precious and as long as we have manpower, any miracle can be achieved' (Mao 1965, pp. 601–3). Hence he did not sanction a policy of population control. Mao's view was criticized by an academic, the President of Beijing University, Ma Yinchiu, and as a result a vigorous debate on China's population policy was ensured in the late 1960s. The debate ended with victory to Mao's thought. Ma was severely criticized as a rightist and was fired as President of the university in 1960.

The failure of GLF was a severe blow to Mao's population policy, as between 14 million and 30 million people were reported dead from starvation because of agricultural failure. Confronted with this grim reality, a population control policy was formally initiated in the early 1970s. Measures introduced to reduce the birth and fertility rate include (a) the encouragement of late marriage; (b) the encouragement of late childbearing (that is, the deferring of first delivery); (c) prolonging the time between births via the use of an intrauterine device (IUD) after the first birth, and finally (d) encouragement of fewer births by requiring sterilization of one partner after the second birth (see Bannister 1997, p. 342; Liu 1984, p. 157). But, the birth control policy was never effectively enforced during Mao's lifetime. It was not until after his death in the late 1970s that the government stepped up its effort to restrict population growth. In 1979 a coercive one-child policy was officially initiated under which urban Han Chinese couples are allowed to bear only one child; whereas rural Han Chinese couples are subject to different rules in different locations (Banister 1997, p. 342). In general, most couples are required to stop childbearing after one or two births. Beginning with Sichuan Province in 1979, all municipalities and provinces had implemented this policy by 1982. The success of the policy is evidenced from the steep decline of the Chinese fertility rate after 1970. The Chinese fertility rate dropped from a high of almost 6 in the early 1970s (Liu 1984, p. 157) to a low of 1.9 in the late 1990s (Banister 1997, p. 343), which is below the replacement level of fertility.

India

The Indian government adopted a birth control programme much earlier than China, namely, back in the early 1950s, but the policy was not effectively implemented until the mid-1960s (Krishnamurty 1984). By and large, the major difference between India's birth control policy and that of China was that the former's was non-coercive with the exception of the period of 1975–77 when a coercive birth control programme was in place to enforce sterilization targets. After 1977, the government birth control programme attempted to avoid coercion of any kind. As a result the sterilization targets were constantly underachieved (see Table 7.3).

Hence the Indian birth control programme is normally characterized as good in intention but poor in achievement (see Krishnamurty 1984). The ineffectiveness of the non-coercive Indian birth control programme is mainly due to the difficulty of implementing the programme in rural areas

Table 7.3   Indian birth control programme: achievement as a % of target

Method of family planning	1974/75	1976/77	1978/79	1980/81
Sterilizations	67.5	192.1	37.0	68.6
IUD insertion	71.7	50.9	91.7	76.2
Equivalent conventional contraceptive users	72.0	78.7	86.8	67.5
Total	70.5	123.7	64.30	68.7

Source: Krishnamurty 1984, p. 175.

as three-quarters of the Indian population still lived in rural areas. It is well known that the fertility rate is generally higher in rural areas where illiteracy and poverty are rampant and marriage at an early age is still widely practised, especially among the Muslim population, which numbers more than 100 million.

UNEMPLOYMENT

High population pressure in China and India makes it difficult for both governments to provide jobs for a large number of people, thus leading to unemployment. Unemployment causes income inequality and poverty, and generates social instability. In the following we will examine (a) how both governments tackled the issue of unemployment in the past, and (b) to what extent they have succeeded.

China

Unemployment occurs when the supply of labour exceeds the demand of labour. The total supply of labour at a given time is determined by the backlog of unemployment and the new entrants to the labour force. The latter, in turn, is determined by the working age population multiplied by the labour force participation rate. China had been relatively successful in solving the unemployment problem during the pre-reform period. In the early 1950s, China inherited a huge backlog of unemployed from the old regime. In addition, new entrants to the workforce were increasing at a speed higher than the rate of total population increase. Consequently, China was confronted with a massive unemployment problem in the urban area at that time. In the rural sector at the same time, each farmer had only 119 workdays each year as compared to the full employment norm of 250 workdays. However, by the mid-1970s, China had succeeded in reducing urban unemployment and raising the agricultural labour requirement to approximately 250 annual mean days per year. Rawski (1979) shows that this impressive employment record was achieved through a combination of measures. These included strict controls on rural–urban migration, the sending down of urban-educated youths to the countryside, the enlargement of the capacity of agriculture to absorb surplus workers through the intensification of cropping practices and cycles, and a shift to labour-using farm activities, including rural construction works.

Table 7.4 compares the growth of the labour force and unemployment during both the pre-reform and the post-reform periods. It shows that during the pre-reform period, the working-age population grew at a rate of

*Table 7.4   Growth of labour force and employment in China (annual %
            rate)*

	Pre-reform period	Post-reform period
Working-age population	2.10[1]	2.00[3]
Total employment	2.60[2]	2.50[4]
Economic growth	5.00	9.40[4]
Employment elasticity of growth	0.51	0.27[4]

Notes:
1. 1953–82.
2. 1952–78.
3. 1982–2000.
4. 1978–2003.

Source: *ZGTJNJ* 2004, pp. 97 and 121.

*Table 7.5   Percentage share of employment growth by economic sectors in
            China*

	1952–78	1978–2003
Total employment growth	100.0	100.0
Agriculture	57.0	24.0
Non-agriculture, of which:	43.0	76.0
Industry	27.9	27.0
Service	15.1	49.0

Source: *ZGTJNJ* 2004, p. 121.

2.1 per cent faster than the growth rate of total population, of 1.9 per cent.
The strong growth of the working-age population was more than offset by
the even higher rate of growth of employment at, 2.6 per cent, generated
during this period, which enabled China not only to employ the tens of millions of new entrants to the labour force each year but also absorbed the
backlog of surplus labour which had been inherited from the old regime.
    Table 7.5 shows the creation of employment by different economic sectors
in both the pre- and the post-reform periods in China. During the pre-
reform period, employment growth occurred primarily in the agricultural
sector. Agriculture was responsible for almost 60 per cent of the total
employment growth. In the non-agricultural sector, the main new job
provider was urban industry which accounted for two-thirds of the new

employment in this sector. Since the industries were almost 100 per cent publicly owned, it can be concluded that in terms of ownership type, most new jobs during the pre-reform era stemmed from the collective owned agriculture sector and the public owned urban industrial sector.

During the post-reform period, as a result of liberalization and privatization, the Chinese unemployment problem has worsened (Tisdell and Chai 1998, pp. 31–3). As shown in Table 7.4, the rate of growth of the working-age population during the post-reform period was about 2 per cent per year, which is similar to that in the past, but the demand for labour grew at a much higher rate of 2.8 per cent a year thanks to the higher economic growth rate of 10 per cent during this period. Hence, China has little problem in providing jobs for the new entrants in the labour force. As can be seen from Table 7.5 in contrast to the pre-reform period, most of the new jobs created, almost 80 per cent of them, were in the non-agricultural sector. Within the non-agricultural sector, most of the new jobs created were concentrated in rural township and village enterprises (TVEs) sectors in the 1980s; in the 1990s the main sources of new job creation shifted to both the rural and urban private industry including foreign invested enterprise sector (Naughton 1996, p. 285).

Despite the impressive growth of demand for labour under the reforms, the problem of unemployment and underemployment in China worsened due to the pressure to fire surplus workers in both the agricultural and the non-agricultural sector as a result of liberalization and privatization. Surplus labour or disguised unemployment are defined either as those workers employed with a value of marginal product of labour close to zero or negative or less than the wage rate. Post-reform China inherited a massive disguised unemployment from pre-reform China. In the mid-1990s, it was estimated that in the rural sector surplus labour amounted to about 27 per cent of the rural workforce (Tisdell and Chai 1998, pp. 31–2). In the urban area, disguised employment or surplus labour amounted to 20 per cent of the urban labour force.

Chinese surplus labour was traditionally kept in the work units instead of being laid off. However, starting in 1994, a massive lay-off has occurred in China which has swollen the army of unemployed. At the same time, despite the rapid economic growth of the Chinese economy, the employment elasticity of growth has dropped from 0.5 during the pre-reform period to 0.37 in the post-reform period, due to the structural change of employment. Thus rapid growth in recent years generated only a slightly higher growth rate of employment of 2.8 per cent as compared to 2.6 per cent in the past. This rate, however, was sufficient to absorb the demand for jobs by new entrants into the labour force but has not been sufficient to absorb the massive backlog of surplus labour, and, hence, the unemployment problem worsened. This is evidenced by the increased number of registered unemployed persons in urban areas, which shot up from 2.7 million in 1983 to 5.7 million in 1998 (*ZGTJNJ* 1998, p. 133). It should be noted that these' unemployment statistics only relate to those with urban residence registration and so does not include statistics for the floating rural population seeking jobs in urban areas. Furthermore, not all unemployed urban residents (with registered households in urban areas) register at the local labour bureaus. It is believed that this group amounted to about three-quarters of the registered unemployed (Tisdell and Chai 1998, p. 33). Hence the real rate of urban unemployment in urban areas is two or three times the official rate of about 3 per cent. Consequently, in 1998, 9 per cent of the urban workforce in the late 1990s were unemployed.

India

As in China, the Indian government in the early 1950s was also facing an uphill battle to find productive jobs for a massive backlog of unemployment, which it had inherited from the old regime, and the rapidly growing number of the new addition to the labour force. Initially, the government relied on a trickle-down effect, that is, through the maximization of the economic growth rate to reduce unemployment. But, due to the sluggish growth rates during the 1950s–1960s and the low employment elasticity of growth due to preferential development of capital-intensive heavy industries, this trickle-down effect did not work either. Since 1973, many Unemployment Alleviation Programmes (UAPs) were introduced to reduce the unemployment. But, according to the study by Bhole (1994, pp. 173–85), UAPs did not work either. This is evidenced by the increasing number of people on the registers of employment exchanges, which jumped from 5 million in 1970–71 to 37 million at the beginning of reform in 1991–92 (Bhole and Dash 2002, fig. 3). As in China, the official number of unemployed is an underestimate of the true number of unemployment as many unemployed do not take the trouble of registering themselves with an employment exchange.

Table 7.6 presents data on official rates of unemployment for the period 1972–73 to 1999–2000 based on nation-wide sample surveys. As Table 7.6 shows, the rate of unemployment was quite high during the pre-reform era. It varied between 5.6 per cent and 9 per cent in the rural area, 10.1 to 11.9 per cent in the urban area and 8 to 10 per cent at the all-India level during the period between 1972–73 and 1987–88. During this period the main labour absorbers were the unorganised sector or informal sector and the organized agricultural and organized urban public sector.

Table 7.7 presents the estimated employment in the organised public and private sector between 1960–61 and 1985–86. It can be seen from Table 7.7

Table 7.6   *Number of people unemployed per thousand persons in the labour force in India[1]*

	Rural area	Urban areas	Total
1972/73	90	108	99
1977/78	81	119	100
1983	82	101	91
1987/88	56	104	80
1993/94	56	85	70
1999/2000	71	83	77

Note: 1. Based on National Sample Surveys. Unemployment is measured on current daily status (CDS) and refers to the total person-days of unemployment of all people in the labour force during the reference week.

Source: Bhole and Dash 2002, p. 283.

Table 7.7   *Estimated employment in India's organized public and private sectors during the pre-reform period (millions)*

	Public sector (1)	Private sector (2)	Total (3)	(1) as % of (3) (4)	(2) as % of (3) (5)
1960/61	5.877	6.213	12.090	48.6	51.4
1970/71	8.852	8.639	17.491	50.6	49.4
1980/81	13.447	9.433	22.880	58.8	41.2
1985/86	15.493	9.564	25.057	61.8	38.2

Source: GOI, *Economic Survey*, various issues.

that total employment in the organized sector increased by about 13 million between 1960–61 and 1985–86. Seventy-four per cent of this increase was due to the public sector. Hence, the major responsibility of making provision for employment in the organized sector rested with the public sector. Columns 5 and 6 show that during the pre-reform period, while the share of the public sector in the creation of employment has continuously increased, that of the private sector has declined.

During the post-reform period, despite the increased rate of growth of GDP, the study by Bhole and Dash (2002) finds that both the magnitude and structure of unemployment in the organized sector as well as in the entire economy worsened rather than improved. This is evidenced from the rising number of unemployed registered with employment exchanges, which jumped from 37 million in 1991–92 to more than 40 million in 2004 (Overdorf 2004, p. 29). As per the National Sample Survey Organization (NSSO) figure (see Table 7.6), the rate of unemployment also increased between 1993–94 and 1999–2000, albeit only slightly. The worsening of unemployment problems can be attributed to several factors. To begin with, the stock of labour to be employed during the reform period is huge. The backlog of unemployment reached a massive scale of 40 million in the early 1990s. In addition, the country's rapidly expanding working-age population generates an increasing number of new entrants into the workforce.

At the same time, as evidenced by Table 7.8, the new job growth rate in the public sector declined from 4.2 per cent during the period between 1970–71 and 1975–76 to 0.19 per cent between 1996–97 and 1998–99. While the new job growth rate in the private sector has increased only modestly from 0.2 per cent in the first half of the 1970s to 1.31 per cent in the second half of the 1990s, this rate of increase is too small to offset the rate of decline in the public sector. As a result the annual average rate of increase in total employment declined from 2.75 in the first half of the 1970s to 0.7 per cent in the second half of the 1990s. The declining rate of employment growth in spite of stronger economic growth during the post-reform period resulted in a declining employment elasticity of growth which dropped from 0.53 during the period between 1970–78 and 1983 to 0.38 during 1997–2002 (Bhole and Dash 2002, p. 278). The main reason why growth during the post-reform period generated less employment than that in the pre-reform period is, according to one analyst, largely the result of a high-tech strategy which emphasized the development of a capital and technology intensive sector such as IT. Hence, very limited employment growth was generated (Overdorf 2004, p. 29).

Table 7.8   Annual average rate of increases in employment in India in different quinquenniums (%)

	Public sector	Private sector	Total
1970/71–1975/76	4.20	0.20	2.75
1976/77–1980/81	2.62	1.74	2.33
1981/82–1985/86	2.71	−0.05	1.83
1986/87–1990/91	1.52	0.83	1.31
1991/92–1995/96	0.42	2.09	0.88
1996/97–1998/99	0.19	1.31	0.72

Source: Bhole and Dash 2002, p. 276.

Unorganized and informal sectors

Since India's employment situation, discussed in the previous section, explains mainly employment in the organized public and private sectors in the country, the discussion presents only a partial picture of India's labour market and labour absorption sectors. We comment below on these issues.

India's informal sector, which does not operate in accordance with the rules and regulations set for the organized sector, is commonly known as the unorganized or unregistered sector consisting of firms with electricity but under ten workers or without electricity and over 20 workers. In practice, however, most firms with labour force numbers in excess of that which allow them to remain unregistered, employ a considerable number of casual labourers not officially declared and, hence, continue to remain outside the purview of the Factories Act (Harris-White 2004). Bhowmik's (1998) study suggests that the proportion of unorganized labour in various corporations stands somewhere between 40 and 85 per cent.

Only 8 to 9 per cent of the total workforce in the country is employed in the organized sector (GOI, *Economic Survey*, 2004/05). On the basis of this estimate, at the end of 2001–02, the total organized sector employment stood at 27.2 million and the workforce at 327.7 million (an estimated 8.3 per cent of the total workforce are employed in the organised sector). This means that 91.7 per cent of the workforce is employed in the unorganized informal sector. But the actual size of India's total workforce would be higher than the official figure of 327.7 million in 2002 and would be closer to Harris-White's (2004) estimate of 390 million because millions of female labourers who migrate to towns and cities in search of jobs along with their families, work as cooks and maids in middle-class families, street vendors selling vegetables and artefacts, or in building construction and so on. All these who are in urban slums are not captured by the NSSO's surveys (Srivastava and Sashikumar 2003). A very substantial proportion of this workforce migrates from rural areas to urban centres, capital cities and all metropolises throughout the country. However, it is virtually impossible to get a correct estimate of the number of migrants from rural to urban centres as the characteristic features and motivations of different groups of migrants are different and, accordingly, many of them remain outside the ambit of NSSO surveys. Hence, the study of India's informal economy and its labour force, which according to a recent estimate (Sinha et al. 1999) account for 60 per cent of net domestic product, 68 per cent of income, 60 per cent of savings, 31 per cent of agricultural exports and even 41 per cent of manufactured exports, is made more complex because the researcher had to collect information from innumerable localized pieces of evidence obtained, for the most part, from field research (Harris-White 1998). Roy et al. (2002), in their study of rural–urban migration and poverty in South

Asia, found that the Harris-Todaro model (1970) can only partially explain the motives behind the decision of poor families in West Bengal to migrate from their village to the Calcutta slums. The 'push factor' appeared to be a very important factor in their decision. The push factor was also an important factor for poor persons without families to migrate to cities.

Among all the members of families that migrated from rural Bengal to one Calcutta slum it was found that most female members quite easily obtained employment in the informal sector as cooks and housemaids. However, as Srivastava and Sashikumar's (2003) study shows, these migrants work longer hours, live in poor living conditions, in social isolation and with poor access to basic amenities. On the other hand, there are many male members of rural families who migrated to major cities in their own states to work to earn money to send the major part of their income to their families living in rural areas. There are still others who live permanently in villages not too far away from the urban centres but migrate to urban areas for work only for a few months during the agricultural slack season in villages. Thus labour mobility is closely linked to social and economic changes taking place in the villages (Mahesh 2004). Apart from all these, the number of interstate and intercity migrants is also not very small. However, this informal economy in which the vast majority of poor migrants live and work is a socially regulated economy. The state has very little direct control over this economy and this labour force. As we have pointed out earlier in this book, any development requires the rule of law, but in India the regulative law is unimportant as much of the economy is not regulated by law and socially influential and respectable people appear to be convinced that they are entitled to be above law (Harris-White 2004).

The conceptions of economy and the polity that currently prevail in mainstream economics and in other social sciences are inapplicable in India's vast socially regulated economy (Harris-White 2004). In recent years, the agents of political parties have been trying to bring this informal labour force under the control of unions affiliated to their respective political parties. Currently, only 7 per cent of India's labour force are on regular wages and salaries, and of this small proportion only half are unionized. Even this minute proportion of India's labour force caused havoc in India's organized industrial sector during the 1970s and 1980s. Even if the political party mafias become partly successful in their attempt to bring this labour force under the control of unions, the capacity of the informal sector and its labour force to contribute to the Indian economy would be badly impaired.

8.   Growth and human development

Growth is a necessary but not significant condition for improving the living standards of large numbers of people in poor countries, which have low per capita income. However, with an increasing population, if there is no growth, it would be difficult to improve peoples' economic and social condition even by transfer of income and assets to the impoverished sections of the community. In poor countries, there may be some very rich people, but the scope for redistribution is usually limited. Hence economic growth is necessary because it enables most members of society to become better off without someone becoming worse off (Perkins et al. 2001).

The overall economic performance of India and China during the second half of the 20th century, although inadequate for their needs, has been impressive in many respects. The economic growth rate has been quite respectable and several important human development indicators have exhibited an upward trend. What is more important is that such growth and human development have taken place within a reasonably stable macro-economic environment devoid of runaway inflation. We now illustrate, below, the principal features of both countries' economic growth and human development.

ECONOMIC GROWTH

Table 8.1 shows the average annual growth rates in net national product and per capita national product during each Five Year Plan period in India.

It can be seen from this table, that during all plan periods except the First Plan and Third Plan, at constant prices, the income recorded very indifferent growth rates. During the Third Plan, the net national product recorded −4.7 per cent average annual growth rates. The tremendous dislocation in production and interruption in economic activities resulting from severe draught and the war with Pakistan in 1965 would certainly have contributed significantly to such a decline in growth rate. The growth started to pick up during the Fifth Five Year Plan but there was a significant decline in growth during 1979–80. During the Sixth and Seventh Plans, the growth rate reached 5.5 per cent and 5.8 per cent respectively. For the entire pre-reform period (1950/51–1990/91), the national income at constant

Table 8.1   India: average annual growth rates of net national product (%)

Year		Net national product at constant prices	Per capita national product at constant prices
First Plan	1951–56	3.6	1.8
Second Plan	1956–61	4.0	2.0
Third Plan	1961–66	−4.7	−6.8
Three annual plans	1966–69	3.7	1.5
Fourth Plan	1969–74	3.3	1.0
Fifth Plan	1974–79	5.0	2.7
Annual plan	1979–80	−6.0	−8.2
Sixth Plan	1980–85	5.5	3.2
Seventh Plan	1985–90	5.8	3.6
Two annual plans	1990–92	2.5	0.4
Eighth Plan	1992–97	6.6	4.6
Ninth Plan	1997–2002	5.6	3.7

Source: GOI, *Economic Survey*, various issues.

prices recorded an annual average growth of 4 per cent, the so-called Hindu rate. But after the opening up of the Indian economy in 1991, India's growth rate reached 6.6 per cent during the Eighth Five Year Plan. This was the highest rate of growth at constant prices during the entire period of Five Year Plans. It should further be noted here that despite the inconsistent growth rate recorded during the Five Year Plans, this performance in both national income and per capita income growth represents a distinct improvement in any historical period for which information is systematically available. It certainly represents an acceleration of growth recorded during the first half of the 20th century (Bhagwati and Desai 1971).

China's economic growth rate during the pre-reform period is much higher than that of India. The real national income grew at an annual average of 6 per cent during the pre-reform period (1952–80) according to Chow (1993). During the post-reform period (1979–98), according to China's official statistics, GDP was up by 490 per cent in real terms with an annual average growth rate of almost 10 per cent (Wu 2000). However, it is generally agreed that the official data overstates the actual growth of China by 1.2 per cent because the GDP deflator used underestimates of the actual rate of inflation in China during this period. Nonetheless, even if one adopts the lower rate of growth of 8.8 per cent, China's economic growth rate during the post-reform period is significantly higher than that of India of 6.6 per cent.

CHANGE IN INDUSTRIAL STRUCTURE

To what extent has this process of expansion of national income been accompanied by marked shifts in industrial structure in both countries?

Table 8.2 records the available data on the relative distribution of net national product by sector of origin at 1980–81 prices in India. The table shows that the contribution of net income from agriculture has declined substantially from 46.5 per cent in 1970–71 to 23 per cent in 2002. The share of industry increased from 22.3 per cent in the early 1970s to 27 per cent in 2002. The share of service rose from 35.2 per cent to 51 per cent during the same period.

Table 8.3 presents the percentage distribution of employment by industries in India. The figures in this table are estimates from the World Bank as official figures on labour force distribution refer to the organized sector only, to the exclusion of the unorganized sector.

Table 8.3 shows that up to 1980, 70 per cent of Indian workers were still employed in the agriculture sector, whereas industry employed only about 13 per cent of the country's workforce.

Economic growth has also been accompanied by a rapid structural change in China. In 1952, China was still an agrarian economy, as agriculture accounted for over 58 per cent of its GDP. By 1980 the percentage share of agriculture in Chinese GDP had been reduced to 30 per cent. At

Table 8.2   India's distribution of national income by industries (%)

Year	A	M	S
1970/71	46.5	22.3	35.2
1980/81	39.0	23.1	37.9
1984/85	36.5	25.7	37.8
1990/91	32.7	28.0	39.3
1992/93	32.0	26.8	41.2
1996/97	27.6	28.9	43.5
2002	23.0	27.0	51.0

Notes:
A = agriculture which include forestry and fishery.
M = industry which includes mining and quarrying, electricity, gas, and water supply as well as construction.
S = services which include trade, hotels and restaurants, transports and communications, finance insurance, real estate, business services as well as community, social and personal services.

Source: GOI, *Economic Survey*, various issues; World Bank, *World Development Indicators*, 2004, table 4.2.

Table 8.3   India: distribution of labour force by industries (selected
              years, %)

Year	A	M	S
1960	73	11	16
1977	73	11	16
1980	70	13	17

Note: For A, M and S see notes to Table 8.2.

Source: World Bank, *World Development Report*, various issues.

Table 8.4   China: industrial structure (%)

Year	National income			Employment		
	A	M	S	A	M	S
1952	58	23	19	84	7	9
1980	30	49	21	69	18	13
2000	16	51	33	50	23	27
2003	15	52	33	49	22	29

Note: For A, M and S see notes to Table 8.2.

Sources: OECD 2002, p. 11; *ZGTJNJ* 1989, pp. 32 and 105; 2004, pp. 54 and 121.

the same time, the share of industry shot up from 23 per cent in 1952 to 49
per cent in 1980. Thus, by 1980, China's industry's share was almost twice
that of India. After the reform, China's industry's share continued to rise
and reached 51 per cent by 2000 (see Table 8.4).

In terms of labour share, the degree of industrialization in China is less
than that, as indicated by its income share. As in India, until very recently,
or at least up to 1980, almost 70 per cent of its labour force was still tied up
with agriculture. Even by 2003, half of Chinese workers were still engaged
in the agricultural sector.

It is well known that economic growth is accompanied by a shift of the
industrial structure towards service industry at the latest stage of development. The service sector had been neglected in China prior to reforms.
Hence, its income share stagnated at 20 per cent during the pre-reform
period. After the reform, its share did increase to 33 per cent, but it is still
much less than that of 44 per cent for India. Thus, it appears that the path
of development of the two countries differs in terms of structural change,
especially during the post-reform period. While China is still industrializing

and has not been transformed into a service economy, India appears to have skipped the stage of industrialization and leapfrogged directly from an agrarian economy into a service economy during the post reform-period.

PER CAPITA INCOME

The living standard of a country can be measured by its per capita income. As shown in Table 8.1 during the pre-reform period from 1950/51 to 1990/91 India's per capita income at constant prices grew slowly at an annual average of 1.7 per cent as a result of a moderate rate of growth of national income and a high rate of growth of population. Growth of per capita income in India, however, accelerated during the post-reform period. From 1990 to 2002, real national income per capita increased at a rate of 4 per cent a year (UNDP, *Human Development Report*, 2004, p. 186). This was the highest rate of growth during the entire period of India's Five Years Plans. In 1950 India's per capita income measured in terms of purchasing power parity adjusted US dollars is $619 (Maddison 2001, p. 215), and by 2002 it had risen to $2670 (UNDP, *Human Development Report*, 2004, p. 186).

As a result of higher economic growth and lower population growth, China's per capita income grew much faster than India's during both the pre- and post-reform period. According to Chow (1993), China's annual average rate of growth of income per capita is 4 per cent during the pre-reform period, which is almost two and half times that of India during the comparative period. During the post-reform era, between 1980 and 2000, China's annual average rate of growth of income per capita is about 7.8 per cent (OECD 2002, p. 11). Again this rate is 70 per cent higher than that of India during the comparative period.

The level of China's per capita income measured in terms of purchasing power parity adjusted exchange rate in 1950 is only $439 (Maddison 2001, p. 215), which is 30 per cent lower than that of India during the same period. Fifty years later, by 2002, China's per capita income in terms of purchasing power parity adjusted exchange rate hit $4580 (UNDP, *Human Development Report*, 2004, p. 185), which is almost 72 per cent higher than that of India. Thus, the living standard gap between the two countries has widened significantly during the second half of the 20th century.

HEALTH AND EDUCATION

The living standard of a country's resident is determined not only by his or her material welfare but also by qualitative aspects of life which are hard to

Table 8.5   India: expansion of health services (numbers)

Item	1951	1961	1971	1981	2003	% increase between 1951 and 2003
Hospitals and dispensaries	9 209	12 500	16 042	23 533	38 031	413.0
SC/PHC/CHC[1]	725	2 565	33 601	57 363	163 195	22 509.7
Hospital beds	117 198	230 000	348 655	569 495	914 543	780.3
Doctors	61 840	83 756	151 129	268 700	605 840	979.7
Nurses	18 054	35 584	80 620	143 887	832 000	4 608.4

Note: 1. Sub-centres, primary health centres and community health centres.

Source: as for Table 8.1.

quantify and can only be inferred indirectly from such indicators as health and education standard, availability of social and economic security, and the extent of income inequality. The United Nations considers these indicators together with the per capita income as the basic indicators for human development.

First, let us consider the health and education standard. In Table 8.5, we present the expansion of health services in India. It can be seen from the last column of the table that there was expansion in all aspects of health care service. The largest increases were, however, recorded in the number of community health centres and primary health centres. During the 52-year period between 1951 and 2003, the number of community and primary health centres increased by over 22 509 per cent. These centres play an invaluable role in rural health care. There were also considerable improvements in access to improved water sources and to sanitation facilities, as Table 8.6 illustrates.

As Table 8.6 shows, in 1998 nearly 93 per cent of the rural population and around 90 per cent of the urban population were supplied with drinking water facilities. But the access to sanitation facilities of rural population increased to only 8 per cent in 1998 during a 33-year period from only 0.7 per cent in 1965. But the access of urban population to sanitation facilities also increased to only 49.32 per cent from 28.4 per cent during the same period. By 2001, about 78 per cent of total households in the country comprising 90 per cent of urban households and around 73 per cent of rural households had access to safe drinking water (GOI, *Economic Survey*, 2004). By mid-1999, only 57 per cent of urban households had latrines or a connection to a septic tank or sewerage, whereas only about 18 per cent

Table 8.6   India: population with drinking water and sanitation facilities (% on 31 March)

Item/area	1965	1990	1995	1998
Drinking water supply				
Rural	56.30	73.90	82.80	92.50
Urban	72.90	83.80	84.33[1]	90.20[2]
Sanitation facilities				
Rural	0.70	2.40	3.59	8.10
Urban	28.40	45.90	49.91[1]	49.32[2]

Notes:
1. On 31 March 1993.
2. On 31 March 1997.

Source: as for Table 8.1.

of rural households had used latrines. But by March 2004, 95 per cent of the rural population throughout the country had access to safe drinking water (GOI, *Economic Survey*, 2004).

Table 8.7 presents some of the main indicators of improvement in Indian education facilities. As column 8 of the table shows, higher economic growth enabled the country continuously to improve the supply of education services for building up the social overhead capital necessary for accelerating the pace of economic growth. However, it appears that least emphasis has been placed on, and therefore least improvement was recorded in the expansion of primary education, which is now recognized as one of the most important prerequisites to achieving higher economic growth and development. On the other hand, most emphasis was placed on, and therefore largest increase in enrolment was recorded in, generalist tertiary education. The enrolment in BA, BSc and BCom degree courses increased by 3687.02 per cent and the enrolment in diploma and certificate courses increased by 3044.70 per cent, although the contribution of generalist education in the formation of human capital will not be as strong as that of primary education. The third largest increase in enrolment was recorded in degree courses in education. Enrolment in engineering and technical degrees also increased significantly. By 2000–01, the total enrolment at Primary (Class I to V), middle and upper primary (VI to VIII) and high secondary/pre-university schools reached 113.8 million, 42.8 million and 27.6 million from 100.9, 35.6 and 20.4 million, respectively, in 1991–92. Student enrolment in higher education for generalist degrees, diplomas and certificates rose from 4.83 million in 1991–92 (Table 8.7) to 9.2 million in 2002–03 (GOI, *Economic Survey*, 2003/04).

Table 8.7   India: growth in education services

Items	1950–51	1960–61	1970–71	1980–81	1990–91	1991–92	% increase between 1950/51 and 1991/92
1	2	3	4	5	6	7	8
Number of students in primary schools	19 154 457	34 993 829	57 045 441	74 194 739	97 375 300	100 939 202	+427.04
Number of students in middle schools	3 119 958	6 704 810	13 315 170	20 724 364	34 025 987	35 647 631	+1046.00
Number of students in high/higher secondary schools	1 441 254	3 345 197	7 600 543	11 871 161	19 057 399	20 338 186	+1311.11
Number of students enrolled in generalist courses:							
(a) BA, BSc and BCom	100 687	348 496	1 435 909	1 913 126	3 566 107	3 813 042	+3687.02
(b) MA, MSc and MCom	18 484	52 836	144 023	238 916	395 994	423 416	+2280.52
(c) Research	1 434	4 674	11 177	27 398	16 486	17 864	+1145.74
(d) Diploma/certificate	1 199	3 632	18 788	23 089	35 265	37 705	+3044.70
Number of students enrolled in professional education courses:							
(a) Education	4 135	19 005	56 922	71 204	117 231	125 345	+2936.31
(b) Engineering/technical	12 094	42 405	87 257	128 937	244 007	260 905	+2057.30
(c) Medicine	15 260	32 238	89 569	110 020	165 812	177 288	+1061.78
(d) Agriculture	3 131	10 057	27 195	39 231	54 561	58 339	+1763.27

Source: as for Tables 8.1 and 8.3.

Increased availability of health care, education and family welfare services resulting from higher economic growth has contributed to the reduction of the Indian death rate, birth rate and infant mortality rate, as well as to an increase in life expectancy at birth and the literacy rate. These indicators are illustrated in Table 8.8.

It can be seen from Table 8.8 that as per capita NNP rose continuously, the life expectancy at birth increased from 32.1 years in 1951 to 63 years in 2002, the literacy rate increased from 18.3 per cent in 1951 to 76 per cent in 2002, and the birth rate and death rate declined from 39.9 and 27.4 in 1951 to 25 and 8 per thousand in 1997. Finally, during this period, the infant mortality rate declined by more than 50 per cent from 146 to 65 per thousand.

In terms of human development, Chinese performance during the pre-reform period was most impressive owing to the Maoist approach of a broad-based development strategy, under which development efforts are targeted on raising the standards of living at all social economic levels and especially the standard of living of the poor. According to a UNDP *Human Development Report* (1990, pp. 51–2), China's human development index by 1978 approached that of developed countries with an income per capita several times that of China.

With respect to health care and education services, China operated an enterprise-based financed social welfare system, under which basic necessities and public goods such as health care and education services were distributed in an egalitarian way to all residents, including the poor and the socially disadvantaged, through the communes in rural areas and through the SOEs in urban areas. The equal access to health care facilities enabled China to reduce mortality, morbidity and malnutrition (World Bank 1983b). As a result there was a dramatic rise in average life expectancy from 36 years in 1949 to 64 in 1979. The equal access to education services increased the adult literacy rate from 20 per cent in 1949 to 66 per cent in 1979.

During the reform period, Chinese average life expectancy continued to rise. By 2001, according to a UNDP *Human Development Report* (2003, p. 239), Chinese average life expectancy reached 70.6 years. China's adult literacy rate also continued to climb during the post-reform period. By 2003, the rate reached 84.2 per cent (UNDP, *Human Development Report*, 2003, p. 122).

ECONOMIC SECURITY

Individual well-being is also affected by the degree of economic security, which can be threatened by inflation and unemployment, both of which lead to a substantial decline in real income. Unemployment problems in India

Table 8.8 India: basic indicators of human development

Year 1	Per capita NNP (at constant prices, Rs) 2	Life expectancy at birth (years) 3	Literacy rate (%) 4	Birth rate (per thousand) 5	Death rate (per thousand) 6	Infant mortality rate (per thousand) 7
1951	1 131.15	32.1	18.3	39.9	27.4	146
1961	1 352.70	41.3	28.3	41.7	22.8	146
1971	1 505.95	45.6	34.5	36.9	14.9	129
1981	1 661.45	50.4	43.6	33.9	12.5	110
1991	2 198.65	59.4	52.2	29.5	9.8	80
1996	8 733.15	62.4	NA	27.5	9.0	72
1997	9 097.80	NA	62.0	27.5	8.9	71
2002	10 774.20	63.0	76.0[1]	25.0	8.1	65

Note: 1. 2000/01.

Sources: as for Table 8.1; World Bank, *World Development Indicators*, 2004, table 2.19.

and China were discussed in the previous chapter, and showed that both countries suffered from increased unemployment pressure during the post-reform period. With regard to inflation, during the first 12 years of India's planned development, the rate of inflation on average did not exceed 2 per cent (Bhagwati and Desai 1971). This was an impressive performance of price stability. However, under the reform the country experienced increased price instability. Table 8.9 presents India's annual average inflation rate based on the Consumer Price Index (CPI) from 1980 to 2003.

As Table 8.9 shows, during 1980–2000 the annual average rate of inflation has increased to around 8 to 10 per cent, with four years (1980/81, 1991/92, 1992/93 and 1994/95) registering double-digit rates of inflation. Table 8.10 presents China's official statistics on annual changes in indexes of workers and employee cost of living, rural retail prices and free market prices.

These price indicators show that, as in the case of India, China had little or no open inflation during the pre-reform period. As the study by Tsakok (1979) demonstrates, this impressive performance of price stability was mainly achieved, not through price controls, but by government intervention

Table 8.9   India: average annual inflation rate (%)

Year	Consumer Price Index	
	IW	AL
1980–88	9.8	7.3
1985–90	8.0	7.5
1990–95	10.4	10.9
1995–2000	8.6	7.7
2000–03	4.1	NA

Notes:
IW = industrial workers.
AL = agricultural workers.

Source: GOI, *Economic Survey*, various issues.

Table 8.10   China: annual average increase in consumer price (%)

	1957–78	1978–90
Worker cost of living	0.7	6.9
Rural retail prices	0.1	5.9
Free market prices	3.5	6.9

Source: *ZGTJNJ* 1991, pp. 230, 243 and 248.

in the supply side of the consumer goods market. The government placed a high priority on ensuring that an adequate supply of basic necessities was available to all. More importantly, it designed institutions to ensure supplies at affordable prices.

Since the introduction of the market-orientated reforms in the late 1970s, China, like India, experienced increased price instability. The annual rate of inflation during the reform period from 1978 to 1990 averaged 6 to 7 per cent (see Table 8.10). Compared with India, China's rate of inflation during the post-reform period is low, but it is generally agreed that the Chinese official price indexes underestimate the real rate of inflation, so it may have been higher in recent years than is suggested by these figures.

INEQUALITY

Individuals tend to judge their own level of economic well-being by the living standard enjoyed by their neighbours. Thus, if income is distributed fairly evenly, people are less likely to feel deprived than if distribution is uneven. There is a lack of official statistics on income distribution in India. Table 8.11 presents the World Bank's estimates of income distribution for India.

The well-known Kuznet's inverted u-curve of inequality versus growth suggests that inequality tends to rise in the early stages but falls in the later stages of a country's economic development. The inequality data in Table 8.11 suggests that, owing to the government welfare programme of offering financial and other assistance to the socially disadvantaged (GOI, *Economic Survey*, 2000/01, pp. 202–3), India has been relatively successful to escape from Kuznet's inverted u-curve relationship between inequality and economic growth. Inequality measured in terms of the ratio between the income share of the richest 20 per cent of the households and that of the poorest 20 per cent of the households has decreased during the pre-reform period. The ratio in the mid-1960s was relatively high as it stood at 7 to 1. However, on the eve of the reform in the late 1980s, the ratio was brought down to 4.693 to 1. Another measure of income inequality is the Gini coefficient. In the mid-1970s the Indian Gini coefficient was 0.416, however, by the early 1990s it had dropped to 0.338.

During the post-reform period, no consistent trend in inequality can be found. The ratio between the income share of the richest 20 per cent to that of the poorest 20 per cent at first increased to 5.012 to 1 in the early 1990s; but it has since declined to 4.272 to 1 in 1994 and later on it increased once again to 4.674 to 1 in 1999/2000.

As in India, China during the pre-reform period has been very successful in preventing Kuznet's law from being operative in China. Inequality

Table 8.11 India: percentage share of households' income by percentile groups of households

Year	Lowest 20%	Second quintile	Third quintile	Fourth quintile	Highest 20%	Highest 10%	Ratio of highest 20% to lowest 20%	Gini Index
1964–65	6.7	10.5	14.3	19.6	48.9	35.2	7.299	NA
1975–76	7.0	9.2	13.9	20.5	49.4	33.6	7.057	0.416
1983	8.1	12.3	16.3	22.0	41.4	26.7	5.111	NA
1984–85	7.8	11.2	15.0	20.6	45.6	31.3	5.846	NA
1989–90	8.8	12.5	16.2	21.3	41.3	27.1	4.693	NA
1992	8.5	12.1	15.8	21.1	42.6	28.4	5.012	0.338
1994	9.2	13.0	16.8	21.7	39.3	25.0	4.272	0.297
1997	8.1	11.6	15.0	19.3	46.1	33.5	5.691	0.378
1999–2000	8.9	12.3	16.0	21.2	41.6	27.4	4.674	0.325

Sources: World Bank, *World Development Report*, various issues; *World Development Indicators*, 2004, table 2.7.

first declined after the land reform in the early 1950s. Later, China has been successful in preventing it from rising despite the relative high rate of growth (Adelman and Sunding 1987). As a result, inequality in China in the late 1970s was one of the lowest in the world, and much lower than that of India.

After the introduction of market-orientated reforms, inequality began to rise again. The Gini coefficient rose from 0.288 in 1981 to 0.388 in 1995 (World Bank 1997). As a result, China's record of inequality exceeded that of India in 1997. The increase of inequality during the recent years was caused by several factors. According to the World Bank's study, 50 per cent of the increase was due to the widening of the rural–urban income gap, another 33 per cent was due to increased regional income disparities, and the rest of the increase was due to increased intra-rural and urban inequality.

LEVEL OF POVERTY

Together with the overall economic growth, the anti-poverty and employ-ment generation programmes targeted at the poor have helped to reduce the incidence of poverty over the long run in India. The poverty ratio declined from 56.4 per cent in 1973–74 to 37.3 per cent in 1993–94 in rural areas and from 49.0 per cent in 1973–74 to 32.4 per cent in 1993–94 in urban areas. For the country as a whole, the poverty ratio declined from 54.9 per cent in 1973–74 to 36 per cent in 1993–94. These figures are shown in Table 8.12.

Current estimates of the poverty ratio are not available yet as the latest large-sample NSSO survey of consumer expenditure, on the basis of which poverty ratios are estimated, was completed only in July 2000.

Table 8.12   India: number and percentage of population below poverty line

Year	Rural sector		Urban sector		Combined all India	
	Number (millions)	Poverty ratio (%)	Number (millions)	Poverty ratio (%)	Number (millions)	Poverty ratio (%)
1973/74	261	56.4	60	49.0	321	54.9
1977/78	264	53.1	65	45.2	329	51.3
1983	252	45.7	71	40.8	323	44.5
1987/88	232	39.1	75	38.2	307	38.9
1993/94	244	37.3	76	32.4	320	36.0
1999/2000	193	27.1	67	24.0	260	26.1

Source: as for Table 8.1.

However, even in 2001, 35 per cent of the total population were below US$1.00 per day (UNDP, *Human Development Report*, 2003). Thus although the reduction in the overall poverty ratio in India from 55 per cent to 36 per cent during a period of two decades is significant, India's performance in poverty reduction has been poor compared with some of the East Asian countries. The success of China in achieving higher growth and development led to a faster decline in the poverty ratio in that country. Hence the solution to the problem of poverty reduction lies in the creation of opportunities for broad-based economic development and higher growth. To this end, various existing schemes of employment and poverty alleviation have been incorporated into the integrated rural development programme (IRDP) in the Ninth Five Year Plan (1997–2000) (GOI 1999a). There has been a shift in the IRDP's approach to implementing a poverty alleviation programme from the individual beneficiary approach to a group and/or cluster approach under which the formation of self-help groups has been the catalyst for organizing the poor. This cluster approach has focused on the identification of a few specified viable activities based on local resource endorsement and occupational skills of the people of that area. The IRDP has also aimed at diversifying the high-value-addition sectors and non-traditional activities, which have market potential. Along with other growth-promoting activities this is also expected to improve the rate of economic growth.

China's poverty incidence in both the pre- and post-reform period was much lower than that of India. Prior to the reform, poverty was almost completely eradicated due to the egalitarian distribution of basic necessities and public goods through the enterprise-based social security system. Under the market-orientated reform, poverty incidence increasingly depends on the rate of economic growth and income distribution. Though inequality during the post-reform period was on the rise, thanks to its very high economic rate China has been able continuously to reduce its poverty incidence. According to a UNDP *Human Development Report* (2003, p. 23), during the 1990s, the proportion of people living on less than US$1 a day in China dropped from 33 per cent in 1990 to only 16 per cent in 2000. The comparative figures for India in 1993–94 and 2001 were 42 and 35 per cent respectively. Thus, by the beginning of the 21st century China's rate of poverty was less than half that of India.

SOME COMMENTS

The indicators presented here on progress achieved in human development and poverty reduction in India may not reflect the real situation because of a number of factors. First, there is the problem of reliability of statistics that we obtain from the international organizations and respective governments in South Asian countries. For example, in India the central government obtains the relevant statistics from the respective state governments, which in turn collect the relevant data from the district administrators, which in turn collect the information from local governments in towns and villages. It is at this local government level that information may not be collected properly. Local government officials or their appointed agents may make up some fictitious figures and send these to the higher authority.[1]

Second, even if the data is properly collected and forwarded to the higher authorities by local government officials, the indicators may still not reflect the real situation. Take the example of school enrolment ratios. The information available from the government of India on school enrolment ratios indicate that in 2001–02, the enrolment ratios at lower primary level (class I to IV) stood at 86.9 per cent for girls and 96.3 per cent for the total boys and girls (GOI, *Economic Survey*, 2003/04). But, it is common knowledge in villages, where 70 per cent of Indians live, that very few girls from landless and land-poor families, from families belonging to scheduled castes and scheduled tribes, attend primary school. Hence the 86.9 per cent enrolment ratio for girls in reality refers to the presence of the names of the girls in school registers but not to their physical presence in their schools and to their active participation in class activity. Hence the figures for girls' actual attendance at primary schools would be considerably lower than the expected attendance figure, if the 87 per cent enrolment ratio for girls at the lower primary level meant that such a percentage of girls were actually attending schools and taking lessons.

Third, even in these village primary schools where boys and girls attend primary level classes, the teachers do not always attend schools and perform their duties responsibly, although they continue to draw high salaries. A similar situation exists in public health care facilities in rural India where doctors and nurses continue to draw their monthly salaries but there are no medicines or equipment to treat the patients, although officially in government ledgers large sums of money have been recorded as being spent on these items. So the only conclusion that one can draw is that the money must have disappeared as rents to powerful groups of people.[2]

In such a situation, spending large amounts of money on primary education and higher education will not achieve the desired goal as a substantial proportion of the money allocated for expansion of primary, secondary and higher education is likely to end up as rents to state administrative apparatus, its informal agents and political party leaders. Thus the transfer of an increasingly larger amount of money to bankrupt provincial governments (Rao 2004) for expenditure on education, health, safe drinking water supply and other social sector projects does not *ipso facto* guarantee that the entire amount received by the provincial governments will be spent effectively on human development projects. Nor does it automatically ensure a genuine improvement in human development indicators – as a considerable amount of that money is directed towards meeting other more pressing needs such as payment of salaries and wages and allowances to excessively large unproductive but highly unionized public sector employees and as a handsome amount is likely to disappear as rents. Hence, if out of a $100 public transfer to the provinces for expenditure on human development programmes only $50 is actually spent and the other $50 is transferred to meet other needs including rent payments, then to ensure that $100 is actually spent, $200 needs to be transferred. Therefore the better policy should be to reduce the level of transfers from the centre to the states so as to force them to manage their budget more responsibly. The amount of money that is currently being directed to social services, including education and health, in terms of absolute amount, increased from Rs 332.5 billion in 1990–91 to Rs 1372.9 billion in 2001–02. Of this, the amount spent on education increased from Rs 170.9 billion in 1990–91 to Rs 680.7 billion in 2001–02 (GOI, *Economic Survey*, 2003/04), but much of this money has gone towards the payment of salaries of staff at educational institutions. Bardhan's brilliant commentary on India's political economy (2004), democracy (1986) and governance (1984) aptly described how corruption permeated India's political institutions, which in turn corrupted all other institutions in Indian society.

Hence, although like Sen (1986; 2004) he also expressed the need for placing greater emphasis on education and health and better targeting of expenditure within the broad fields of education and health, simply the increase in the level of expenditure alone without improving the governance of these sectors will not achieve the goals of human development. The first and the most fundamental precondition for human development is the removal of poverty and hunger. The best way to achieve poverty reduction is by raising the income of the poor by raising the rate of economic growth rather than by attempting to reduce inequality in income, as it would require an enormous adjustment in the distribution of income to achieve the same addition to living standards for the poor as 1 per cent more of sustained growth. Thus a clear link exists between growth, poverty alleviation, human development and gender empowerment. In this chapter we have shown that the level of poverty estimated on the basis of the headcount method has declined considerably in India in recent years. But Sen (1992) argues against relying on poverty percentage or the headcount approach. For Sen, poverty is not low well-being but the inability to pursue well-being because of a lack of economic means. Poverty, according to Sen, is a failure of basic capabilities to reach minimally acceptable levels. So what does capability stand for?

To Sen, a small number of basic requirements, which indicate attainments, such as being adequately fed, clothed and sheltered, being able to appear in public without shame and being happy and free, are central to the well-being of individuals. But GNP per capita which measures capabilities fails to correlate closely with those functionings. Thus, even if a person's per capita income rises above poverty-line income, the basic capability of that person even with the rise in income may fail to reach a level at which he or she can pursue his or her well-being. For example, the poverty of a family does not end immediately after the family's income rises above the poverty line by one extra dollar (Blackwood and Lynch 1994). Hence, Sen argues that in addition to the Head Count Index (H) there is also the need for an Income Gap Approach (I) which measures the additional income needed on per capita terms to bring the poor up to the level of the poverty line. If both measures are used to estimate the level of poverty in India, the level of poverty would appear to be considerably higher than the headcount measure has shown.

It has to be noted here that the failure of a person even with adequate economic means to pursue well-being, which in Sen's terms consist of a vector of interrelated functionings such as being adequately fed and nourished, and being happy and free, can be due to the failure of basic capabilities which are greatly conditioned by the institutional parameters within which that person pursues his/her well-being. So, apart from economic poverty, people, particularly women, suffer also from social poverty. Hence Sen continues to emphasize the need for the government to provide high-quality education and health care to the people to improve their capabilities, but he believes that these goals can be better pursued in a friendly economic climate rather then in a fierce political regime (2004).

At the theoretical level, Sen further elaborated his concept of capabilities in his book, *Commodities and Capabilities* (1999a), in which the argument, in assessing personal well-being and advantage, focused on the capability of individuals to function (that is, to be able to do what the person wants to do and to be what the person wants to be). In his theory, a person's motivation behind choice is treated as a parametric variable which may or may not coincide with the pursuit of self-interest. But Sen continues to stress the need for India to achieve a higher rate of growth to enable the country to remove economic poverty, improve the quality of human lives and to improve the capabilities of individuals. In conclusion, we can say that, despite the shortcomings in the collection of data on human development and population below the poverty line and on the method used in the estimation of the level of poverty, there is a clear indication that India has recorded slow but steady improvement in human development and reduction in poverty.

NOTES

1. This was revealed to the present authors by villagers in a private conversation with them during their fieldwork in Eastern India in January 2004.
2. This situation was narrated to the present authors by health officials and village community members in private conversations with the authors when they visited several rural health centres in Eastern India in January 2004.

9.　Women's empowerment

Although poor women in India and China work longer hours than men, many of their activities are not socially visible and therefore not socially recognized. Therefore, their status within the family remains inferior. They experience widespread anti-female bias in institutional arrangements. In recent years there has been increasing recognition in government circles of the importance of raising productivity and income of poor women as a more general growth and poverty alleviation strategy. The government's programmes for women's empowerment aim to realize this objective. This chapter discusses these programmes and evaluates their results. It highlights the shortcomings of the government measures and reaffirms the need for community education and social reforms to modify traditional values and norms as well as social institutions, which perpetuate gender inequality in both countries.

RELEVANT ISSUES AFFECTING WOMEN'S SOCIO-ECONOMIC STATUS

There are a number of issues relevant to the socio-economic status of women in most Third World countries. Poor women in a rural area are the major providers of sustenance to their families. Their contributions are not duly rewarded by society and the government. A number of institutional deterrents impede women's progress towards economic independence and empowerment. Since women spend long hours doing household duties, they have less time available to spend on farms and on non-farm activities. Hence, if it is possible to reduce women's time spent on household tasks, then that time could be spent on income-generating activities. Women's access to income is more likely to pay welfare dividends for the community at large (especially for children) than men's incomes. The advantage of targeting women for achieving development goals is that women's productivity and potential for income-generation may be raised with minimum capital outlays (Kandiyoti 1992). Reducing the time women spend on household work does not mean doing away with these jobs. It means doing the same work in a less time-consuming way. The income-generating activities also include upgrading those areas in which women are already involved and those newly created opportunities in small-scale rural industries such as fruit-canning, soap-making, textiles, brick-making and so on.

An increase in women's direct control over resources including cash income is necessary to enhance the immediate welfare of families as well as the health and nutritional status of their children. There is evidence to suggest that the same improvements in welfare may not take place with an increase in men's income as a considerable part of men's income is usually spent on personal habits, domestic goods and leisure (Hunger and Morris 1973; Roy and Tisdell 1996; Roy et al. 1993; Young 1978).

It is therefore important to recognize that women of poor households, whether male- or female-headed, bear a significant responsibility for the family's subsistence. However, the fulfilment of this responsibility is strongly constrained not only by the unequal sharing of the household resources, but also by women's unequal access to earning opportunities and to agricultural lands, and by the decline in common property and forests. As a response to these problems faced by women, there has also been a shift in policy discussion from an equity-orientated approach in matters of assistance to women, which stressed the widening gap created by development policies, to a poverty-orientated approach, which documents the importance of raising the productivity and income of poor women as a more general growth and poverty alleviation strategy (Kandiyoti 1992). In other words, the implication is that the removal of difficulties faced by women due to unequal sharing of household resources, unequal access to earning opportunities and to agricultural land would reduce poverty and promote growth. Any type of policy undertaken to improve women's economic condition should include measures (1) to protect women's existing sources of livelihood; (2) to eliminate discriminatory legislation in the ownership and control of productive assets; (3) to ensure equitable access to agricultural inputs, credits, extension services and education; (4) to provide support of extra household forms of organization of women's labour; and (5) to provide encouragement for enhancing capacity for political empowerment and organization (Kandiyoti 1992).

EQUITY AND PROTECTION OF WOMEN'S RIGHTS IN INDIA

India's concern for safeguarding the rights and privileges of women found its best expression in the Constitution. Article 14 confers equal rights and opportunities on men and women in the political, economic and social spheres, Article 15 prohibits discrimination against any citizen on the ground of sex, religion, race, caste, and so on, and Article 15 (3) empowers the state to make affirmative discrimination in favour of women.

Similarly, Article 16 provides for equality of opportunities in the matter of public appointments for all citizens. Yet, Article 39 mentions that the state shall direct its policy towards providing men and women equally with the right to a means of livelihood and equal pay for equal work. Article 42 directs the state to make provisions for ensuring just and humane conditions of work and maternity relief. Article 51 (a) and (e) imposes a fundamental duty on every citizen to renounce the practices derogatory to the dignity of women to make this *de jure* equality into a *de facto* one, special legislation having been enacted from time to time in support of women.

Government's Approach to Women's Empowerment

In the early post-independence period, efforts to improve the situation of women began with the Community Development Programme (CDP) which was launched in 1952 to provide agricultural development and villages with welfare services. Initially, the programme did not include any special provision for women but halfway through the First Five Year Plan, in 1954, a decision was made to include two 'Gram Sevikas' (female village-level workers) in each development block, working under the guidance of a female social education organizer (later designated as 'Mukhya Sevika' or main female workers). Each village was to have a Mahila Mondal, or women's group, which was to be the village-level forum for organizing women. Hardly any attempt was made to make women economically independent. The reason was that the CDP clearly considered women as housewives and marginal workers. The Central Social Welfare Board (CSWB) was established in 1953 to fund and support the activities of voluntary organizations in the field of social welfare.

In 1954, the CSWB introduced the Welfare Extension Project (WEP). Services under the WEP included child care, supplementary feeding for children and pregnant women, a nutrition and health care programme, arts and crafts training and 'social education'. The scheme was implemented at the village level through Project Implementing Centres (PICs) that were run by a Gram Sevika, who was in charge of the centre, and a midwife.

The scheme viewed women of rural families as middle-class housewives, not their need of economic independence and, therefore it focused on the physical welfare of women. As a result, it proved to be a failure. Other reasons for its failure was shortages of funds and personnel, and poor training of CDP workers.

During the same period, the state policy for the empowerment of poor women consisted of a series of stopgap measures to tackle hunger and malnutrition and so on (Kandiyoti 1992). In the 1950s and 1960s, poor rural women and other members of their families were provided with temporary relief work in the dry season for a few months during a year. The work consisted mostly of construction of roads and canals in rural areas. But the amount of money spent on such schemes was small and the families involved were few.

However, during the 1970s, there was a definite shift in the approach from 'welfare' to 'development' that started recognizing women as participants in development. The 1980s adopted a multidisciplinary approach, with a special thrust on the three core sectors of health, education and employment. Accordingly, priority was given to the implementation of programmes for women under different sectors of agriculture and its allied activities such as dairying, poultry, small animal husbandry, handlooms, handicrafts, small-scale industries, and so on. Recognizing the role and contribution of women to development, the early 1990s made a beginning in concentrating on training cum employment cum income-generation programmes for women, with the ultimate objective of making them economically independent and self-reliant (GO1 1999a).

Current Situation Relating to Women's Status

State programmes in both women-specific and women-related sectors implemented during the Five Year Plans have brought forth perceptible improvement in the socio-economic status of women.

Women's health

Considerable gains in women's health status have been recorded. Expectation of life at birth for females has risen steadily from 31.7 years in 1951 to 63 years in 2002. Female life expectancy overtook male life expectancy during 1981–85 period. These are illustrated in Table 9.1.

Marriage

The mean age of marriage for females has also increased from 15.6 years in 1951 to 18.3 years in 1981, while the effective age of marriage stood at 19.4 years in 1995. The prevention of child marriage by the Child Marriage Restraint Act of 1976 and the pursual of higher studies by increasing numbers of girls have played an important role in lifting their age at marriage, as Table 9.2 illustrates.

Maternal deaths

While Crude Birth Rate (CBR) declined from 40.8 in 1951 to 27.5 in 1996, the Crude Death Rate (CDR) has declined from 15.6 in 1970 to 8.9 in 1996.

Table 9.1   Life expectancy at birth in India, 1951–2002 (years)

Year	Male	Female
1951	32.5	31.7
1961	48.9	40.6
1971	46.4	44.7
1981–85	55.4	55.7
1987–91	58.1	58.6
1989–93	59.0	59.7
1998	62.0	64.0
2002	64.0	63.0

Source: Government of India 1999a; World Bank, *World Development Report*, 2000–01; UNDP, *Human Development Report*, 2004, pp. 218–19.

Table 9.2   Mean age at marriage in India during 1951–95 (years)

Year	Female	Male
1951	15.6	19.9
1961	15.5	21.3
1971	17.2	22.4
1981	18.3	23.4
1991	19.5	NA
1995	19.4	NA

Source: as for Table 9.1.

Similarly, the total fertility rate also has declined from about 6 in the early 1950s to 3.2 in 1998. But the maternal mortality rate which stood at a very high rate of 437 per 100 000 live births in 1993 declined only to 410 per 100 000 live births at the end of 1998 (World Bank 2001). The causes of this high rate of maternal mortality are mostly related to the problems that arise during pregnancy and during childbirth. The major causes that account for 75 per cent of total maternal death appears to be bleeding during pregnancy and puerperium (28.9 per cent), abortion (17.6 per cent), anaemia (17.0 per cent), puerperium sepsis (8.5 per cent) and malposition of the child (4.0 per cent) (GOI 1999b), all of which are treatable.

Sex ratio
The sex ratio illustrates that the survival rate has been exceptionally unfavourable to women. The ratio has been declining since 1951 except for

Table 9.3 Sex ratio in India, 1951–91

Year	Sex ratio
1951	946
1961	941
1971	930
1981	934
1991	927

Source: as for Table 9.1.

Table 9.4 Literacy rates in India, 1951–2002

Year	Female	Male
1951	8.86	27.16
1961	15.34	40.40
1971	21.97	45.95
1981	29.85	56.50
1991	39.19	64.13
1998	43.00	67.00
2002	46.40	69.00

Source: as for Table 9.1.

a marginal rise between 1971 and 1981. This is illustrated in Table 9.3. Two of the major problems that women suffer from are chronic energy deficiency and anaemia both of which can be prevented by providing better nutrition to women.

Literacy rates

Literacy rates for females are illustrated in Table 9.4. As the table shows, the literacy rate for females has risen continuously from 8.86 per cent in 1951 to 46.4 per cent in 2002. This rate of increase is considerable. Nevertheless the literacy level of women is still quite low.

Work participation rate

According to the 1991 census, the total female work participation rate increased from 14.22 per cent in 1971 to 22.27 per cent in 1991. But it was much lower than the male work participation rate in both rural and urban differentials. The total participation rate for women increased further to 45 per cent in 2002 (Table 9.5).

Table 9.5   Workforce participation rates in India, 1971–2002

Years	Category	Females	Males
1971	Total	14.22	52.75
	Rural	5.92	53.78
	Urban	7.18	48.88
1981	Total	19.67	52.62
	Rural	23.06	53.77
	Urban	8.31	49.06
1991	Total	22.27	51.61
	Rural	26.79	52.58
	Urban	9.19	48.92
2002	Total	45.00	86.80

Notes: Excludes Assam and Jammu and Kashmir.

Source: 1971–91: as for Table 9.1. 2002: World Bank, *World Development Indicators*, 2004, table 2.2.

Table 9.6   Labour force in the organized and unorganized sectors in India in 1991 (millions)

Sector	Female		Male		Total	
	Actual	%	Actual	%	Actual	%
Organized	3.78	4.20	22.95	10.20	26.73	8.50
Unorganized	85.99	95.80	201.41	89.80	287.40	91.50
Total	89.77	100.00	224.36	100.00	314.13	100.00

Source: as for Table 9.1.

Distribution of women in the workforce

Table 9.6 illustrates the distribution of the female workforce in the organized and unorganized sectors in 1991. It can be seen from the table that in 1991, of the total female workforce of 89.77 million, which accounted for nearly 29 per cent of the total workforce, their share in the organized sector is only 4.2 per cent. Hence nearly 96 per cent of the female workforce works in the unorganized sector. In 2001 the number of women working in the organized sector reached 4.9 million which constituted 17.8 per cent of the total organized sector employment in the country (GOI, *Economic Survey*, 2003/04).

Table 9.7   Representation of women in Parliament in India, 1952–98

Year	Lower House (Lok Sabha)		Upper House (Rajya Sabha)	
	Male	Female	Male	Female
1952	475	22	201	15
1980	514	28	209	24
1991	486	39	221	24
1998	543	41	218	18

Source: as for Table 9.1.

Representation of women in premier services

While the representation of women in the government accounts for only 13.7 per cent, the representation at the decision-making level through these premier services – namely, Indian Administration Service (IAS), Indian Police Service (IPS) and Indian Foreign Service (IFS) – accounted for only 5.8 per cent in 1987. In 1997 this share marginally increased to 7.5 per cent. In terms of actual numbers in 1997, the total female representation stood at 650 out of a total male and female representation of 8611.

Representation of women in Parliament

There has been a definite improvement in women's participation in grass-roots democracy through the Panchayati Ray Institutions (PRIs) and other local bodies, but in the state legislatures the number of women members increased from 102 and accounted for 2.5 per cent of total members in 1977, to only 162 and accounting for 3.9 per cent in 1997. In Table 9.7, the representation of women in the federal Parliament is shown.

It can be seen from Table 9.7 that in the lower house of the federal Parliament in 1952 the number of women representation is only 22 and it accounted for only 4.4 per cent of total members of the lower house. In 1998 this number and the percentage increased to only 41 and 7.5 per cent respectively.

Thus, while the measures taken by the Indian government to empower women have been to some extent successful, more needs to be done to make women reasonably well empowered.

Limitations of the Government's Women's Empowerment Programme in India

The government of India's programmes for women's empowerment have been designed on the assumption that the provision of employment for women will enable them to earn income, which in turn will allow them to become economically independent, exercise influence on the family's decision-making process, gain control over their own lives and gain the freedom to move outside the confines of their homes. Making women economically independent on a long-term basis is of crucial importance in this empowerment issue. However, the government programmes have failed to realize this goal. There are several reasons behind the failure. To begin with, the government schemes, by providing credit, were designed to help poor women become self-employed and thereby earn income. But the provision of credit to a woman to buy inputs for cultivation, or for petty trading, is of no help to her when there is no food in the house. So the money obtained to purchase inputs goes towards the purchase of foods and other necessities. Hence for any self-employment scheme for poor women to work, the credit for input ought to be accompanied by reasonable provisions of food to poor women's families. This has not happened.

However, even if a woman earns a certain amount of income, does that enable her to exercise influence on the family's decision-making process and to gain control over her own life? Recent research suggests that the answer is 'no'. The results of the analysis of data obtained from a fieldwork in 1999 in rural West Bengal in India (Tisdell et al. 2000) suggests that wives earning cash in the fields of others does not significantly empower them within their own family. Furthermore, wives working outside their home are subject to increased restriction on their ability to join female groups. They suffer even more social restriction than those who do not work in 'outside fields'. They appear to have significantly less involvement in decisions about the future of their children than women who do not work in the fields of others for cash. The results also suggest that there is no significant increase in control over cash by wives in families with higher perceived economic status, but there is some weakly significant increase in their involvement in family decisions and in decisions about the future of their children. The social restriction for wives seems to intensify with increases in perceived economic status of their family. Social restrictions on women embodying an 'ideology of seclusion' are greater in higher castes than in lower ones, particularly in Northern and Eastern India. Increases in income, therefore, appear to result in greater restrictions on social choices of females and not to increase women's influence on the family's decision-making process. The situation could change in the long term with a pattern akin to Kuznet's curve emerging.

A similar situation appears to be prevailing in Tamil Nadu in Southern India. Lakshmanaswamy's study (2002) suggests that women's non-labour income has a different but weak effect on household resource allocation. If the separate non-labour income of the spouses is used as a measure of the independence and control of females over their families resources, then the results of this study lend only marginal support to the economic empowerment of women within the household. Similar conclusions have also been drawn by Haddad and Hoddinot (1992) and others. Thus it seems that independent income for women has increased neither their bargaining power nor their threat of power within their households.

Is income, then, not important? The continuation of gender restriction on women within and outside the family sphere, despite the increasing contribution of women to their family's income, does not mean that women's earning is not important to their empowerment. Some contribution by a woman to the family's income may prevent her social status within the family from deteriorating.

If a woman's contribution to the family's income is substantial and also vital for the survival of that family, then that woman can exercise significant influence on the family's decision-making process. She can also use threatening powers to extract better treatment from other family members. Hence, the level of contribution that a woman makes to the family's income seems to be more important than any income contribution for women's empowerment. This point seems to have been missed in most of the studies that tried to analyse the effect of women's contributions to family's income on their family's decision-making process.

The important point to be noted is that the ideology of seclusion embodying gender restrictions on women are culturally ordained in India. Hence, irrespective of whether a woman contributes to her family's income or not, these restrictions are imposed on them by their family and the village elders. Therefore, the lessening of the forces of the ideology of seclusion is also crucially important for women's empowerment. This can be achieved only through community education of all adult family members, including the elderly. But the state has not implemented any such scheme yet. Thus, income alone, in absence of community education, cannot facilitate women's empowerment. However, since gender restrictions are culturally ordained, the forces of such restrictions are easily weakened.

While Sen has consistently argued that the provision of education and health care for women is crucial to achieving success in empowering women, the important role played by sociocultural institutions in the empowerment process was implicitly recognized in his theory of entitlement exchange and poverty alleviation (Sen 1981). Although the primary objective of the theory was to explain the causes of famines, a decomposition of the theory extends its application to women's empowerment and raises the possibility of institutions preventing women from alleviating economic poverty and attaining empowerment.

In the vast rural hinterlands of India, the sociocultural perception of girls being a burden to the family results from the following factors:

1. Investment in a daughter in the form of food, clothing, education, health care, and so on will bring no return to the parents but only to her marital home, as her parents will be required to arrange for her to be wedded to a suitable groom.
2. The cost of a wedding, including that of a dowry to the bride's family, will rise the higher the level of education of the girl and the older the marriage age is.
3. Parents are under social pressure to discharge their principal responsibility to their daughter as quickly as they can by marrying her off to someone.
4. Like the Chinese, Indian parents also have a very strong preference for boys who will carry forward the family name and look after their parents in the latters' old age.

Hence these factors, combined with population pressure and a greater earning power of men, have contributed in rural India to inter-family discrimination against girls and women (Dreze and Sen 1989), the neglect of baby girls and to the abortion of foetuses, and have eventually led to the failure of women to be able to be what they want to be. Also the number of dowry-related deaths of young married women are rising in India. In many cases women commit suicide, while in other cases they are killed by their in-laws, sometimes in collaboration with their husbands.

While the severity of discrimination against girls and women in rural India may have lessened somewhat, as we observed during our field studies in Bengal and Orissa in December 2003 and January 2004, discrimination has not disappeared.

Dreze and Sen (1989) in their original study on male–female ratios and missing women, found that about 95 million women were 'missing' worldwide according to normal male–female ratios. While subsequent studies (Coale 1991) have revised the number downward, the problem is still serious. The estimate of Dreze and Sen suggests that in the late 1990s the number of missing women in China and India stood at 44 and 36.9 million, respectively. However, in recent years the female–male ratio for India has been rising in favour of women. China has planned to outlaw the selective abortion of female foetuses to correct the imbalance in the ratio of boys to girls that has grown since the one-child policy was introduced more then 25 years ago (*The Telegraph* 2005).

The problems outlined above are the manifestations of cultural poverty and they continue to persist in India because of the failure of institutions to provide adequate and effective freedom to women. The importance of social, economic, political and judicial institutions in enabling human beings to utilize their capabilities have been brought out clearly by Sen in his landmark work, *Development as Freedom* (1999b), in which he argues that in individual freedom lies the capacity for political participation, economic development and social progress. Hence freedom is the efficient means of realizing general welfare. Again the same need for freedom and the role of institutions are presented more forcefully by Dreze and Sen (2002) in their analysis of the role of public action in eliminating deprivation and expanding human freedom in India. They have placed human agency at centre stage and have stressed the roles of different institutions (economic, political and social) in enhancing effective freedom. This effective social, economic and political freedom, which is crucial to women's empowerment, is hopelessly lacking in India, even in the 21st century.

Recent Government Action

The government's increasing awareness of the importance of the role of women in the nation's development has led the government to adopt in the Ninth Five Year Plan (1997–2002), the strategy of the Women's Component Plan, under which no less than 30 per cent of funds will be earmarked in all related sectors, for women-specific programmes. The Tenth Five Year Plan (2002–07) aims to empower women through translating into action the National Policy for Empowerment of Women (adopted in 2001) and also through ensuring survival, protection and development of the children's rights-based approach.

The major strategies of women's empowerment include social empowerment, economic empowerment and gender justice. Education is accepted as a tool for social empowerment of women and schemes are implemented to reduce the school dropout rates. The government's measures to spread education among women and children throughout the country consist of 'Saarva Shiksha Abhijan' (universal education campaign) and 'Mahila Samahshya' (visibility of women). However, it is quite well known that these schemes do not achieve any genuine result as a large percentage of money earmarked for these schemes flows as rents to the agents implementing programmes in rural areas. Women simply sign the form stating that they have attended the education programme. Such schemes were implemented also in the past, with limited results. Furthermore, the 'ideology of seclusion' and lack of spare time prevent women in rural areas from joining such programmes. Hence breaking the social barrier to women's freedom of movement and honest and efficient agents for implementing programmes are crucial to achieving success in these programmes. Apart from these, the government has also been implementing other programmes, such as an integrated project for the development and empowerment of women through self-help groups (SHGs) with an emphasis on covering services, developing access to micro-credit and promoting micro-enterprises; developing the Development and Empowerment Project for rural women with an emphasis on women's access to resources for better quality of life; and the provision of better health care, education and skills for income-generating activities, as well as a few other programmes. On the legislative front, bills have been introduced to protect women from domestic violence (GOI, *Economic Survey*, 2003/04) and to give daughters equal rights with sons by birth to ancestral property or property in the hands of the father (*The Statesman Weekly* 2005).

During 2002–03, the first year of the Tenth Five Year Plan, the total expenditure by the central government on gender-specific schemes accounted for only 15.6 per cent of total central government expenditure on its own consumption and capital formation, but when we include the expenditure on transfer to the provinces in the total central government expenditure, then the share of gender-specific expenditure in this total expenditure declines to only 4.5 per cent (GOI, *Economic Survey*, 2003/04). At the global level, India ranked 124th out of 173 nations in terms of the United Nations Development Programme's (UNDP's) Human Development Index (HDI) and was classified in the Medium Human Development Group with an HDI of 0.577 for the year 2000 compared with 0.439 in 1992. For the same year in 2000 in terms of the Gender Development Index (GDI) and the Gender Empower Measure, India's scores were 0.560 and 0.240 compared with 0.401 and 0.226 in 1992 (GOI, *Economic Survey*, 2003/04). Records of Indonesia, China and Sri Lanka are considerably superior to those of India in these respects. Hence we can say that India has made progress in the area of women's empowerment, but it has been quite slow.

STATUS OF WOMEN IN CHINA

Compared with India, China has been relatively more successful in improving the status of its women. Tables 9.8 and 9.9 present several indices of women's status in India and China which show that women's status in China is much higher than that in India.

Table 9.8 shows that the ratio of female to male life expectancy in China is higher than that of India. The percentage of income earned by women is also higher than that of India. Similarly, China's ratio of male to female literacy rates and school enrolment are much higher than those in India.

Table 9.9 presents further indicators of the low status of women in India as compared to China. It shows that Chinese women held more seats in Parliament and more administrative, managerial, professional and technical positions than their Indian counterparts.

Table 9.8   UNDP's gender-related development indices in India and China, 2002

	India	China
1. GDI rank		
(Range 0 to 1, the higher the better)	0.572	0.741
2. Ratio of female to male life expectancy at birth	1.02	1.06
3. Ratio of female to male adult literacy rate (%)	0.67	0.91
4. Ratio of female to male combined primary,		
secondary, tertiary school enrolment rate	0.77	0.93
5. Ratio of female and male earned income	0.38	0.68

Source: as for Table 9.1; UNDP, *Human Development Report*, 2004, pp. 218–19.

Table 9.9   UNDP's gender empowerment indices in India and China, 1997

	India	China
1. GEM rank (out of 94 countries, 1 = best)	86.0	28.0
2. Seats held in Parliament (% women)	7.3	21.0
3. Administrators and managers (% women)	2.3	11.6
4. Professional and technical workers (% women)	20.5	45.1

Source: as for Table 9.8.

Why has China been more successful than India in enhancing the status of women? What are some of the major factors behind China's relative success? To shed light on these questions, let us look at the status of rural women in China and its development during the post-war years.

Rural Chinese Women's Empowerment

According to a World Bank (2001) study, the relative status of women or gender equality is conditioned by three sets of factors. At the household level, the most important factors are the incentive system, which govern intra-household allocation of resource based on sex difference. At the national level, the basic factors are institutions and economic development. Institutions include legal, social and economic organizations, which govern different male and female rights of access to resource use, control and ownership. Economic development in terms of industrialization, urbanization and growth of per capita income are important for women's empowerment because it expands the opportunities and resources and relaxes constraints for women and girls.

Unlike India, there are no specific government women's empowerment programmes targeted at rural women in China. There are some organizations developed at grass-roots level in the rural areas in the form of women's workers' co-operatives and women-credit co-operatives sponsored by the All-China Women Federation and other international agencies to improve rural women's access to resources such as land, credit, jobs, training and information (see Chen 1999). However, these are mainly voluntary organizations with little government involvement. Despite the lack of government direct intervention, Chinese rural women have been able to improve their status over men in the last 50 years or so largely due to the change in the aforementioned three sets of factors.

To begin with, China has a long-established legal institution, which guaranteed equal rights for women. The Chinese legal institution is guided by Marxian ideology, which believes that women are the same as men. The Chinese marriage law of 1950 eliminates arranged marriage, polygamy, bride price and child-marriage. Women are given the right to choose their partners, demand a divorce, inherit property and share control of their children (World Bank 2001, p. 118).

Legal reforms since 1979 have further enhanced the rights of Chinese women. The Chinese Constitution adopted in 1982 guarantees that women enjoy equal rights with men in all spheres of life, and that the state protects the rights and interests of women, applies the principle of equal pay for equal work to men and women alike, and trains and selects cadres from among women. These promises were further affirmed by the Women's Rights Protection Law in 1992 (Woo 1994, p. 280).

During the Maoist period rural Chinese women's status was enhanced by the commune system. The commune strengthened the incentive system of intra-household allocation of resources toward more gender equality. In a commune, inter-household distribution of income was based on work points. To maximize individual household work points, and hence its share of collective income, women were motivated to enter the workforce en masse and even take up jobs which traditionally are held by men (Gao 1994, pp. 81–4). Since women earned work points and contributed to household income, their status in the household rose. To ease women's entry into the workforce, collective dining halls, nurseries, sewing collectives, laundries, hair salons, shoemaking shops and knitting shops were established to relieve women of some of their household responsibilities. In addition, the government deliberately trained a group of women as model workers and activists, some of whom were promoted to administrative departments at all levels (Gao 1994, p. 81).

The economic reforms and the open-door policy introduced during the late 1970s have further enhanced the status of rural women in China. Initially, the abolition of communes and the restoration of the household farming system saw rural women slipping back to their traditional role: women were left to work on farms while men gained access to newly created off-farm jobs (see Parish et al. 1995). But later, rural economic reforms coupled with the open-door policy saw rural China experiencing rapid industrialization and urbanization, which further enhanced rural women's status.

Rural industrialization created opportunities for women to work in export-processing industries such as textile, clothing, electronics and food processing as well as tourism industries along the coastal areas. Women received fixed wage, gained financial independence and reduced their reliance on their husbands. Remittances to parents have also increased daughters' status in the family, giving them a greater sense of control of their lives (World Bank 2001). Some enterprising women using their own talent and skill even set up their own business and became successful business women (see Gao 1994, p. 86).

Rural China also experienced rapid urbanization after the economic reforms, with the share of urban population increased from 18 per cent in 1978 to 31 per cent in 1999 (*ZGTJNJ* 2000, p. 95). Women made up an increased share of rural–urban migrants because many of them moved to cities and towns for reasons of marriage or to accompany husbands, and a significant proportion of them moved to engage in business and study. Rapid urbanization also offered increased jobs for rural women in jobs many city dwellers were unwilling to enter, such as cleaning, domestic service and so on (see Gao 1994, p. 87). Urbanization also reduced family size and accelerated the trend towards a nuclear family because of a shortage of housing in Chinese cities and towns. The trend towards a nuclear family eroded the base of the traditional patriarchal system. The relationship between husband and wife has become primary and women's position in the household has risen accordingly.

Economic reforms also introduced competitive market practice in hiring labour. Under market practice, a worker is hired according to his or her productivity contribution instead of sex difference. Hence, it reduces gender wage discrimination. This is confirmed by several studies (World Bank 2001). These studies compare the gender wage gap between employees whose jobs were assigned through an administrative practice and those who found their jobs through a competitive job market, and found that the proportion of wage gap due to discrimination is higher among workers in assigned jobs than among those in jobs obtained competitively.

Though China has been relatively successful, compared with India in improving the status of their rural women, it has not completely eradicated gender discrimination. In some respects its record of gender discrimination is even worse than that of India. For instance, China has a higher level of discrimination against girls than in India. The sex ratio (male to female) at birth in China is much higher than in India. While India's ratio of males to younger females for each five-year birth cohort remained most of the times during the post-war years under 1.00, China consistently exceeded 1.00 (Dasgupta and Li 1999). Moreover, the level of discrimination against girls has risen in recent years, with the sex ratio jumping from 1.07 in 1980 to 1.14 in 1993 (see World Bank 2001, p. 47). It has been estimated that there are 60–100 million fewer women alive or missing today than there would be in the absence of gender discrimination. As a result, there is a sharp contrast between China and India in the marriage market. While there is a long-term shortage of women in China, India has experienced a long-term surplus of women (Dasgupta and Li 1999).

Why has China a higher child mortality rate for girls? This has much to do with the traditional practice of son-favouritism. There are at least three main factors, which contribute to the son-favouritism. First, under the Chinese rigid patrilineal and patrilocal kinship system, lineages are defined in terms of the male alone (Dasgupta and Li 1999, p. 621). Sons are favoured because sons inherit the family surnames or lineage, whereas girls must marry and their descendants belong to another surnamed lineage. Second, Chinese rural villages are usually made up of several large single-surname lineages and, as land is scarce, villages restrict outsiders from moving in.

Land is periodically redistributed or contracted out to households for cultivation under the households responsibility system. The criterion used to distribute the land is the number of people in the household. Daughters must marry and move to another village. This causes their family to lose another portion of land. However, with sons, when they marry, their wives move in and are regarded as conceptually their own lineage and all their descendents are welcome as parts of the lineage and hence also receive a portion of village land. Thus having a son enables a family to gain another piece of land when the son marries. Third, with the disbandment of the commune system the rural social welfare system has also collapsed (see Roy and Chai 1999). As a result, the sons are increasingly relied on by their parents to care for them during their old age as sons live near their parents. Hence, peasants value sons more than daughters.

The age-old son-favouritism in rural China has serious consequences for gender equality. It led to high child mortality rate for females under the one-child policy. Since each family is allowed to have only one child, parents who prefer male children, tend to abandon female children or choose sex-selective abortion, or neglect daughters (World Bank 2001, p. 47).

Furthermore, son-favouritism has also led to increased gaps between *de jure* and *de facto* rights for women. Even though marriage and inheritance in China are legislated to give daughters and sons equal privileges as heirs, patrilineal inheritance has continued to be practised in rural China. Rural residences, for example, have consistently been passed on to sons, not to daughters (Gao 1994, p. 95).

SUMMARY AND CONCLUSION

In India even when a woman makes significant contributions to the family's total income her status within the family may not improve and she may not have any control over her income nor any voice in the family's decision-making process. It is also true that her status within the family may deteriorate if she does not make any significant contribution. Therefore, the generation of employment for women on a long-term basis is of paramount importance. But this effort must be combined with measures to lessen the force of the 'ideology of seclusion' that keeps women in an inferior position inside and outside their homes.

The attempt by the Indian government to empower women has been mainly directed at creating some employment opportunities. The shortcomings of the government measures have been pointed out, but the government has not done anything to undertake programmes of community education that are necessary to reduce the power of the 'ideology of seclusion'. Hence the government programmes for women's empowerment have not produced significant beneficial results for women.

Compared with India, China has been relatively more successful in empowering its rural women. Although there are no specific government empowerment programmes targeted at rural women, Chinese rural women have been able to improve their status over men during the last 50 years thanks to Marxian ideology, the Maoist experiments with the commune system and, more recently, the economic reforms and the rapid industrialization and urbanization of the Chinese countryside. Nonetheless, China has failed to eliminate gender discrimination. China's level of discrimination against girls is higher than that of India thanks to the age-old patrilineal and patrilocal kinship system coupled with the one-child policy. It has been estimated that there are 60–100 million fewer women alive today than there would be in the absence of gender discrimination. Thus, to reduce discrimination against girls, the Chinese government, like its Indian counterpart, needs to undertake programmes of community education to modify the traditional Chinese value, norms and social customs which perpetuate gender inequality in China.

10. Environment in planned development

Rapid economic growth in post-war India and China has been accompanied by increased environmental degradation. The purposes of this chapter are to examine the nature and extent of environmental problems in both countries, and to evaluate the performance of the environment policies of both governments.

EXTENT OF ENVIRONMENTAL DEGRADATION IN INDIA

Forest Cover, Land Degradation and Deforestation

India's total forest cover as a percentage of total geographical area stood at only 21.6 per cent in 2000, as Table 10.1 illustrates.

This 21.6 per cent compares very unfavourably with the 33 per cent target set by the National Forest policy of 1988 (GOI 1999a). Even within the total forest cover of 63.34 million hectares, only 36.7 million hectares, or 11.2 per cent of the country's total land area, comprises dense forest with a crown density of more than 40 per cent. Land and soil degradation have adversely affected the productive resource base of the economy. Out of a total geographical area of 329 million hectares, 175 million hectares are considered degraded (GOI, *Economic Survey*, 1998/99). However, out of these 175 million hectares, slightly over 141.3 million hectares are subject to water and wind erosion. Hence wind and water erosion appear to be the two major causes of land degradation in India.

Thus the spread of the Green Revolution, with its increased dependence on an intensive mode of cultivation and irrigation, has resulted in soil erosion, loss of micronutrients, alkalization and water-logging in irrigated areas. Leaching from extensive use of pesticides and fertilizers has been an important source of contamination of water bodies. Soil erosion by rain and river in hill areas has caused landslides and floods. Overgrazing, traditional agricultural practices, mining and incorrect citing of development projects in forest areas have resulted in opening up these areas to heavy soil

Table 10.1   India: forest cover estimates, 1981–2000

Period	Total forest cover (million hectares)	% of geographic area	% of area under dense forest	Open forest
1981–83	64.08	19.5	—	NA
1985–87	63.88	19.4	59.1	40.2
1987–89	63.94	19.5	60.2	39.1
1989–91	63.94	19.5	60.2	39.1
1991–93	63.89	19.4	62.2	39.0
1993–95	63.34	19.3	58.0	41.3
2000	NA	21.6	NA	NA

Source: GOI, *Economic Survey*, various issues; World Bank, *World Development Indicators*, 2004, table 3.4.

erosion. Also, shifting cultivation has been an important cause of land degradation. Currently 4.9 million hectares of land are subject to shifting cultivation. In the arid west, wind erosion has caused the expansion of desert dust storms, whirlwinds and destruction of crops, while moving sand covers the land and makes it sterile.

Deforestation and Loss of Biodiversity

Forests play a vital role in enhancing the quality of the environment by influencing the ecological balance and life support system (checking soil erosion, maintaining soil fertility, conserving water, regulating water cycle and floods, and balancing carbon dioxide and oxygen content in the atmosphere). However, the capacity of the forest to play its role effectively is declining due to overgrazing, overexploitation, encroachment, unsustainable practices, forest fires and indiscriminate citing of development projects in forest areas.

The current annual withdrawal of fuel wood from the forests is estimated at 235 million cubic metres (GOI, *Economic Survey*, 1999) compared with the sustainable capacity of about 48 million cubic metres. Similarly, the annual demand for industrial wood is about 28 million cubic metres compared with the production capacity of 12 million cubic metres. Also, the area affected by forest fires ranges from 33 per cent in West Bengal to 99 per cent in Manipur. With only 2.4 per cent of the total land area of the world, the known biodiversity of India contributes 8 per cent of the known global biodiversity. It is one of 12 mega biodiversity centres in the world. Currently India holds the 10th position in the world and 4th in Asia in plant diversity. It ranks 8th and 10th in the world in terms of endemic species of higher vertebrates and mammalian species. It stands 7th in the world for the number of species relating to agriculture and animal husbandry. But the overexploitation of forests and the consequent loss of habitat is leading to the extinction of various plants, animals and other species. Over 1500 species are now endangered and about 79 mammals, 44 birds, 15 reptiles, three amphibians and several insects are endangered (GOI, *Economic Survey*, 1998/99).

The problem of the loss of biodiversity is being addressed. Approximately 4.2 per cent of the total geographical area of the country has been earmarked for extensive *in situ* conservation of habitats and ecosystems. *Ex situ* conservation is also being undertaken through a network of botanical gardens and wildlife preservation centres.

Water Quality – Rural and Urban Sectors

Although the Green Revolution has made India self-sufficient in food grains, the negative impacts of the use of agricultural chemicals, often indiscriminate, on water and the environment are now being felt. Fertilizer $(N+P_2Q_5+K_2O)$ consumption has increased from 7.7 million tonnes in 1984 to 13.9 million tonnes of nutrients in 1995–96. Use of technical good pesticides has increased from 24305 tonnes in 1971 to 85030 tonnes in 1994–95 (CSO 1977). Fertilizer run-off leads to nutrient enrichment in the receiving water bodies, resulting in eutrophication. Pesticides accumulate in the food chain, with increasing concentration along the food chain (biomagnification). This in turn affects various species in the food chain, including human beings. Soil erosion and deforestation also affect water quality in rural areas.

Apart from agricultural run-off, the two other major sources of water pollution in both the rural and urban sectors are domestic wastewater and industrial wastewater which contain organic pollutants, chemicals and heavy metals, and are the cause of many severe water-borne diseases. The organic loading of water bodies is enormous due to the extremely limited availability of sewage treatment plants in rural as well as urban areas. Domestic and municipal effluents are estimated to constitute about 75 per cent of India's wastewater by volume (MOEF 1992). Class I cities generate more wastewater than class II cities.

In 1988 the two mega cities, Mumbai and Delhi, generated more wastewater than that generated by 241 Class II towns (Parikh 1999). Facilities to treat wastewater are totally inadequate. In Class I cities only 5 per cent of the total wastewater is collected and out of this only 25 per cent is treated. More than half of the cities have no sewers. Estimates of wastewater generated in the rural sector are not available, however, only 14 per cent of the rural population have access to sanitation services (GOI, *Economic Survey*, 1998/99).

Of the 2901 large polluting industrial units discharging effluents into rivers and lakes, only 841 (29 per cent) have adequate effluent treatment plants (ETP), 2026 units (9.8 per cent) do not have adequate treatment facilities and the remaining 34 have been closed down (MOEF 1997).

Atmospheric Pollution

The main factors contributing to urban air quality deterioration are growing industrialization and increasing vehicular pollution. The problem of pollution has been aggravated by developments that have occurred as India has tried to industrialize: growing cities, rapid economic development and industrial growth, all of which are associated with higher energy consumption. Industries such as petroleum refineries, textiles, pulp and paper, industrial chemicals, iron and steel and non-metallic mineral products, small-scale foundries, chemical manufacturing, brick-making and thermal power plants, are all important sources of air pollution in the country.

Vehicular traffic is the most important source of pollution in all mega cities. India's vehicle population registered phenomenal growth from 2.1 million registered vehicles in 1973 to 25.2 million registered vehicles in 1993 (Ministry of Surface Transport 1993). Vehicular emission loads in 1994 are estimated at 3596.8 tonnes per day in 12 major Indian cities. Of all the registered vehicles, two- and three-wheelers constitute 75 per cent of total vehicles and cause more than 50 per cent of total pollution (GOI, *Economic Survey*, 1998/99). Six of the ten largest cities in India – Mumbai, Calcutta, Delhi, Ahmedabad, Kanpur and Nagpur – have severe air pollution problems with annual average levels of suspended particular matter (SPM) at least three times higher than World Health Organization (WHO) standards. In Delhi, Calcutta and Kanpur, these levels are over five times the standard.

Noise Pollution

Ambient noise levels in most of the big cities exceed the prescribed standards. The sources of noise are vehicles, diesel generators, loudspeakers, construction activities and the bursting of firecrackers. An attempt is being made to control the noise pollution by notifying the standards and by monitoring their compliance through local authorities. In Table 10.2 we present the ambient noise levels in the six largest cities in India.

It can been seen from Table 10.2 that the ambient noise levels in residential, commercial and industrial areas, both day and night, are worse in

Table 10.2   India: ambient noise levels in cities, 1999

	Residential		Commercial		Industrial	
	Day	Night	Day	Night	Day	Night
Prescribed standards	55	45	65	55	75	70
Bangalore	59–79	37–59	68–81	46–64	63–86	42–65
Calcutta	76–86	58–76	70–90	57–78	75–82	53–70
Chennai	57–84	45–50	74–80	69–71	69–76	63–69
Delhi	53–71	NA	63–75	NA	65–81	NA
Hyderabad	56–73	40–50	67–84	58–73	44–77	42–70
Mumbai	45–81	45–68	63–81	60–75	73–79	56–72

Note: All values expressed in decibels.

Source: GOI, *Economic Survey*, 1998/99.

Calcutta than in other cities. Both Bangalore and Hyderabad, the two smallest cities of the largest six, have less noise pollution than in the largest cities.

Causes of Environmental Degradation and the Indian Situation

The major causes of environmental degradation can be grouped under three headings – (1) poverty, (2) ignorance and (3) institutional failures, which include market failure and government failure (Gillies et al. 1992).

Tropical deforestation is primarily attributable to poverty; shifting cultivation practised by hill tribes in the north-eastern hill region of India has contributed to widespread deforestation in this region. Also in other regions of India, the desperate search for fuel wood by poor people has contributed to denudation of forests.

Ignorance is also to blame for deforestation. Utilization of tropical forest and timber resources for industrial and other activities has continued in India since the second half of the 19th century amid virtually complete ignorance of the ecology of the tropical forest. Ignorance and greed have also been responsible for the illegal felling of trees in large tracts of forests for private gain since the beginning of India's planned development programme in 1951. Commercialization of Indian agriculture after the introduction of Green Revolution technology in Indian agriculture since 1967, combined with increased demand for food resulting from population growth, greatly increased the demand for land in India's rural hinterland. Once again, greed and ignorance led to the gradual encroachment by powerful egocentric villagers on state forests, and on such village commons as village forests, pastures, graveyards and canals, to the extent that such commons have virtually become extinct (Roy and Tisdell 1993a). The effect on the environment has been dramatic.

The increase in the intensity of flooding in villages and the large-scale destruction of crops are the direct consequence of the disappearance of canals and drainage systems from the villages after the implementation of Green Revolution technology in Indian agriculture. Furthermore, ignorance is the principal reason for the contamination of water in village ponds and in paddy fields, and the consequent disappearance of fish populations, due to the spraying of pesticides in rice fields and washing of pesticide containers in village ponds. Contaminated waters also affect the health of women who frequently work in the fields and use the water in village ponds. Also the extinction of the bee population from the forest due to pesticide infection has significantly reduced the supply of flowers and the supply of bees in the forest, which in turn has considerably reduced the supply of honey. Water and environmental pollution in urban slums in all major cities in India are also due to poverty and ignorance.

Institutional failure is the other important factor in environmental degradation. To economists, institutions are viewed in two ways. First, institutions can be the rules of the same governing decision-making by individuals as producers, consumers or voters. Second, institutions can be organizations, especially public organizations, for example, the state apparatus affecting the operation of the economy. Institutions affect individual and social choices by shaping incentives, by influencing the availability of information and resources, and by establishing the basic rules of social transactions (Arkadie 1989).

The most important economic institutions, which are the principal focus here, include the system of property rights, the contract systems and markets, including those for capital goods and labour, all of which mediate the interaction of demand and supply. In many instances, the environmental problems can be traced directly to the failure of such institutions as property rights, contract systems and state apparatus. The denudation and destruction of natural forests are primarily due to the failure of the system of property rights in natural forests and rule of land tenure for disturbed forests.

Throughout the tropics in the developing world, the central governments have appropriated property rights to vast areas of forest from local people. About 80 per cent of closed forest area in developing countries is owned by governments (Repetto and Gillies 1988) rather than by local people who possess intimate knowledge about the forest ecology and want to ensure the continuation of the flow of economic and social benefits emanating from the forest by maintaining productive services, such as wood, non-wood and other forest products, and protective services, such as control of floods and erosion and provision of animal and plant habitats in intact or lightly perturbed forests.

Since central and state governments in many developing countries, including India, have generally lacked the means, and often the interest, to enforce the forestry regulations in remote regions, local people have often been powerless to resist opening up access to the forest for virtually uncontrolled exploitation. The forest, as a result, has become an open access or common property resource to which everyone has free access. This type of institutional failure has occurred widely in India. Illegal encroachment on and exploitation of forests have been allowed to continue by corrupt public officials. Hence the government is also responsible for institutional failure.

Honest forest department officials are unable to enforce the forest protection laws because the illegal exploiters of forests happen to have friends in the political party in power. Hence, it would appear, that the government is allowing the destruction of forests and natural resources to continue unabated.

In cities and urban centres in India, the air and water pollution are also caused by institutional failure. Unroadworthy cars and heavy vehicles are allowed to ply the streets as they possess legitimate roadworthy certificates. The requirement to install pollution control devices in motor vehicles cannot be enforced on the owners of vehicles as the public officials in charge of enforcing this rule are routinely bribed. In this same way, unhygienic slums also continue to expand.

In cities, markets for environmental services such as clean air and water do not exist. In India as in other countries, since forests are public goods, degradation continues. Deforestation caused by land clearing for agriculture and by logging has involved considerable external costs in the form of diminished watershed protection, soil erosion and sedimentation, and has increased the vulnerability of forest to disastrous fires, costing the country millions of dollars.

Environment in India's Development

The objectives of India's development plans were first raised in the Second Five Year Plan (GOI 1956). These are as follows:

1. a sizeable increase in national income so as to raise the level of living in the country;
2. rapid industrialization with particular emphasis on the development of basic and heavy industries;
3. a large expansion of employment opportunities; and

4. reduction of inequalities in income and wealth and more even distribution of economic power.

Since rapid industrialization of the country was accepted as the major objective of India's development plans in the early years of planning, the planners should have been conscious of the need to preserve the environment, as industrialization does cause considerable damage to the environment. But it can be seen that there is no mention of the need for preservation of the environment in this statement of objectives.

Planning in India began in 1951 but environmental issues were first raised in plan documents in 1972, that is, 20 years after the planning for development began. The Department of Environment was set up in 1980. It was made a Ministry of Environment in 1985. The Environmental (Protection) Act came into force in 1986, that is, 35 years after the planning for development began.

Before 1986, the viability of a project was determined on the basis of the following economic and technical criteria:

1. whether it is possible to maximize economic returns;
2. whether the implementation of the project is technically feasible.

Therefore it can be said that only from 1986 were environmental issues taken into account in making decisions regarding the implementation of development projects.

Management of Environment

The Ministry of Environment and Forests (MOEF) within the government, is responsible for protection, conservation and development of the environment. The Environmental (Protection) Act 1986 is the key legislation governing environmental management. Other important legislation in the area includes the Forest (Conservation) Act 1980 and the Wildlife (Protection) Act 1972.

The Environmental (Protection) Act 1986 empowers the central government to decide emission standards, restrict industrial sites, lay down procedures and safeguards for accident prevention and handling of hazardous waste, and to conduct investigations and research on pollution issues and on-site inspections, establish laboratories and collect and disseminate information. The Environmental Impact Assessment (EIA), introduced in 1994, empowers the central government to impose restrictions and prohibitions on the expansion and/or modernization of any activity or new project unless an environmental clearance is granted.

Projects must submit an EIA and an environmental management plant. It has been made mandatory for all major polluting industries to submit annual environmental audits to the concerned pollution boards. The objective is to make industries accountable and self-monitoring so that the burden on the pollution board will be reduced.

Thus the present approach to control pollution in India is to use regulatory instruments along with a system for monitoring the prescribed standards to achieve the government's policy goals. Thus standards for ambient and point of source emissions and discharges are set by various Acts of the government. Compliance is mandatory and provisions for penalties are made in the Acts. Central and state pollution control boards monitor these. A legal framework and, occasionally, fixed incentive schemes for implementation and compliance of the standards support the regulatory approach.

The result

No perceptible improvement in the quality of air and water in many parts of the country suggests that the policies have not worked. This obviously implies that legislation is either not properly implemented or cannot be implemented. Since the mid-1980s the pollution control boards have initiated many thousands of cases against polluting industries and have obtained only a few convictions. In the state of Rajasthan, out of nearly 7000 cases, only two convictions have been obtained.

On the one hand, the pollution control boards are poorly staffed, lack technical facilities to measure and monitor, and have meagre financial resources. On the other, they are subject to political pressures. Furthermore, some dishonest officials of the boards do not instigate cases against polluting industries. Hence, apart from meagre financial resources, the institutional failure is also to blame for failure of policies to work.

Allocations of Resources to Environment under Various Plans in India

Prior to the Seventh Five Year Plan (1985–90), there was no mention of environment among the heads of development for which financial resources were allocated. In the Seventh Plan, science and technology were added to environment for allocation of plan outlay. In Table 10.3 we present the allocation of plan outlay by heads of development.

It can be seen from Table 10.3 that the total share of environment, science and technology in total plan outlay increased from 1.4 per cent in the Seventh Plan to 2.1 per cent in the Eighth Plan. However, the share of the environment and forests together accounted for 1.1 per cent out of 2.1 per cent allocated to environment, science and technology in the Eighth Plan. In the Ninth Plan the total share of environment, science and technology in

Table 10.3   India: plan outlay by heads of development

	Total outlay (Rs billion)	Environment, science and technology (Rs billions)	Share of 2 in 1 (%)
Seventh plan (1985–90)	1800.00	24.60	1.4
Annual plan (1990–91)	583.69	7.59	1.3
Eighth plan (1992–97)	4341.00	90.41	2.1
Ninth plan (1997–2002)	8592.00	184.58	2.1

Source: GOI, *Economic Survey*, various issues.

the total plan outlay remained unchanged at 2.1 per cent. Hence, financial resources allocated in these development plans for the preservation of the environment have been very small. Again, the vast proportion of this meagre outlay went to the forestry sector. Thus, very little resources were made available by the government for controlling water, air and noise pollution. According to a 1992 estimate (GOI, *Economic Survey*, 1999), the annual cost of urban air pollution, soil erosion, land degradation and deforestation stands somewhere between US$1 billion to US$13.8 billion. This represents a share of 4.5 to 6 per cent of GDP.

Nevertheless, since 1986, prior environmental clearance of development projects based on impact assessment has been increasingly emphasized. Such clearance has been made mandatory for a large number of development projects. Public hearings have been made mandatory for all these projects prior to submission of project proposal to the Ministry of Environment and Forests to decide on environmental clearance.

ENVIRONMENT DEGRADATION IN CHINA

Water Shortage and Pollution

China's key environment problem is a shortage of water and water pollution. China's fresh water resources per capita is next to last in the world as it has less than one-third of the world average (United Press International 2004). In general, countries with less than 2000 cubic metres of water per capita are considered by the World Bank as having serious water problems, especially in the drought period, and those with less than 1000 cubic metres per capita are considered to be facing a chronic water problem (Tisdell 1997, p. 4). China's fresh water per capita in the early 1990s was 2484 cubic metres but, given predicted population growth, fresh-water resources per capita are predicted to fall to less than 1500 cubic metres by 2025 (World Bank, *World Development Report*, 1992). The distribution of water resources is very uneven in China, with Northern China especially water poor as the region currently has only one-fifth of the per capita water resources of Southern China and just 750 cubic metres per capita (United Press International 2004).

China's water is also heavily polluted. Much of the coastal waters and many of the major rivers, such as the Yangtze, are badly polluted. Both the surface and ground waters in many parts of China are also contaminated. The main source of water pollution in urban China is the industrial wastewater, which include nitrates, sulphates, arsenic and cyanide, only one-third of which is treated. Municipal sewage, the rate of treatment of which is even lower, is the other main contributor to urban water pollution.

In rural areas, the main source of water pollution is the agricultural pollution from pesticides and chemicals used in the countryside. Heavy fertilizer use contributes to the poor water quality through the leaching of nitrates into the ground water and run-off into streams. China's TVEs are another main contributor of rural water pollution. These enterprises, set up along the river banks, employ outdated technology and produce a lot of industrial wastewater which is rarely treated before it is flushed into the river system.

Air Pollution

Air pollution is China's second vast and growing environmental problem. The air quality of most of China's largest cities is lower than the standard set by the WHO. For example, in 1995, more than 50 per cent of the 88 cities monitored for sulphur dioxide (SO_2) exceeded the WHO guideline, and all but two of the 87 cities monitored for TSPs (total suspended particulates) far exceeded the WHO's guidelines, with some cities having as much as ten times the WHO's recommended SO_2 level (*United Press International*, 29 January 2004).

China's emission of greenhouse gas has also grown rapidly since the late 1980s as the coverage rate of consumer durables such as refrigerators and air conditioners in households increased. In the late 1980s, China ranked third in the world in terms of greenhouse gas emissions, after the USA and the Soviet Union (Tisdell 1997, p. 5). However, with the rapid increase of car ownership, it is expected that China will become the largest emitter of greenhouse gases by 2020 (Bingham 1993, p. 12; Smil 1993, p. 191).

The major cause of air pollution is the use of coal. Coal accounts for roughly three-quarters of China's total energy consumption and production. However, less than 30 per cent of coal in China is used for electricity generation while the rest is burnt directly, and about 80 per cent of the coal consumed is not washed before combustion and, hence, has high emission levels (Chai 1997, p. 202). It is estimated that some 90 per cent of the annual sulphur emission comes from burning coal.

Land Degradation and Deforestation

Another key environmental problem in China is land degradation and deforestation. Cultivatable land in China is very scarce because of population pressure. In terms of cultivatable land per farmer, China ranks the lowest in the world. Yet, owing to rapid industrialization and urbanization, Chinese farm land is disappearing at a rate of 0.53 million hectares a year (Strizzi and Stranks 2000, p. 77).

In urban China, solid wastes generated by industries create a serious problem for land degradation. About 55 000 hectares of land is covered with untreated solid waste, and much of it contains metal and toxic substances (Tisdell 1997, p. 302). In rural China, soil erosion caused by intensive cultivation, through the increased use of chemical fertilizers and plastic sheeting, to meet the food requirement of the growing population has affected more than 10 million hectares of farm land (Chai 1997, p. 202).

Deforestation has also occurred at an alarming rate. According to the estimates of the World Resources Institute, the area of forest and woodland decreased by 61 per cent between 1979 and 1991 (Tisdell 1997, p. 5). As result, by 1992, only 13.6 per cent of China was covered by forest and woodland. Thus, China's forest coverage is significantly lower than that of India which had 19.4 per cent in 1992/93.

Deforestation contributes to desertification of farm land in the northern and western regions. It also contributes to biodiversity loss as it destroys the natural habitat of a large number of species of mammals, birds and plants.

All in all the total economic loss caused by the above-mentioned environmental pollution is much higher in China than in India as it ranges as high as 7 per cent of the Chinese GDP per year (Roberts 2003). The breakdown of this total cost is as follows: 44 per cent is attributed to water pollution, 33 per cent to air pollution and 23 per cent to pollution from solid waste and pesticides (Tisdell 1997, p. 5).

Causes of Environmental Degradation in China

The causes of environmental degradation in China are somewhat different from those of India. Unlike India, China is not a typical developing country. During the pre-reform period, the main cause of China's environmental problem was the systemic inefficiency. Pre-reform China was operating under a planned economic system. There was an absolute lack of property rights to scarce natural resources such as clean water, air and forest. These resources were allocated to the enterprises and households as 'free goods' hence overuse of these resources was inevitable. Furthermore, under such a system, the enterprises were motivated to fulfil a physical, planned output target without due regard to cost and efficiency in resources use, let alone environmental consideration. The excessive use of resources is evident from the high energy and resources intensity of Chinese GDP, which in general was 2–3 times higher than their Asian neighbour. For example, the energy consumption per unit of GDP in China in 1979 is found to be 2.7 times that of India (Chai 1990, p. 358).

The lopsided industrial structure is another important cause for China's environmental problems in the pre-reform period. Under the strategy of preferential development of heavy industry, industrial structure was biased towards capital- and resource-intensive heavy industries, while the light industry and service sector were neglected. As a result, the share of heavy industry in total industrial output shot up from 26 per cent to 57 per cent during 1949 to 1978; whereas the share of light industry decreased from 70 per cent to 43 per cent during the same period (SSB 1984, p. 11). As a comparison of the pollution intensities of Chinese industries shows, heavy industries such as iron and steel, non-ferrous metals, chemical, petroleum processing, coking, and so on are in general among the most pollution-intensive industries (see Table 10.4). Light industries such as textiles and garments, on the other hand, have relatively low pollution intensities. Thus, the increased share of the dirty heavy industry accompanied by the decreased share of the cleaner light industry during the pre-reform period must have made the overall Chinese industry dirtier over the years.

Like India, environmental issues did not catch the attention of the government until the early 1980s after the initiation of the reform policy. In 1984, China set up for the first time the Environmental Protection Commission to look after its environment. Similar institutions were also established at the local levels (Tisdell 1997, p. 10). By 1998, there were 9937 environmental protection agencies in China, which employed more than 112000 people (*ZGTJNJ* 1999, p. 768). Since the early 1980s the government has also enacted a large number of laws and regulations dealing with environmental protection. Discharge fees were also introduced in the late 1970s basically at the same time as Chinese economic reform began. Since then these have been widened and strengthened (Tisdell 1997, p. 17).

So far, the performance of Chinese environment policies have been mixed. On the one hand, the government effort to control pollution did achieve a certain degree of success. A study by Chai (2004) reveals the pollution

Table 10.4   Pollution intensities of Chinese manufactures, 1993 and 1997

Branches	Pollution intensity (tons per million RMB)		Change (%)
	1993	1997	
Food, beverage and tobacco	56.5	22.4	−60.4
Textile and garment	28.7	17.2	−40.1
Leather, fur and down	21.9	8.6	−60.7
Pulp and paper	238.1	143.7	−39.7
Petroleum and coal	109.2	26.3	−75.9
Chemical	219.9	97.3	−55.8
Medicine	40.1	20.6	−48.6
Rubber products	28.9	18.9	−34.6
Non-metallic mineral products	146.1	95.7	−34.8
Iron and steel	528.5	364.7	−37.8
Non-ferrous metals	386.5	197.1	−49.0
Metal products	18.9	11.2	−40.7
Machinery, equipment and instruments	16.4	8.1	−50.6
Average			−47.7

Source: Chai 2004, p. 307.

intensities of the Chinese manufactured sector have been significantly reduced in recent years.

Table 10.4 compares the pollution intensities of China's manufactured industry between 1993 and 1997. The reason why these two years have been chosen is that pollution intensities data for the manufacturing branches are not available prior to 1993. As Table 10.4 shows, between 1993 and 1997, all manufacturing branches experienced a decrease in pollution intensities. The rate of decrease ranges from a low of 35 per cent for rubber products and non-metallic mineral industries to a high of 76 per cent for petroleum and coal. The average pollution intensity of the Chinese manufactured sector has dropped by 47.7 per cent over the four-year period. Other studies, such as Wheeler (2001), also confirm that air pollution in China's major cities in the last few years has also significantly decreased.

On the other hand, as mentioned earlier, China's pollution level is still significantly higher than the world average. This suggests that the effectiveness of these policies is still very limited. There are several reasons for this. To begin with, China is still a transitional economy where, on the one hand, the decision-making has been decentralized from the central to the local and individual levels and price signals are increasingly used as the basis of their decisions. On the other hand, the property rights to most of the resources are still very ill defined. Furthermore, markets for resources are still underdeveloped and, hence, the most common resources such as air and water either have no price or are underpriced. The inadequate specification of ownership rights coupled with the undervaluation of resources within a decentralized decision-making framework encourages the overuse of natural resources, leading to their lack of maintenance and conservation.

Second, due to funding constraints imposed by the government, declining budget revenues and competing demand for scarce capital, the government budget for environmental protection is very limited. During the period 1995–2000, the government allocated less than 1 per cent of China's GDP to clean up China's polluted environment.

Third, because the pollutant charges and fines for an enterprise breaking anti-pollution laws are too low, amounting to only a small percentage of China's annual industrial output, they make no difference to the decisions of the management.

Fourth, most of the key enterprises are still under government control, hence the government is both the principal polluter and the environmental regulator. Consequently, it is difficult for the regulators to carry out reviews of the state enterprises, or to take opposing position (Strizzi and Stranks 2000, p. 78). For example, the Ministries of Construction, Land and Resources and Agriculture regularly overrule the less powerful state Environmental Protection Agency (EPA) when projects are slowed by land use and emission regulations (Roberts 2003).

Fifth, the increased autonomy of local government also increases the difficulty for the Environmental Protection Agency to enforce its regulations. For example, pollution-intensive factories facing stiff new anti-pollution laws in the rich coastal regions often shifted their manufacturing to the poorer inland region, where authorities are more concerned about jobs and tax revenues than they are about the environment (Roberts 2003).

Finally, the increased number of small but less easily regulated private enterprises which exist across all of China also pose a serious obstacle for the EPA to enforce its regulation.

11. Democratization

Successful economic reforms cannot be sustained without accompanying successful political reforms. However, whether democracy, which was developed in the West, is suitable for China and India is debatable. This chapter reviews the progress of democratic development in both countries and analyses the major hurdles it faces.

INDIA

The Indian sub-continent, after remaining under British rule for nearly 200 years, was split up by the British into two states – India and Pakistan – which gained independence as separate states in August 1947. India became a sovereign secular democratic republic with a parliamentary form of government. The constitution which governs the republic was adopted by the constituent assembly on 26 November 1949 and came into force on 26 January 1950. The Indian Constitution is federal in structure with some unitary features, but within the federal structure the states enjoy considerable state rights. Although the President is the head of the Executive of the Union, the real executive power vests in the Council of Ministers with the Prime Minister as head. The President is elected by members of an electoral college consisting of elected members of both Houses of Parliament and Legislative Assemblies of the states in accordance with the system of proportional representation by means of a single transferable vote. The Council of Ministers is collectively responsible to the Lower House of the Parliament, the House of People (Lok Sabha). Members of this lower house are elected by the people under a system of universal adult franchise. The elected members of the majority party elect their leader, who becomes the Prime Minister and in turn selects other ministers.

Similarly in the states, the Governor is the head of the Executive but it is the Council of Ministers with a Chief Minister as the head in whom the real executive power vests. The Council of Ministers of a state is collectively responsible to the Legislative Assembly.

At the local government level also, multiparty democracy prevails. Elections are held to elect representatives to run the administration of corporations, municipalities and village panchayats. Elections are held every five years to form governments at all levels throughout the country.

Aims of India's Democratic Republic

The Indian constitution lays down the following directive principles of state policy which are fundamental in democratic governance of the country; it is the duty of the state to apply these principles in making laws:

1. The state shall strive to promote the welfare of the people by securing and protecting as effectively as it may, a social order in which justice – social, economic and political – shall prevail in all institutions of national life.
2. The state shall direct its policy in such a manner as to secure the right of all men and women to an adequate means of livelihood, equal pay for equal work and within the limits of its economic capacity and development, to make effective provision for securing the right to work, to education and to public assistance in the event of unemployment, old age, sickness, and so on.
3. The state shall also endeavour to secure for workers a living wage, a decent standard of living and full involvement in management of industries.
4. The state is to direct its economic policy in such a manner as to secure the distribution of ownership and control of resources of the community to subserve the common good and to ensure that the operation of the economic system does not result in concentration of wealth and means of production to common detriment.

Some of the other important directives relate to provision of opportunities for children to develop in a healthy manner; free and compulsory education for all children up to the age of 14; promotion of educational and economic interests of secluded castes, secluded tribes and other weaker sections; separation of the judiciary from the executive; promulgation of a uniform civil code for the whole country and protection and improvement of the environment (GOI 1992).

Implications of These Directive Principles of State Policy
The implications of these directive principles are that the state shall endeavour to secure social, economic and political justice for all its citizens. Only a democratic policy with democratically elected government can make sincere attempts to implement these objectives in practice. In theory, the greatest good of the greatest number can only be achieved in democracy

if a democratic government is formed by the people and the policies are designed and implemented by the people through their democratically elected representatives. In other forms of state, the elite minorities ruling the country will try to preserve and foster their own interests at the expense of the vast majority of the people.

In reality, however, even in a representative democracy, the political parties represent the interests of different groups of people. In a two-party system of democracy, the party which wins absolute majority in the election and forms the government, will try to protect and foster the interests of the groups that support the party. Hence, the interests of the groups that support the minority party are likely to be neglected and the number of people in those groups may be very large. Nevertheless, for formulating economic and social policies to subserve the natural interests and to effectively implement these policies, it is necessary for the ruling party to have a substantial majority in a two-party system of government.

Democratization Process in India

To discuss how the democratization process has worked in India to promote economic growth and economic and social development, it is necessary first to illustrate some of the essential prerequisites to the successful functioning of democracy and whether these prerequisites are present in India.

1. Election process: for a democracy to work effectively, the members for the Lower House of Parliament and for the state legislature have to be elected by the people. The process of conducting an election has to be fair so that people can cast their votes freely without any fear of intimidation and torture by the political party in power.
2. The Electoral Commission must have the power and authority to call on the federal police to ensure that elections are held in respective states freely and without any disturbance. To ensure that this happens, it is necessary for the law enforcement agencies (police force) of individual states not to be aligned to any political party and to be able to enforce the rule of law during the election time in respective states where the election for the members of both the federal Parliament and state legislatures are held.
3. In a federal state in a democratically elected government, one party will need to have an absolute majority in the federal Parliament and an absolute majority in the state legislatures. Only then can it be ensured that the appropriate national policies on economic, social and environmental issues can be framed and effectively implemented throughout the country. Such an absolute majority at the federal and state

levels is also necessary to ensure that any amendment to the constitution deemed necessary in the national interest can be carried out.

4. Bureaucrats and ministers need to be efficient, honest and impartial, and to work for the national interest. In implementing policies, bureaucrats must not have any bias towards the state or the region they come from and must not be influenced by the vested interests of the minister and the party in power.

5. The trade unions' primary responsibility would be to not only ensure that workers receive a fair reward for the work they perform, but also to ensure that production units and capital survive and grow. In other words, there should be no violent industrial action, frequent strikes and disruption to normal economic activities.

These are some of the essential prerequisites for the successful functioning of a democracy. However, none of these prerequisites are fulfilled in India.

The election process in recent years has not been fair in several states. During election time, political parties systematically use their cadres or gangsters to force people to vote in favour of their political parties. Ballot box capture and booth capture by the cadres of the party in power are quite common occurrences in several states. This has been happening because the elections of members to the state legislature are held in individual states, therefore, the state police force remains in charge of maintaining law and order. Many state governments have routinely used the police force to gain advantages over their opponents prior to and during the election. In one state where the Marxists have been in power for more than two decades, a substantial majority of the police force belongs to a union affiliated to the party in power. Hence opposition parties are at a disadvantage during the election. Therefore, to ensure that elections are held properly, one view is that an emergency needs to be declared and the President's rule needs to be imposed in every state where the election is being held. But, for this to happen, Article 356 of the Indian Constitution needs to be amended. To check this abuse of the state administrative machinery by the ruling party during State Assembly elections, if there is unanimity among all political parties, the federal government can bring legislation so that State Assembly polls are held under the President's Rule. But this unanimity can very rarely be achieved in India's political culture (*The Statesman Weekly*, 20 July 2002).

Judicial activism is playing an increasingly important role to ensure that democratic institutions function properly, that the government's inaction on vital economic, social, political and environmental issues is prevented, property rights of individuals and businesses are protected and constitutional obligations are met. However, the judicial decree has to be given effect by the police force in the states. But the police force is not always honest, efficient and impartial in all states. Hence, judicial activism becomes meaningless.

The National Election Commission has an office in the capital city of each state to oversee the process of electing members of Parliament and state legislature. However, at the time of election of members for state legislature, the state government and the party in power in many states systematically use their influence to convince the Election Commission officers to turn a blind eye to the irregularities that take place in the election process. So the National Election Commission does not get a true picture of the election process in individual states.

At the centre, currently, there is a coalition government of many minority parties, each of which is interested in furthering its own sectarian interest, at the expense of national interest, to retain its power and influence among its electorate. One recent example is the transfer, after 150 years, of the headquarters of the Eastern Railway from Calcutta in West Bengal state to a little-known place in Bihar by the current railway minister, who comes from Bihar, the neighbouring state of West Bengal. This means that the new railway office will not have the same wealth of knowledge and expertise that the Calcutta office possessed in managing the operation of Eastern Railway for 150 years. Also without any infrastructure in existence, the new headquarters at Hajipur will be in charge of managing five divisions.

So why did the central Cabinet support this action of the railway minister? Because this was the only way of neutralizing the damage caused by the departure from Bihar state of one minister who foretold a loss of Dalit (untouchables) votes in the forthcoming 2004 parliamentary elections. As for the gain of the railway minister, this move will reap rich political dividends and has already portrayed him as the minister most dedicated to furthering the interests of Bihar. Also this bifurcation of Indian Railways into 16 zonal railways will, according to the railway experts, make it economically, operationally, strategically and personnel-wise unviable, and eventually will spell its doom. The Chinese Railway, having an identical structure to Indian Railways, has in the last decade, reduced the number of its bureaus and divisions by 30 and 45 per cent respectively (*The Statesman Weekly*, 27 July 2002). The experts also say that things would not have come to such a pass if successive chairmen and members of the Railway Board did not act as 'hatchetmen' of railway ministers. They willingly complied with orders they knew to be wrong and unethical. If they did not barter away their professionalism for lucrative post-retirement benefits, the Indian Railway would not be balkanized in the 150th year of its founding (*The Statesman Weekly*, 27 July 2002). This is an example of how bureaucracy in Indian democracy works sometimes willingly in pursuance of its own interests and sometimes under political pressures from its ministers.

The coalition government in power at the centre is not in power in many states, which are ruled by the Congress Party (the main opposition party at the centre) and many regional parties. As a result, the chances of any economic or social policy being implemented uniformly at the state level are considerably reduced.

In the past, during the rule of the Congress Party, although the party in power at the centre was also in power in an overwhelming majority of states, the states with greater political influence were able to extract greater economic advantages from the centre than other states (Bhagwati and Desai 1971). This contributed to the unbalanced development of states which has adversely affected India's overall growth performance. The same trend is continuing today. This has been one of the major drawbacks of India's federal democracy.

Bureaucrats at the centre tend to favour their own states for disbursing development project grants, directing foreign investment, and so on. This has further accentuated the bipolarism in Indian development. Sometimes bureaucrats have been forced to act in such ways by ministers.

In East Asian countries, bureaucrats are highly paid, enjoy a very high social status and have tremendous job security. Therefore, ministers' influence on bureaucrats is very limited.

On the industrial front, militant unions resorted to violence to force employers to accede to their demands for higher wages. This led to the closure of many production units throughout the country. Inability of successive governments to curb union excesses allowed these unions to wield enormous power. This union militancy has been one of the principal factors adversely affecting India's industrial production and growth, inflow of foreign capital and preventing the government from implementing its programme of privatization of public enterprises. One recent example of union power is the failure of the West Bengal government to enter into a joint venture agreement with the French hotel group, Accor Asia Pacific, to run its hugely loss-making hotel, Great Eastern Hotel of Calcutta, due to the demand by the hotel's Marxist affiliated union that none of the 400 employees can be sacked. Now that the hotel has accumulated substantial liabilities and the West Bengal government is unable to subsidize the hotel to cover its losses, the government plans to float a global tender for a 30-year lease of the hotel with the clause that the lessee must take on all the liabilities of the hotel, not retrench any of the 400 employees and not remove any of the shops on the hotel's ground floor (*The Statesman Weekly*, 27 July 2002). Needless to say, no foreign investment will take place in any venture in which militant unions wield so much power.

Thus it would seem that some of the most essential prerequisites to the successful functioning of a democracy do not exist in India. What we have in India is a framework of a political democracy which provides a legitimate cover for minority groups' political party in power to pursue vested interests through undemocratic means. Hence the impact of this façade of political democracy on the performance of the economy has been disastrous.

Economic Policy and Applications

Indian socialism has fragmented and destroyed India's economy and social life (Roy 1984; Rudolph and Rudolph 1987; Shenoy 1971). Comprehensive and pervasive social controls on the private sector, combined with centralized planning and public sector control of the 'commanding heights' of the economy, stunted economic growth in a land of tremendous human and natural resource potential. Confiscating tax rates combined with escalating controls in the 1960s produced one of the world's largest and most thriving underground economies, accounting for about 50 per cent of economic activity. Also government control of the broadcast media and educational and social policy has gone hand-in-hand with the unrestrained growth of a bureaucratic redistributive state in order to achieve a socialistic pattern of society (Kamath 1993a).

India's jungle of bureaucratic red tape is said to be one of the largest and most complex in the world. For example, the permission to open a hotel involves around 45 applications, which are reviewed by over 25 different government agencies. Before the economic reform programme began, it took anywhere from 27 to 63 months to obtain government clearance for any medium or large private sector industrial projects (Jagannathan and Guhathakurata 1991). Throughout the period of its development history, in the world's largest functioning democracy, adoption of statist policies led to the systematic suppression of voluntary exchange and market activities and other private voluntary activities. Also private property rights are severely attenuated and circumscribed (Lal 1988a; 1988b). Due to the suppression of market forces, while the economy could manage to achieve a growth of around 1.8 per cent annually on a per capita basis until the early 1980s, it contributed to rising expectations resulting from increasing population pressure, and the growth of political and other rent-seeking special interest groups.

The government's economic reform package implemented in 1991 was neither comprehensive nor complete. It had been politically easy since it did not threaten the special interests created by the permit-licence Raj (Kamath 1993a). In fact, the Congress Party was never interested in the proper implementation of the reform package as it was apologetic about reform and it brought back the old populist policies and programmes discarded in 1991. The opposition political parties were also against the implementation of any economic package that would harm their political interests. Hence, what happens in regard to the implementation of any economic policy in India's democracy is as follows.

When the politicians need support of the people they tend to proclaim a move to the left in economic policy. This generally happens on the eve of the election, when the votes of the poor are solicited. But once the politicians gain power, their leaning to leftism in policy terms slowly begins to wear off. Intense desire to stay in power drives them to look for funds to meet the expenses of the next election. The time is ripe then for a swing to the right in policy stance, which lasts until the treasury of the political party in power is filled. Thus economic policies in India move in a cycle – sometimes to the left, but not enough to be called leftist, and sometimes time to the right, but not enough to be called rightist. The reason for these opportunistic turns in politics, according to Khatkhate, is the concentration of political power at the centre. As a solution to this problem, like many other economists, he suggests diffusion of political power among the state units and even lower down the ladder among district units (Khatkhate 1991; 1997).

However, one has to note that there has already been considerable decentralization of power to the states but further decentralization may eventually lead to the disintegration of the country as one federal democratic state. On the other hand, many of the vital areas in which the state governments have exclusive jurisdiction should be brought under concurrent list (that is, under the equal jurisdiction of both the central and the provincial governments) so that, for the sake of successful functioning of the democracy, the centre can also have jurisdiction over vital areas such as law and order. Currently several state governments have used the state police force to systematically maim opposition forces and destroy democratic principles in governance. For the Indian democracy to function properly, the democratic principles have to be applied in governance at the centre and, more importantly, at the state level. Unfortunately, further decentralization of power will not achieve this. India's development has already been regionalized due to the systematic neglect of the entire Eastern and North Eastern regions, and parts of Northern India, by the central government and its bureaucracy. Any further neglect would make Indian democracy dysfunctional.

The programme of privatization of loss-making public enterprises has not made any progress at all due to opposition from the bureaucracy and public sector unions (Joshi and Little 1994). As a result many of the other items in the reform agenda have also not been implemented properly. All these have significantly affected India's economic growth.

There has been considerable discussion in economic literature about the relationship between democracy and economic growth and about the performance of Indian democracy in terms of achieving important goals such as high growth, poverty alleviation and human development. Sen (2004) admits that the hypothesis that there is no relationship between democracy and economic growth seems hard to reject but, on Indian democracy, his view is that the real problem is not that India has too much democracy, but that in some ways it has too little of it. His primary concern here is violation of civil rights and of individual liberties, on the grounds of combating terrorism or preventing separatist extremism. These are, of course, matters of genuine concern. Commenting on advantages of democratic India over autocratic China, he argues that the freedom of people to voice their grievances and the freedom of the press in India have contributed a great deal to the prevention of famine in India; whereas in China, the absence of these freedoms was a factor in the severe famine in 1958–61 which cost the lives of about 30 million people.

Basu (2004) supports this view. We certainly agree with Sen that the freedom of the press, freedom of speech and freedom to organize public meetings would have forced the government to take appropriate action to prevent famine. Our view is that in India there is a democratic structure which has been extensively used by all political parties in power – at the centre and at the provincial level since Indira Gandhi assumed power at the centre in 1967 – to adopt corrupt and undemocratic means to stay in power. Thus a democratic structure has been used to prevent a genuine democracy from taking hold in India. The objectives of every dominant political party has been to win the election and to stay in power for five more years. Hence, in a province, a party in power which has been able to establish a strong network of party agents and mafias within its territorial jurisdiction and bring the police force under its control, can use all means, such as intimidation of people, preparation of a false electoral roll and vote rigging on a massive scale, to win all elections.

A government winning an election in this way does not need to bother about any adverse comments made by opposition political parties, their supporters or by the press about the performance of the government. This is why the communists and other minor left-orientated parties are the greatest champions of India's democratic structure. Bardhan's (1984; 1988; 2004) works explain in great detail how India has evolved since independence and how it has been functioning. We are in complete agreement with his view that the politics of buying support with patronage and of accommodating the conflicting demands of a large and heterogeneous coalition of interests has had serious implications for the pace and pattern of economic growth in India. At the same time, he feels, that a lack of autonomy at state and local levels will act as a binding political constraint on economic performance in spite of the new economic policy and that the 'Panchayati Raj' system (democratically elected rural government) has worked reasonably well to improve socio-economic conditions in the village.

Basu (2004) also holds a similar opinion regarding the 'Panchayati Raj' (democratic system of government at villages) system. However, as we mentioned earlier, greater devolution of power to provinces and to local governments in the rural sector may simply enlarge the scope of collecting a larger amount of rents from a larger population by political party leaders, ministers, bureaucrats, party agents, party mafias and local government representatives. In a country, democracy cannot work to foster economic growth and development where the judiciary and the police force have lost their independence and power to enforce the rule of law and to protect property rights, and individual freedom, due to skulduggery by political party leaders and their informal agents within the boundaries of each state.

Note the following comments of Bardhan (2004, p. 57):

> In large parts of the country the judiciary (particularly at the lower end) is almost completely clogged up by the enormous backlog of cases. The legal system is largely paralysed by delay and corruption, and the institutional independence of the police and criminal justice system is regularly undermined by politicians of whichever is the ruling party. As a result the rule of law which is as much the foundation stone of a regime of market reforms as of political democracy is sadly missing. Hence market reformers, instead of trying to organise the retreat of the state, should devote a large part of their energies to the cause of reform of the state machinery, to administrative and judicial reform to make the state more accountable to the common people, and to prevent the hijacking of the police and the criminal justice system by the politician – criminal nexus.

Hence, following Bardhan's arguments we also are compelled to argue that democracy cannot work without a powerful and independent judiciary and police force but, in India, the political institution has been systematically incapacitating that judicial institution. In the rural sector, the 'Panchayati Raj' system delivers benefits mostly to the supporters of the political party in power.

In one state the current state committee secretary of an opposition party commented that during the present chief minister's regime, there is total politicization of administration. In all districts except two, all the Zilla Parishads (District Legislative Bodies or District Boards) are under the control of the major political party in power. Over 90 per cent of Gram

Panchayats (village governments) are controlled by the party in power at the provincial government level and, in such a situation, the bureaucrats have hardly any independence. The district magistrates, who are experts in administration and who can take an impartial and politically neutral decision on any administrative matters, are dictated to by the chairman of the district board and are required to have their decisions ratified by the local leaders of the party in power at the provincial level. A recent attempt in the same state by the government to pass a bill to establish a 'Salisi Board' (village court) to deal with village-level legal disputes aims to take away from the subdivisional level judiciary virtually all judicial powers and to vest these powers in the hands of political party members at the village level. For a democratization process to succeed it has to be successful at the provincial level because India as a country exists in provinces.

Unfortunately it is in these provinces that Bardhan's (1984) dominant proprietary classes rule and use the provinces as their private fiefdoms. The practice of democracy involves (1) the selection of candidates by various parties to contest the election; (2) ensuring free and fair polls and (3) the election of a leader of a legislative party, if it commands a majority by itself, or of the leader of a coalition of parties elected to the assembly for the formation of government.

Out of these three steps, only the polling and declaration of results are free, fair and democratic in India. However, as we mentioned earlier in this chapter, the election commission makes judgement on the fairness of polling on the basis of the reports of election commission representatives stationed in each province. Unfortunately, political party mafias ensure the maintenance of a show of free and fair poll and the Election Committee Reports rarely represent the facts. Hence, following Douglas North (1987), we can say that for democracy to succeed, the people carrying out the business of governance need to share some conviction about the appropriateness of the society and the economics system within which they are acting.

This conviction requires the presence of some ethical values among the ruling class and in the community at large. Unfortunately, that value system has been disappearing from the ruling class and from the community at large in Indian democracy. Perhaps if the democratization process had begun in India at the provincial level during the British rule and progressed slowly right up to 1947, it would have prepared the country well for a successful transition from a colony of the British Raj to a better-functioning democracy. Unfortunately, the structure of a multiparty instead of a two-party federal democracy was adopted immediately after India's independence.

CHINA

Merits of Democracy

According to UNDP (*Human Development Report*, 2002, p. 3), democracy is better than an authoritarian regime in many respects. To begin with, democratic governance is valuable in its own right, as enjoying political freedom and participating in the decisions that shape one's life are fundamental human rights and hence an integral part of human development. Second, democracy increases the efficiency of the government as it holds the government fully accountable to the voters. Third, democracy is also better than an authoritarian regime at managing conflict as it provides open space for political opposition so that military conflict can be avoided and peaceful handover of power is possible. Fourth, democracies are better at avoiding catastrophes and at managing a sudden downturn that threatens human survival.

Sen (1995), for example, provides evidence which show that in the post-war years, India performed better at managing political catastrophes than China. In the Great Famine of China during 1959–61, casualties reached almost 30 million. In contrast, in post-war India, despite several crop failures, famine has been averted as elected politicians responded with public works programmes for famine-affected people (UNDP, *Human Development Report*, 2002, p. 3). The recent spread of SARS (Severe Acute Respiratory Syndrome) in China and other parts of the world is another glaring example of failure of an authoritarian regime. The disease was allowed to spread so quickly because the media was prevented from publicizing the condition of the disease and the political leadership, shielding information about the disease, was slow to act.

Optimal Democratic Standard

Though UNDP (UNDP, *Human Development Report*, 2002) provides an excellent exposition of the virtue of democracy, it does not answer the fundamental question which a developing country nowadays is facing, namely, should it strive for a maximal democratic standard regardless of its cultural background and stage of economic background? The answer to this question is no, for each country has its own optimum democratic standard giving its cultural background and stage of economic development. It is inequitable for Western nations to impose its democratic norm on other developing countries.

Democratic standard can be considered a local public good. The optimal level of democratic standard is determined by the demand and supply for democratic standards. The demand curve for democratic standard represents the sum of individual derived marginal benefits (MB_i) for a given democratic standard. The supply curve of a democratic standard represents the marginal cost (MC) of maintaining democratic standard.

The optimal level of democratic standard is determined by Samuelson rule, according to which

$$\sum_i MB_i = MC \tag{11.1}$$

In Figure 11.1, $\Sigma_i MB_i$ is the demand curve and *MC* is the supply curve of democratic standard. The optimal level of democratic standard, therefore, is determined by the intersection of the supply and demand curves. The optimal level of democratic standard for a developing country is likely to be lower for two reasons. First, for a typical developing country without democratic tradition, democracy is perceived as a luxurious good and hence its perceived benefits to the general population is likely to be lower and can be represented by a lower demand curve for democratic standard $\Sigma_i MB_i^1$. On the other hand, the perceived *MC* of maintaining a given democratic standard is likely to be higher. This is because the opportunity cost of resources used in maintaining a given level of democratic standard is higher because the resources in developing countries are relatively scarce. Furthermore, additional cost may be incurred as a result of maintaining a higher democratic standard. As UNDP studies (UNDP, *Human Development Report*, 2002) show, though there is no empirical evidence to

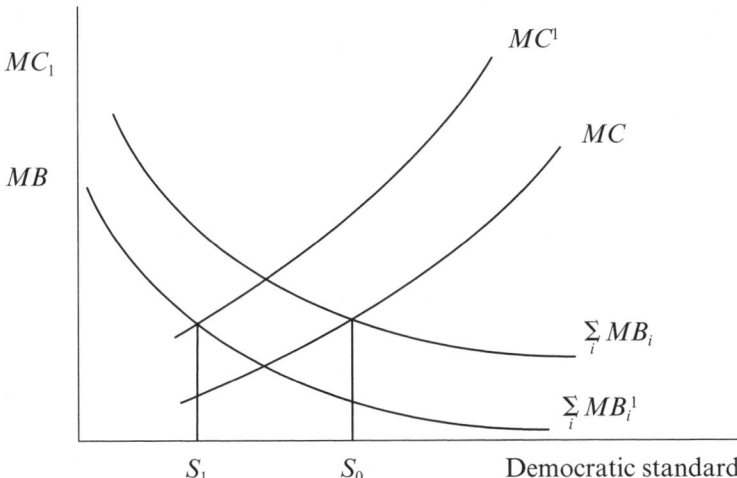

Figure 11.1 Determinants of an optimal level of democratic standard

support the hypothesis that democracy costs economic growth, there is evidence to show that democracy increases the degree of political instability in forms of frequency of demonstrations and riots which may cause capital flight. Hence, the additional cost of democracy can be measured by the decline in the supply of capital that results from an increased democratic standard, $-\Delta K$, multiplied by the net value of an additional unit of this capital for a country in the form of higher income and employment foregone, t. Thus, if this opportunity cost of higher democratic standard is taken into account, the MC of maintaining a given level of democracy becomes $MC - t\Delta K$. With capital outflow being treated as an opportunity cost for maintaining a higher democratic standard, the supply curve of democracy will be higher, that is, it becomes MC^1. Consequently, the optimal level of democratic standard for a developing country would be settled at S_1, much lower than S_0. Thus, if a Western nation imposes a higher democratic standard on the developing countries at S_0, it implies that MC is larger than MB_i. Hence, the higher democratic standard is not welfare-enhancing but welfare-diminishing for developing countries.

Four Ideal Types of Political Regime

Diamond and Myers (2000, pp. 365–86) distinguish two main types of political systems in the world, namely, democracy and an authoritarian regime. An authoritarian regime is defined as a regime without political opposition and individual rights. Democracy is further subdivided into three ideal types, namely, electoral democracy, liberal democracy and pseudo-democracy.

Electoral democracy is a political system under which the legislative and chief executive officers are filled through regular, competitive multiparty elections with universal suffrage. Liberal democracy is an electoral democracy with the following additional attributes: extensive individual and group freedom, and vigorous pluralism in economic, political, organizational and intellectual life (the so-called four market places) and finally, a strong rule for laws. Pseudo-democracy possesses a formal democratic institution and also holds regular multiparty elections, but a single party dominates the political system.

India's political regime can be regarded as a liberal democracy as it satisfies the condition of both electoral and liberal democracy, whereas China's political system is undoubtedly an authoritarian one. The fact that India is much more advanced than China in terms of democratic development is confirmed by the findings of a world opinion survey carried out by international agencies such as Freedom House and the World Bank as well as other organizations such as the University of Maryland, the result of which is presented in Table 11.1.

Table 11.1   Indicators of democratic governance, 2000

	China	India
Democratic institution[1]	−7	9
Civil liberties[2]	6	3
Political rights[3]	7	2
Press freedom[4]	80	42
Voice and accountability[5]	−1.11	0.66
Rule of law[6]	−0.19	0.23

Notes:
1. This indicator is developed by the University of Maryland which reflects whether laws and institutions allow democratic participation. The score ranges from −10 to 10, the higher the better.
2. This indicator is developed by Freedom House. The score ranges are as follows: 1–12, free; 3–5, partly free; and 6–7, not free.
3. This indicator is developed by Freedom House. The meaning of the score is the same as in note 2.
4. This indicator is developed by Freedom House. The scores range from 0–30, free; 31–60, partly free; and 61–100, not free.
5. This indicator is developed by World Bank. Score ranges from −2.5 to 2.5, the higher the better.
6. This indicator is developed by World Bank. The meaning of the score is the same as in note 5.

Source: UNDP, *Human Development Report*, 2002, pp. 39–40.

Table 11.1 measures the degree of democracy of each country in terms of six indicators, namely, democratic institution, civil liberties, political rights, press freedom, voice and accountability, and rule of law in the year 2000. As evidenced from Table 11.1, India is well ahead of China in all six indicators.

Political Liberalization without Democratization

Though China has not experienced any real progress in democratization over the last 50 years, it has experienced a significant extent of political liberalization in the recent years. Zhao (2003) provides an excellent survey of political liberalization in China in recent years. The purpose of this political liberalization, according to Zhao (2003) is to make single party rule of the Chinese Communist Party (CCP) more efficient or to provide it with more of a legal base. The content of political liberalization in China, according to Zhao, consists of the following.

First, there has been a significant reduction of the state's interference in the daily life of Chinese people. This has manifested itself in the greater freedom of belief, expression and consumption as well as employment and residential choices.

Second, China has made a small step towards electoral democracy at the grass-roots level via the introduction of an election for the village committee in the township's people congress. After the disbandment of communes in 1982, township, town and village were re-established at the lowest level in the government hierarchy (Chai 1997). In 1998, there were 26 400 townships and 19 100 towns and 740 000 villages in China (*ZGTJNJ* 1999, p. 17). A township is governed by the township's party committee, the township's people's government and the township's people's congress, and the village is governed by a village committee. Grass-roots democracy in the form of an election for the village committee was started by peasants in Guangxi Province in the early 1980s (see O'Brien and Li 2000, p. 463) and was later adopted nationwide. A formal village committee election was adopted in 1987 (Lum 2000, p. 143) and institutionalized in 1998 with the passage of organic law of Local People's Congress and Local Government. This law requires that all village committee candidates be directly nominated by villagers and that the election be conducted with multiple candidates and secret ballots. Estimates of the proportion of Chinese villagers who had held democratic elections ranged from 10 to 60 per cent in the mid-1990s (O'Brien and Li 2000, p. 485).

The purpose of an election for the village committee was originally designed to increase mass support for the party by establishing a self-government programme aiming at rejuvenating village leadership by cleaning out incompetent, corrupt and heavy-handed leaders, according to O'Brien and Li (2000, p. 489). But it is far from clear that the election is carried out freely and fairly, as party village secretaries usually served on (or chaired) the village election committee that supervised village elections. This gives them considerable influence over the election outcome (Diamond and Myers 2000, p. 383). Furthermore, even if the village committee elections are relatively free and fair, they are not meaningful since the real power remains in the hands of the party secretaries in the village as the articles of the Organic Law of the Village Committee stipulates that the party branch in the village is the leadership core in the village (O'Brien and Li 2000, p. 488).

There has also been an attempt to move the electoral democracy higher up to township level. The first experiment with a township election occurred in Nancheng county in Si-Chuan Province without prior approval of the central government in 1998. This was soon followed by other counties (see Li 2002, p. 721). However, fear of loss of party control in local politics prompted the central government to issue the central document No. 12 in July 2001 (Li 2002, p. 721) which has practically halted the experiment. Like the village committee election, the primary purpose of the township election is to stabilize the countryside by stopping township officials acting like a local emperor and mistreating peasants (Li 2002, p. 707).

Third, the role of China's National People's Congress (NPC) has also changed in recent years. The NPC is no longer merely a rubber-stamp Parliament. It has become increasingly assertive and dares to go against party dictates. For example, there have been several occasions in recent years during which deputies have rejected and voted down the government work report and several pieces of legislation proposed by the party.

Finally, to loosen the single party rule by the CCP, several measures have been introduced to separate the party from the government and reduce the party's interference with economic institution (Zhao 2003, p. 345). One of the measures introduced is to bar the party officials such as party secretaries and deputy party secretaries from holding a concurrent position at the same level of government leadership. Another measure introduced is the abolition of the party committee leadership system in economic and academic institutions. Yet another measure is the abandonment of the old system of party control over personnel appointments and the establishment of a new civil service system based on an open and competitive examination. However, so far these measures have not been fully implemented.

Prospects of Democratization in China

Will the political liberalization now going on in China lead to eventual democratization in the near future? Studies on democratic transition in China abound, but most of the findings of these studies appear to be pessimistic (see Diamond and Myers 2000; Hsieh 2003; Lum 2000). Transition from an authoritarian regime to a democratic regime, according to Przeworski (1991), is a game of tug-of-war between those in power and those in opposition. Only when the opposition holds a sufficient amount of resources can one expect the government to make concessions and move down the democratization path. Currently, the opposition in China consists mainly of critical intellectuals who possess little social, economic and political support. The lack of support stems from the lack of public opinion pressure for democracy. For example, evidence from the 1995 Beijing residents survey conducted by two US scholars, Dowd and Cartion, with the corroboration of a Chinese scholar, M. Shen, shows that there is little public opinion pressure for democracy in China (quoted in Zhao 2003, p. 334). This lack of support for democracy in China can be attributed to several factors. One is the Chinese communist success at maintaining social control and political stability. This success can be attributed to their effectiveness in applying peer pressure at the local level and in managing the

Table 11.2   Indicators of efficiency of governance, 2000

	China	India
Graft (corruption)[1]	−0.30	−0.39
Corruption perception index[2]	3.5	2.7
Political stability and lack of violence[3]	0.39	−0.05
Law and order[4]	4	4
Government effectiveness[5]	0.14	−0.17

Notes:
1. Score ranges from −2.5 to 2.5, the higher the better.
2. Score ranges from 0 to 10, the higher the better.
3. Score ranges from 0 to 6, the higher the better.
4. Same as note 3.
5. Score ranges from −2.5 to 2.5, the higher the better.

Source: These indicators were developed by the World Bank and are quoted in UNDP, *Human Development Report*, 2002, pp. 39–40.

economy successfully. The success of Chinese communists in these regards can be seen from Table 11.2.

Table 11.2 compares the quality of the government between India and China in 2000 in terms of four indicators: effectiveness of government, political stability and lack of violence, extent of corruption, and law and order. China's score on the first three indicators is significantly higher than that of India, whereas in the last indicator China's score is on par with that of India. Thus, contrary to the claim of UNDP, democracy has not necessarily produced a high-quality government in India. The main reason for this is that democracy did not work in India because, as discussed in the previous section, the condition for a workable democracy there is still lacking. In contrast though, the Chinese government is undemocratic but it is more efficient that that of India.

Another reason why there is little support for the opposition in China, according to Hsieh, is that there has not been any significant value change in China. Although more and more people in China nowadays embrace individualism as a result of increasing income, education, information and global connectedness, China's culture remains essentially Confucian which is not very democratic, according to Hsieh (2003), as Confucian culture sets up a strongly hierarchical structure for society which consists of a set of dualistic relationships: emperor–subject, father–son, husband–wife, elder brother–younger brother and friend–friend with the superior being expected to set moral examples for subordinates and the subordinates being expected to respect their superiors (Hsieh 2003, p. 380).

Another reason why there is a lack of support for opposition in China, according to Hsieh (2003, p. 384), is that there is an absence of pluralistic social order in China which the opposition can exploit to pursue their agenda. Whereas India's society is characterized by a lively quasi-pluralistic social order as the country is deeply divided along the lines of religion, race, language, culture, and so on, China is a relatively homogenous society with Han Chinese comprising 92 per cent of the population. Furthermore, the country has a common written and spoken language, Mandarin. Hence the prospect for a speedy democratic transition in the near future is not good in China.

12. Conclusion and prospects

The acceleration of the Indian economic growth rate to 8.5 per cent in 2003 has fuelled speculation that India is about to catch up in its growth race with China. Is the Indian cobra likely to join the Chinese dragon in the sun in the near future (*The Economist*, May 2004). The answer to this question depends very much on (a) how big are the existing development and reform gaps between the two economies and (b) whether India can close these gaps with China in the near future. Throughout this book the development and reform gaps between India and China have been examined in detail and in this final chapter the results of these examinations will be reviewed and summarized in order to draw some overall conclusions on this issue.

THE DEVELOPMENT GAP

Currently a significant development gap between China and India exists, however, the size of the gap differs among the various economic sectors.

Macroeconomic Performance and Structure

Table 12.1 compares the current stage of India's macroeconomic performance and economic structure with that of China in terms of ten economic indicators.

The GDP per capita (item 1 of Table 12.1) is considered to be the summary indicator of a country's level of economic development. India's 2002 per capita GDP in terms of purchasing power parity adjusted US\$ was \$2670 (Table 12.1), which was only 59 per cent of that of China. The Indian 2002 level of GDP is comparable to that reached by China in 1994 (UNDP, *Human Development Report*, 1997, p. 147). Hence, in terms of GDP per capita, India trails China by about eight years.

Economic development is accompanied by a declining share of the primary industry and a corresponding rise of manufacturing in both GDP and exports (items 2 to 5 of Table 12.1). In 2002, the share of the primary industry in India was still dominant and made up almost a quarter of the GDP, whereas in the same year the share of the primary industry in

*Table 12.1   Selected macroeconomic performance and structure indicators:
India and China, 2002*

	India	China
1. GDP per capita (PPP adjusted in US$)	2670	4580
2. Share of primary industry in GDP (%)	23	15
3. Share of primary industry in exports	22	10
4. Share of manufactured products in exports (%)	75	90
5. Share of manufacturing in GDP (%)	16	35
6. Electric power consumption per capita (kwh)	561[3]	1139[3]
7. Share of high-tech products in manuf. exports (%)	5	23
8. Engel coefficient for farmer (%)	59[1]	46[5]
9. Rate of poverty (%)	35[2]	17[3]
10. Share of IT industry in GDP (%)	3[4]	NA

Notes:
1. 2000.
2. 1999/2000.
3. 2001.
4. 2000. The figure refers to share of IT revenues in GDP.
5. 2003.

Sources: World Bank, *World Development Indicators*, 2004; UNDP, *Human Development Report*, 2004; Singh 2004, p. 225.

China's GDP was only 15 per cent. On the eve of reforms in 1979, China's primary industry's share of GDP was 31 per cent, but it decreased to 25 per cent in 1989. Thus Indian industrial structure was at the level reached by China in 1989.

The share of primary industry in India's exports in 2002 was also still relatively high and amounted to 22 per cent. This is in stark contrast to the situation in China in 2002 where it amounted to only 10 per cent. India's level of development measured on this indicator is similar to China's level in 1991 (*ZGTJNJ* 1998, p. 579).

The share of manufacturing in India's exports in 2002 was 75 per cent compared with China's level of 90 per cent in the same year (*ZGTJNJ* 1999, p. 579). China's manufacturing share in exports declined steadily after the reforms, and by 1990 it had declined to 74 per cent. Thus, India's level of development in terms of this indicator is similar to that reached by China in 1990.

The per capita electric power consumption (item 6 of Table 12.1) is an indicator of the degree of the modernization of a country's industrial structure, as growth in electricity consumption is closely related to growth in the modern sector. In 2001, India's per capita electricity consumption was 561 kwh, whereas that of China was double that, namely, 1139 kwh. In China the electricity consumption was relatively low on the eve of the reform in 1978, but it increased to 545 kwh by 1990 (*ZGTJNJ* 1999, pp. 111 and 251). Hence the development gap between China and India is again about ten years in terms of this indicator.

Thus, based on the above five indicators, India's level of development in the early 21st century is comparable to China's level of development in the late 1980s and early 1990s. Thus the development gap between China and India is about ten years. However, measured in terms of other indicators, the development gap between China and India is greater than ten years. The share of manufacturing in Indian GDP (item 5 of Table 12.1) in 2002 was only 16 per cent, whereas that of China in the same year was 35 per cent. China had reached the 2002 level of India's manufacturing share in 1956 (*ZGTJNJ* 1999, p. 56). Thus, in terms of the share of manufacturing in GDP, the gap between India's and China's economic development amounts to roughly 46 years.

India is also well behind China in terms of its share of high-tech manufactured exports (item 7 of Table 12.1). There are two approaches to measure a country's high-tech exports, namely, the sectoral and product approaches. Because an industrial sector characterized by a few technology products may also produce many low-tech products, the product approach is more appropriate for analysing international trade than is the sectoral approach (World Bank, *World Development Indicators*, 2003, p. 305). Using the product approach, the World Bank finds that the share of high-tech products in Indian exports in 2002 was only 5 per cent, whereas that of China in the same year stood at 23 per cent. According to a study by Lall and Albeladejo (2002, p. 89) the share of Chinese high-tech products in manufacturing exports grew rapidly from the late 1970s and by 1985 it had already reached India's 2002 level. Hence, in this regard, India lags behind China by 17 years. However, it should be noted that most of China's high-tech products originate from the FIEs and not from indigenous enterprises. Hence, China's high-tech manufactured export share may be overestimated.

In terms of the standard of living there is also a big gap between the two countries. One of the best indicators to measure this is Engel's coefficient, which in 2000 was 59 per cent for Indian farmers (item 8 of Table 12.1). In 2003, Engel's coefficient of Chinese farmers was only 45.6 per cent. The 2000 Indian rural Engel coefficient is similar to that reached by China in 1981 (*ZGTJNJ* 1981, p. 437). Thus the gap between China and India in terms of the standard of living of farmers is approximately 19 years.

Another important indicator which reflects a country's standard of living is the rate of poverty measured in terms of the proportion of the population living on under US$1 a day. In India in 1999/2000 this rate stood at 35 whereas in China it had come down to 17 per cent.

However, the comparison is not totally lopsided in all respects for India. On the basis of at least one indicator India was actually ahead of China in the early 21st century. A modern economy is characterized by the increasing share of the new economy, especially the IT sector. The overinvestment in higher education in India, the use of the English language in its higher education system and the ample supply of IT skilled labour have all contributed to a leap in development of the Indian IT sector and its rise in the share of GDP. Between 1994 and 2000, the IT sector grew by a factor of 5, whereas the GDP as a whole only slightly more than doubled over the same period (Singh 2004, p. 225). As a result, the share of the IT sector in India's GDP rose from less than 1 per cent to 3 per cent in 2000. However, it should be noted that the IT figures are not directly comparable to that of GDP as the former is based on revenues rather than value added. Most of India's IT industry is centred on software, which accounted for almost 80 per cent of overall sales in this industry in 2000 (Singh 2004, p. 227). Comparable figures for China are not available but, according to the McKinsey report, China's software industry lags behind India's because of its fragmented structure and poor management (see Jonquieres 2005).

In summary, a comprehensive comparison of the ten economic indicators reveals that, as far as the general macroeconomic performance and the economic structure are concerned, India currently is at the level that China had reached in the late 1980s and early 1990s. Hence, there is roughly a ten-year gap between China's and India's economic development. However, in some sectors, such as in manufacturing, high-tech manufacturing exports and the standard of living, the gap between China and India widened to more than ten years. On the other hand, in the IT industry India is ahead of China.

Human Resources Development

Successful economic development requires the building of human capital through human resources development in terms of investment in education and health care, leading to improved levels of literacy and numeracy as well as a higher level of average life expectancy of the population. In 2002, India's adult literacy rate stood at 61 as compared to 91 in China in that year (items 1 to 5 of Table 12.2). Thus, the Indian literacy rate is now at the level that China had reached in 1964 (SSB 1985, p. 137). In 2002, Indian net primary school enrolment was 83 per cent compared with 93 per cent in China. The 2002 Indian rate is similar to that of China 37 years earlier, namely, in 1965 (SSB 1985, p. 171). Primary school attendance is a critical factor for a country's economic growth because research suggests that five

Table 12.2   Selected indicators of human resource, infrastructure, science and technology development: India and China, 2002

	India	China
Human resource		
1. Adult literacy rate	61	91
2. Net primary school enrolment ratio (%)	83	93
3. Gross secondary enrolment ratio (%)	48[1]	68[1]
4. Gross tertiary enrolment ratio (%)	11[1]	13[1]
5. Life expectancy at birth (years)	64	71
Infrastructure		
Transport		
6. Km of railway per 1000 square km land area	21[2]	6[2]
7. Km of road per 1000 square km land area	1 109.6[2]	145.8[2]
8. Railway traffic density units (traffic units per km)	11 725[2]	30 262[2]
9. Railway employee productivity (traffic units per employee)	467[2]	1 115[2]
10. Goods hauled by road million (ton–km)	958[2]	612 800
11. Aircraft departures (thousands)	152	932
12. Aircraft passengers (millions)	12	83.7
13. Air freight (billion ton–km)	0.4	5
14. Port container traffic (million TEUs)	3.4	44
Telecommunication		
15. No. of phones (per 1000 people)	40	167
16. No. of cell phone subscriptions (per 1000 people)	12	161
17. No. of wire Internet connections (per 1000 people)	16	46
Science and technology		
18. No. of researchers in R&D (per million people)	157[3]	584[3]
19. R&D expenditure in GDP (%)	0.82[4]	1.1[5]
20. Patents granted to residents (per million people)	0[6]	5

Notes:
1. 2001/02.
2. 1996/2001.
3. 1990/2001.
4. 1989/2000.
5. 1996/2002.
6. 2000.

Sources: as for Table 12.1.

to six years' schooling at the primary level is a critical threshold for the achievement of sustainable basic literacy and numeracy skills. Thus, in terms of the above two basic education indicators, the gap between India and China is about 37 to 38 years.

However, in terms of the gross secondary and tertiary enrolment ratio the situation looks much better for India. In 2001/02 its rates were 48 per cent and 11 per cent respectively for secondary and tertiary enrolment. In the same year in China, by comparison, the rates were 68 per cent for secondary enrolment and 13 per cent for tertiary enrolment.

Life expectancy at birth reflects the level of development of health care services. In 2002, the Indian life expectancy at birth was 64 years, whereas the corresponding figure for China was 71 years. Life expectancy had increased in China gradually from 1957 onward, and in the period from 1970 to 1975 it had reached the current Indian level. Thus the gap between the two countries in terms of health care service standards is about 30 years. Thus, as far as human resources development is concerned the gap between China's and India's development is about 30 to 38 years.

Infrastructural Development

Sustained economic growth also requires a well-developed transport and communication infrastructure (items 6 to 17 of Table 12.2). India has a more developed road and railway system than China. In the 1996 to 2000 period India had 21 kilometres of railway lines per thousand square kilometres of land area. In contrast, China had only 6 kilometres per thousand square kilometres of land area in the same period. Similarly, in the same period, India had 1109.6 kilometres of road per thousand square kilometres of land area, whereas China had only 145.8. However, as is to be expected, the intensity of use rate and productivity of these two transportation modes in China are higher than those of India. The intensity of rail usage is measured in terms of traffic unit per kilometre, which is the sum of passengers and freight tons per kilometre. In the period of 1996 to 2001 the intensity of railway use was 11 725 whereas the comparable figure for China was 30 262. This means that the intensity of rail usage in China was more than two and a half times that of India during this period. China's rail system is also more productive compared with India's. Worker productivity in Indian railways in the same period was 467 traffic units per worker. This contrasts with China's figure of 1155, which is again two and a half times higher than India's figure. Similarly, the rate of utilization of China's roads is much higher than that of Indian roads. In the period from 1995 to 2000, goods hauled by road in India was 958 million tons per kilometre whereas the Chinese figure was 621 800 million tons per kilometre. Thus, the intensity of road usage in China was 648 times higher than in India

In terms of other transport modes, however, India is behind China. In aviation, for example, China in 2002 had 923 000 aircraft departures compared with only 152 000 for India in the same year, and the number of passengers carried was 83.7 million in China and only 12 million in India.

Similarly, the ton to kilometre ratio moved by air freight in 2002 was 5 billion in China compared with only 0.4 billion in India. It is much the same picture for water transport. In 2001, for example, the container traffic in Indian ports reached only 3.6 million TEUs (twenty-foot equivalent units) compared to 44 million TEUs in China in the same year.

Despite the rapid development of its IT industry, India is behind China in terms of development of the telecommunication infrastructure; however, the gap is relatively narrower than in respect of other criteria. In 2002 India had 40 telephones for every thousand people whereas China had more than four times that number, namely, 167 per thousand. The 2002 Indian level of development of the telecommunication infrastructure is equivalent to that of China in 1996 (*ZGTJNJ* 1999, pp. 111 and 533). In regard to cell phone coverage, the same picture emerges, for in 2002 India had only 12 cell phone subscriptions per thousand population, whereas that figure for China was 161. Despite India's boom in IT its number of wire Internet connections per thousand population was 16 compared with 46 for China. Hence, the gap between China and India in terms of telecommunication development is about five to six years.

In summary, it can be said that in respect of transport the picture about the relative level of development of the two countries is mixed. While India is behind China in terms of telecommunications, air and water transport, and the productivity and usage intensity of its road and rail coverage, it has a much more developed road and rail system. In telecommunication development, however, India is definitively behind China.

Science and Technology

Modern economic development is increasingly knowledge based. The acquisition of knowledge depends very much on the development of science and technology. With respect to these indicators, India is somewhat behind China, which is evident from a comparison between the two countries in respect of technology base and achievement (items 18 to 20 of Table 12.2). The technology base can be measured in terms of the numbers of people employed in R&D for every million people. In the decade from 1990 to 2001 India's figure for this amounted to 157, whereas China's figure is 584.

The percentage of R&D expenditure in GDP can also serve as an important indicator of the technology base of a country. In the period from 1989 to 2000 India spent only 0.82 per cent of its GDP on R&D, whereas that of China stood slightly higher at 1.1 per cent in the period from 1996 to 2002.

In terms of technological achievement, the same picture emerges. Its level can be measured in terms of the number of patents granted to residents per million population. China was ahead of India in this regard since it had five patents for every million people, while India had none in 2000.

Political and Social Development

Successful economic development also requires the modernization of the political system, and India, with a well-established democratic system since its independence in 1949, is far ahead of China, which still maintains an autocratic political system that only reluctantly allows piecemeal political reforms. As discussed in Chapter 11, India is ahead of China along all six key democracy indicators, namely, development of democratic institutions, civil liberties, political rights, freedom of the press, voice and accountability, and rule of the law.

However, in terms of social development, discussed in Chapter 8, India is still well behind China. It is clear that economic growth cannot be sustained in the long run if its benefits are not shared by the majority of the population. China has achieved a broad-based growth owing to the Maoist legacy of egalitarianism, under which it distributed basic necessities and public goods in an egalitarian way and made such services as health care and education accessible to the whole population. This resulted, as mentioned earlier, in the raising of Chinese life expectancy at birth and of primary school enrolment. India, where much of the caste system remains, had no such egalitarian policies and thus lags far behind China in this regard. Moreover, China's broad-based growth has also been achieved through the elimination of inequality of opportunities between the different social strata as well as between that of men and women. For example, as discussed in Chapter 9, in terms of gender equality, India is way behind China's development, for in 2002, India's gender-related development index was 0.572 whereas that of China stood at 0.741 (Table 9.8).

In sum, a comparison between China's and India's level of development in six key dimensions shows that India lags behind China in most areas. The gap is widest in industrial, human resources and social development, and narrowest in infrastructural development as well as the level of science and technology. However, in terms of the development of the IT industry and in political development, India is way ahead of China.

THE REFORM GAP

Successful economic development requires a modern economic system and industrial organization and, in particular, a market-orientated economy and competitive and efficient industrial organizations and enterprises. Both

China and India have embraced economic reforms to move their country closer to this goal. However, China has the edge over India in this regard, since it started its reforms ten years earlier than India. However, India has the advantage of starting reforms from a more advanced economic system, namely, a mixed economy, while China has to build a market economy from scratch.

Economic reform, in both India and China, involves essentially the triple goals of privatization, liberalization and globalization. The two countries' success at reforming is gauged in terms of the progress made in these three areas.

Privatization

On the eve of India's reforms in the early 1990s, the share of PSEs in GDP stood at 25 per cent (Joshi and Little 2004, p. 174). Privatization in India takes the form of divestiture of the existing public sector enterprises (PSEs). As discussed in Chapter 2, owing to the strong resistance of vested interest groups, the progress of privatization is painfully slow. In the period from 1991/92 to 2000/03 the value of all PSEs that had been privatized was only 13 per cent. Thus the share of the private sector, which had stood at 75 per cent on the eve of the reform, has increased only marginally.

In contrast, China has made great strides in privatizing its economy. However, the situation was quite different because on the eve of the reform its share of the private sector amounted to less than 1 per cent of GDP. Currently, its agricultural sector is *de facto* privatized under the house-hold responsibility (HRS) system. In the non-agricultural sector, owing to the rapid growth of non-state enterprises (NSEs), the share of state-owned enterprises (SOEs) has shrunk as well. In 1998, the share of the private sector in GDP, if the UCEs (urban collective enterprises) and town and village enterprises (TVEs) in the non-government sector are considered as private, was 72 per cent (see Siebert 1999, p. 177; Chai, 2003, pp. 236–46). Thus, in quantitative terms India is only slightly ahead of China in terms of the degree of privatization.

Liberalization

Product market
Liberalization in product market involves the increase of enterprise autonomy, price liberalization and an increase in the ease of doing business for the enterprises.

In its reform period China has made significant progress in increasing enterprise autonomy. Mandatory planning has been completely eliminated, but enterprises in both the agricultural and non-agricultural sectors are still subject to numerous administrative controls. In the agricultural sector, the government still controls the production and marketing of food grain which accounts for two-thirds of China's cultivated area. In the non-agricultural sector, SOEs have gained increased autonomy with respect to input, output, sales and investment decisions, but the government still has much influence over their activities through two channels. First, the appointment and promotion of enterprise managers are still in the hands of the state bureaucracy. Second, certain industrial inputs, such as some materials and energy, and bank loans remain rationed by the authority. Moreover, enterprise autonomy, especially in the SOE sector, is still very restricted in regard to industrial relations and especially in regard to the hiring and firing of workers.

The deregulation of enterprise activities in India involved the abolishment of the Industrial Licensing Department, the de-licensing and deregulation of investment and production in most industries, and the elimination of exclusive reservation of many key industries for the public sector. However, the progress in increasing enterprise autonomy is very slow. Public sector enterprise managers are, as a rule, political appointments. As in China, they continue to require ministerial and bureaucratic clearance for their decisions and they cannot retrench unproductive labour because of section 5–13 in the Industrial Dispute Act. Entry to and investment in certain industries is still restricted. Some 830 products are currently still reserved for SMEs and capacity expansion is limited in sectors earmarked for SME development, McKinsey and Co. (2004).

China has also achieved significant progress in terms of price liberalization as 90 per cent of retail prices are now completely determined by market forces. However, some inertia of its price system remains. The retail prices of energy and utilities as well as the producer prices of food grain are still regulated by the government.

India had a mixed economy on the eve of its reforms, hence most of its prices were already formed by market forces but were subject to a number of government controls. Since the early 1970s the Indian government has moved to reduce and/or to remove these controls, however, its progress is very slow. In the agricultural sectors, as in China, the government still controls the domestic prices of some staple goods, such as rice and wheat, keeping them lower than the prices of other agricultural products but higher than world market prices. The government also provides a minimum support price (MSP) to farmers for a large number of food and non-food agricultural crops. The prices of certain agricultural inputs, such as electricity, water and fertilizers are also controlled and underpriced, inviting an overuse of these inputs.

With regard to the ease of doing business, enterprises in both countries are still facing a lot of administrative and legal hurdles. However, according to the World Bank survey (see World Bank, *World Development Indicators*, 2004, table 5.3), China is well ahead of India because of its head start in administrative reform. The World Bank compares the ease of doing business across countries in terms of the following criterion: entry regulation, contract enforcement and the ease of bankruptcies. In terms of the first criterion, India is well behind China, for in 2003 the time needed to complete all the required procedures to legally operating a business was 88 days as compared with only 46 days in China. Not only is the lead time to start a business longer in India but the costs involved are also higher. In India the cost to register a business measured in terms of percentage of national income per capita was 50 per cent compared with only 14 per cent in China.

In terms of contract enforcement the picture is similar. In 2003, the time needed to enforce a contract was 365 days in India compared with only 180 days in China. Similarly, the costs of contract enforcement were much higher in India. Measured in terms of the percentage of national income per capita its figure in 2003 was 95 per cent, whereas that of China stood at only 32 per cent.

In terms of bankruptcy procedures, India is still much more bureaucratic and has higher hurdles. In 2003 the average time to resolve a bankruptcy in India was 11 years as compared with only 2.6 years in China. However, the costs in India were lower, they amounted to only 8 per cent of the bankrupt estate compared to China's 18 per cent.

Factor market

Land market   The development of the land market in China is still in its embryonic stage. Owing to the lack of clear delineation of property rights in both rural and urban areas, very few land transactions have taken place and there is virtually neither a rural nor an urban land market. In contrast, India has a well-developed land market and land transactions are virtually free. Nevertheless, severe distortions remain. According to McKinsey and Co. (2004) one of these is unclear ownership. The lack of clarity about who owns what makes the Indian land prices in major cities the highest among all Asian nations relative to average income. Other important distorting factors are inflexible zoning, rent control and the protection of tenants, which have the effect of freezing the land available in cities for urban renewal.

Labour market   China's labour market is still developing. In both rural and urban areas the market is subject to many administrative restrictions, with the effect that the rate of labour turnover at the enterprise level is very low. In India the labour markets in the agricultural sector and the informal sector in the urban areas, which employ the 91.5 per cent of the total labour force (Bardhan 2004, p. 53), are virtually free. However, in the urban organized sector, in both public and private enterprises, liberalization has made little progress as the labour market is controlled by militant trade unions. Thus workers have secure jobs even in loss-making PSEs, the nationalized banking sector and, of course, in the bloated state and national bureaucracies (Lal 1995, p. 1480).

Labour market regulation is measured by the World Bank in terms of a composite index of three aspects of labour regulation, that is, flexibility of hiring, conditions of employment and flexibility of firing. The index varies from 0 to 100, with higher figures indicating a better situation. The Indian index stands on 51, whereas that of China is 47 (World Bank, *World Development Indicators*, 2004, table 5.3). Hence, India is only slightly ahead of China in respect of this indicator of development.

Financial market Economic growth requires a well-developed financial market. The financial market includes the banking system and the stock market. At a relatively low level of development, banks dominate the financial system, while at higher levels the stock market tends to become more important.

The financial system in both India and China in the pre-reform period catered in essence to the needs of planned development. In the process of reforms both countries have liberalized their financial markets. What is the current level of financial market development in both countries? In terms of the size and depth of the financial sector, India is still very much behind the development of China. In terms of financial depth, for example the ratio of liquidity assets or broad money (that is, the sum of currency in circulation plus household saving deposits) to GDP, India's figure in 2002 was only 63 per cent whereas China's stood at 178 per cent in the same year (World Bank, *World Development Indicators*, 2004, table 5.5). The structure of the financial market in both countries is similar, that is, it is still dominated by the banking system. However, the growth of the banking system has been faster in China than in India. The ratio of domestic credit, provided by the banking system, to GDP is used to measure the growth of the banking system since it reflects the extent to which savings are financial. In 2002, in India this ratio stood at 59 per cent of GDP, whereas China's was 166 per cent, that is more than two and a half times that of India (World Bank, *World Development Indicators*, 2004, table 5.5). However, in both countries the banking system is still dominated by the nationalized banking sector, with the majority of bank credits going to the government enterprises.

In India in 2000/01 the PSEs' share in such credits was 52 per cent while in China the share of SOEs is even higher with 95 per cent (Laurenceson and Chai 2003, p. 9).

The stock market in both countries plays a very limited role as a source of finance for corporate investment. In China it was developed only relatively late, namely, in the 1980s. In India the stock market has existed since the middle of the 20th century but in the period from 1999 to 2001 corporate investments originating primarily from it amounted to only 4 per cent (Rakshit 2004, p. 98). In China, capital raised from equity issue amounted for only 2 per cent of all business financing in 2004 (*The Australian*, 30 May 2005). However, despite China's relatively shorter history of development, the size of its stock market, measured by market capitalization as a percentage of GDP, is much larger than India's. The respective percentages for China in 2002 were 37 and for India 26. However, the Chinese stock market is much less liquid than India's as the value of shares traded as a percentage of capitalization was only 12 per cent in 2002 as compared with India's 14.1 per cent in the same year (World Bank, *World Development Indicators*, 2004, table 5.4). The relatively low liquidity of the Chinese stock market is mainly due to the fact that the majority of shares are held by the state, or organizations closely controlled by it, and are, therefore, not tradable.

Globalization

Globalization is an essential ingredient to growth as empirical studies have shown that globalization is always correlated with a faster pace of growth (Dollar and Kraay 2004). The degree of globalization of an economy can be measured in terms of the degree of openness and integration of its product and capital market with the world economy. The former depends on the height of a country's average tariff barrier. The simple mean tariff in India is 15 per cent in 2005 as compared to that of China of 10 per cent. China has in the reform period significantly lowered its tariff barriers and in 2001 it stood at 15 per cent (World Bank, *World Development Indicators*, 2004, table 6.6). Thus India lags about four years behind China in regard to this indicator.

Successful trade liberalization should result in an increased share of imports and exports of goods and services as a percentage of GDP (trade shares). In 2002, the trade share of India was only 31 per cent compared with that of China of 55 per cent (UNDP, *Human Development Report*, 2004, p. 194) . India's current trade share is at China's 1990 level (see Table 5.2). Thus, the gap in development between the two countries in regard to this indicator is about 12 years.

The increasing integration of a country's capital market with the world economy should be reflected in a relatively greater share of foreign direct investment (FDI) in its gross capital formation. In 2001, FDI in India made up only 3 per cent of its gross capital formation, whereas the corresponding figure for China in that year was 10 per cent, or more than three times higher (World Bank, *World Development Indicators*, 2003, pp. 262–3). The 2001 Indian share is at the level reached by China in 1990. Thus, in terms of FDI liberalization, the gap between India and China is about 11 years.

Thus, in terms of the above three indicators of globalization, India lags four to 12 years behind China. Since China has opened up its economy ten years earlier than India, a gap of this magnitude between India and China is to be expected.

In summary, on the eve of the reforms the systemic gaps between the two countries was huge, as India operated a mixed system whereas China had a command centralized planning system (that is, an economic system under which resource allocation is planned by the government and the government plan is mandatory for enterprises). China started its reform movement ten years earlier and its implementation ran more smoothly due to it being enforced by an authoritarian regime. After the reforms, the two economic systems became more similar to each other. Currently, both countries have a mixed economic system. They share the following systemic features: the size of their state sector is still relatively large and the state still plays a dominant role in economic activities, the budget restraints of state-run enterprises remain soft, and the product and factor markets are still overregulated. However, there are also some noteworthy differences between the two economic systems. For example, the private sector in India is larger and its factor markets, especially land and labour markets, are more developed and subject to fewer distortions than those in China.

On the other hand, China's economy is more integrated into the world market and the conditions of entry, exit and contract enforcement in the product market in China is subject to fewer restrictions than in India.

THE FUTURE OF THE INDIAN ECONOMY AND POLICY IMPLICATIONS

What of the future of the Indian economy? Will the Indian cobra be able to catch up with the Chinese dragon in the economic growth race? As mentioned earlier, the answer to this question depends on whether the existing development and systemic gap between India and China is surmountable for India. In terms of economic development, the above comparison reveals that, on most key indicators, India is about ten years behind China and this ten-year gap can be simply explained away by China's headstart of ten years in economic reforms. Hence, the gap is not insurmountable for India. However, in regard to some areas, such as human resources and social development, India is so far behind China's development that India's government would have to make a substantial effort to catch up. However, it is precisely because social factors are slower to change and a democracy cannot simply impose desirable changes that it seems unlikely that India will take great strides in this regard in a relatively short time.

In terms of economic systems, currently no significant gap exists between the two countries. India is behind China only in terms of the globalization of its economy and administrative reforms. Since these gaps can be explained by China's headstart in these two areas, they are not insurmountable for India.

In view of the fact that the development gap between China and India in many areas is simply due to the time gap in starting the reforms in their countries, it is imperative for India to accelerate the pace of its structural reforms in the following areas if it intends to catch up with China.

First, India should step up the speed of privatization of its PSEs.

Second, India should continue to liberalize its product and factor markets. For India's product market especially, it is imperative, according to the McKinsey Global Institute (MGI), to remove all remnant licensing and quasi-licensing restrictions which limit the number of players in the affected industries. Moreover it needs to completely eliminate the reservation of products for small-scale enterprises. In the factor market, it is essential to get rid of the distortion in the land market by clearly delineating property rights in urban land and by abolishing the protection of tenants, rent control and irrational zoning laws. In the labour market, it is necessary to repeal section 5–13 of the Industrial Disputes Act in order to get rid of surplus labour in both private and public enterprises and the bloated bureaucracies at national and state government levels. With respect to the financial market, India needs to step up the privatization of its banks and allow entry of foreign banks in order to develop an independent and sufficient banking system. The access of private producers to domestic credit also needs to be considerably improved.

Third, India needs to open the economy more to the world market. It should continue to liberalize its trade and FDI regime and lower the average tariff rate to bring it in line with the level of China, that is, 10 per cent. India also needs to remove the ban on FDIs in the retail sector and allow the unrestricted operation of FDIs in all sectors (McKinsey and Co. 2004).

Fourth, in view of the fact that India is implementing its economic reforms in a democratic political framework it is important to strengthen the popular support for reform. This can be achieved by constructing a minimum social safety net to soften the opposition of the potential losers from the reforms, who come mainly from the previously protected sectors and bureaucracy. In conjunction with this the interlocking interests of politicians, industrialists and bureaucrats in perpetuating the rents generated by the licensing Raj which finance politics need to be broken up. This can be done by creating an alternative source of electoral finance as suggested by Lal (1995, pp. 1485–6) and Bardhan (2004, p. 54).

However, the acceleration of its reforms is a necessary but not a sufficient condition for India to catch up with China's economic development. According to McKinsey and Co. (2004), the acceleration of reforms in India alone would free the Indian economy to grow as fast as China's . However, this view is somewhat simplistic. Considering the huge development gap between China and India in regard to some of the key areas compared, India needs to change its development strategies, especially in the following areas, if it is going to catch up with China in the economic growth race.

Saving and Investment

In order to achieve a relatively high growth rate, a high rate of investment and savings is inevitable. In 2003, while China invested 42 per cent of its GDP the figure for India was only 23 per cent (see Tables 6.1 and 6.2). The gap between China's and India's rate of saving is even larger. In 2002, China's saving rate was 43 per cent compared with that of India of 24 per cent (see Tables. 6.10 and 6.2 respectively). One of the constraints that keeps the Indian rate down is the fiscal deficit of both the state and the national governments. This increased from 7 per cent of GDP in the early 1990s (Basu 2004, p. 25) to 10 per cent in 2003/04 (Wolf 2005). Thus while in the post-reform period in India both the private and corporate savings have increased, the public saving rate has actually declined and become a negative figure (Basu 2004, p. 25). Hence, a fiscal reform is urgently needed to redress the growing fiscal deficits at both the central and the state levels (Rakshit 2004, pp. 103–6) and to provide the conditions for faster economic growth.

According to Rao (2004, p. 142) the following specific measures need to be implemented to address the fiscal crisis of the Indian states. The state needs to restructure the administrative system, downsizing the bureaucracy and prioritizing expenditure allocation to provide infrastructure and create a less inhibitive business environment. The state needs to limit its expenditures on interest payments and the state needs to arrest the slide in revenue and GDP ratio by phasing out loss-making PSEs. In addition, fees need to be increased to cover the costs of running the quasi public and private services.

Human Resources and Social Development

High growth cannot be achieved in the absence of human resources development. As mentioned earlier, India lags far behind China in this area. Hence, India would need to significantly step up its expenditure on education and health care and ensure equal access to these public goods and services for all segments of the population in order to catch up with China in terms of rate of adult literacy, life expectancy and net primary school enrolment.

High growth cannot be sustained if its benefits are not equally shared by the population. To provide conditions for broad-based growth it is imperative to achieve a high degree of social development in terms of equalization of opportunities so that everyone has the chance to be upwardly mobile, or at least to improve their standard of living. As mentioned before, India lags rather far behind China in respect of its social development as it is still left with many of the trappings of the caste system, which inhibit upward mobility, and there is still extensive and systemic discrimination against women. India needs to work hard on improving social development to close the significant development gap with China on this score. It needs to eliminate entrenched patterns of discrimination, such as gender discrimination and landlordism, which prevent India from achieving a broad-based growth strategy like that of other East Asian nations (Sen 1995).

Agricultural Development

As discussed in Chapter 3, India lags far behind China in agricultural development in spite of the fact that its prime agricultural resource, arable land per capita, is much higher than that of China. The Indian economy is currently still very dependent on its agricultural sector, which accounts for one-quarter of its GDP. Moreover, unlike China, Indian agriculture has not been able to stabilize its yield through irrigation. As a result, its yield is still very dependent on variable weather conditions, especially the monsoon. Much of the recent acceleration of India's economic growth can simply be attributed to a few good monsoon seasons. The crucial factors constraining long-term agricultural growth is the neglect by the government of agricultural investment and other infrastructural facilities in rural areas (Rakshit 2004, p. 95). Thus , the government needs to step up its investment in agriculture. In particular, it needs to increase the percentage of land under irrigation and to lessen dependence on the monsoon. It also needs to improve credit access for farmers so that they can buy HYV (high-yield variety) seeds and other related inputs.

Manufacturing Industrial Development

As stated before, India is way ahead of China in terms of IT industrial development but equally way behind China in terms of manufacturing industrial development. As *The Economist* rightly pointed out (Economist Intelligence Unit 2001), the IT sector cannot serve as the only engine of growth as IT labour is highly specialized and the number of jobs the sector can create is relatively limited. Currently about half a million people in India are employed in this sector (Basu 2004, p. 23) which is only a minute fraction of the huge Indian labour force of 460.5 million. As discussed in Chapter 7, despite the higher rate of growth in the post-reform period, the unemployment situation in India has worsened compared with the pre-reform period owing to the declining employment elasticity of growth. The latter, in turn, is partly due to the government's neglect of the development of the manufacturing industry and its overemphasis on the development of the IT sector which is capital and technology intensive but not labour intensive. In view of the fact that India and China are the world's two most populous countries and that the Indian labour force grows much faster than the Chinese labour force – due to China's birth control policies – India can ill afford to neglect the development of its manufacturing industries. Only this sector can provide the broad-based productive employment that India needs to accelerate and sustain its economic growth and promote social development.

Though China currently dominates the world manufacturing market, there is no reason why India could not win a world market share from China, especially since the wage rate in China is rising. Due to the rapid growth of its income per capita, India is fast closing the gap with China in terms of labour cost per unit of value added in the manufacturing sector. During 1980–84 the Indian labour cost per unit of value added in manufacturing was 3.3 times that of China, however, in the period from 1995 to 1998 the ratio had dropped from 1.5 to 1 (World Bank, *World Development Indicators*, 2003, pp. 54–5). As China's wage level in manufacturing rises, it has to shed the more labour-intensive manufacturing and move to more capital-intensive methods of manufacturing. This can provide an opportunity for India to step into China's shoes and specialize in labour-intensive manufacturing exports. Such a development would not only solve the unemployment problem in India but would also enhance India's economic growth through an increase in its labour productivity as currently 92 per cent of the labour force are still employed in low-productivity agriculture and the informal sector.

Infrastructure Facilities

As mentioned earlier, India is relatively better endowed with a modern transport infrastructure, compared with China, such as roads and railways. However, India lags behind in terms of the rate of utilization and efficiency of these transport modes. According to Joshi and Little (2004), Indian infrastructure suffered from both undercharging and underinvestment. Hence there is an urgent need to transfer the management of the existing infrastructure to the private sector and of contracting out the construction and management of new infrastructure to the private sector (McKinsey and Co. 2004).

References

ACFERT (*Almanac of China's Foreign Economic Relations and Trade*), Beijing: Ministry of Foreign Economic Relations and Trade, various issues.

Adelman, I. and D. Sunding (1987), 'Economic policy and income distribution in China', in J.C.H. Chai (ed.), *Economic Development of Modern China*, vol. 2, Cheltenham: Edward Elgar.

Ahluwalia, I.J. (1985), *Industrial Growth in India: Stagnation Since the Mid-Sixties*, New Delhi: Oxford University Press.

Andors, S. (1977), *China's Industrial Revolution*, New York: Pantheon.

Arkadie, B.V. (1989), 'The role of institutions in development', *Proceedings of the World Bank Annual Conference on Development Economics*, Washington, DC: World Bank.

Ash, R. (1976), 'Economic aspects of land reform in Kiangsu', *China Quarterly*, September, 519–45.

Athukorala, P.C. (2002), 'Introduction', in P.C. Athukorala (ed.), *The Economic Development of South Asia*, vol. 1, Cheltenham: Edward Elgar.

Athukorala, P.C. and K. Sen (2002), *Saving, Investment and Growth in India*, Oxford and Dehli: Oxford University Press.

Bajpai, N. and J.D. Sachs (1997), 'India's economic reforms – some lessons from East Asia', *Journal of International Trade and Economic Development*, **6** (2), 135–64.

Bannister, J. (1997), 'China: population dynamics and economic implications', in M.E. Sharpe (ed.), *China's Economic Future*, New York: US Congress Social Economic Committee, pp. 339–60.

Bardhan, P. (1969), 'Agriculture in China and India: output, input and prices', *Economic and Political Weekly*, **4**/1–2, 129–36.

Bardhan, P.K. (1984), *The Political Economy of Development in India*, Oxford: Oxford University Press.

Bardhan, P.K. (1986), 'Dominant proprietary classes and India's democracy', in A. Kohli (ed.), *India's Democracy; An Analysis of Changing State–Society Relations*, Princeton, NJ: Princeton University Press.

Bardhan, P.K. (1988), 'Epilogue: the political economy of reform in India', in A. Kohli (ed.), *The Political Economy of Development in India*, expanded edition, New Delhi: Oxford University Press.

Bardhan, P.K. (1998), 'Corruption and development: a review of issues', *Journal of Economic Literature*, September, 1320–46.

Bardhan, P. (2004), 'Disjuntures in the Indian reform process: some reflections', in K. Basu (ed.), *India's Emerging Economies: Performance and Prospects in the 1990s and Beyond*, Cambridge, MA: MIT Press, pp. 49–58.

Basu, K. (2004), 'The Indian economy: up to 1991 and since', in K. Basu (ed.), *India's Emerging Economies: Performance and Prospects in the 1990s and Beyond*, Cambridge, MA: MIT Press, pp. 3–32.

Bhagwati, J. (1982), 'Directly unproductive profit seeking (DUP) activities', *Journal of Political Economy*, **92**, 988–1002.

Bhagwati, J. (1993), *India in Transition: Freeing the Economy*, Oxford: Clarendon Press.

Bhagwati, J. and P. Desai (eds) (1971), *India, Planning for Industrialisation*, London: Oxford University Press.

Bhalla, A.S. (1992), *Uneven Development in the Third World: A Study of China and India*, London: Macmillan.

Bhalla, A.S. (1998), 'Sino-Indian liberalization: the role of trade and investment', *Economics of Planning*, **31**/2–3, 151–73.

Bhalla, A.S. (2000–01), 'Political economy of Indian development in the 20th century: India's road to freedom and growth', *Indian Economic Journal*, **48** (3), 1–23.

Bhatia, V.G. (1988), 'Asian and Pacific developing economies: performance and issues', *Asian Development Review*, **1**, 1–22.

Bhole, L.M. (1994), 'Unemployment alleviation programmes in India: a review and prospects under the new economic policy', *Indian Journal of Labour Economics*, **37** (2), 173–85.

Bhole, L.M. and P. Dash (2002), 'Employment – unemployment in India', *Indian Journal of Labour Economics*, **45** (2), 273–86.

Bhowmik, S. (1998), 'The Labour Movement in India: present problems and future perspectives', *Indian Journal of Social Work*, **59** (1), 147–66.

Bingham, A. (1993), 'China's phenomenal growth has environmental tag', *Pollution Prevention* (Asia/Pacific edn), **1** (4), 10–22.

Blackwood, D.L. and R.G. Lynch (1994), 'The measurement of inequality and poverty: a policy maker's guide to the literature', *World Development*, **22** (April), 569.

Bose, P.K. and M. Mukherjee (1985), *Mahalanobis: Papers on Planning*, Calcutta: Statistical Publishing Society.

Brandt, L., S. Rozelle, G. Li and J. Huang (in press), 'Land rights in China: facts, fictions and issues', *China Journal*.

Buiter, W. and V. Patel (1992), 'Debt deficits and inflation: an application to the public finances of India', *Journal of Public Economics*, **47**, 171–205.

Central Statistical Organization (CSO) (1977), *Compendium of Environment Statistics*, New Delhi: Government of India.

Chai, J.C.H. (1986), 'The economic system of a special economic zone under socialism', in Y.C. Yao and C.K. Leung (eds), *China's Special Economic Zones*, Hong Kong: Oxford University Press, pp. 141–59.

Chai, J.C.H. (1990), 'International impacts of China's economic reforms', in D. Cassel (ed.), *Wirstschaftssyeteme im Umbruch*, Munich: Verlag Vahlen, pp. 344–62.

Chai, J.C.H. (1991), 'Agricultural development in China, 1979–1989', in E.K.Y. Chen and T. Maruya (eds), *A Decade of Open Economic Development in China, 1979–1989*, Tokyo: Institute for Developing Economies, pp. 4–28.

Chai, J.C.H. (1996), 'Divergent development and regional income gap in China', *Journal of Contemporary Asia*, **26** (1), 46–58.

Chai, J.C.H. (1997), *China: Transition to a Market Economy*, Oxford: Clarendon Press.

Chai, J.C.H. (2003), 'Privatisation in China', in D. Parker and D. Saal (eds), *International Handbook of Privatisation*, Cheltenham: Edward Elgar, ch. 12.

Chai, J.C.H. (2004), 'Globalisation and the environment: the Chinese experience', in C. Tisdell and R.K. Sen (eds), *Economic Globalisation: Social Conflicts, Labor and Environment Issues*, Cheltenham, UK and Northampton, MA, USA: Edward Elgar, pp. 299–313.

Chai, J.C.H. and Haishun Sun (eds) (1993), 'Liberalizing foreign trade: experience of China', *Department of Economics Discussion Paper No. 135*, Brisbane: The University of Queensland.

Chai, J.C.H. and C. Tisdell (1999), 'Hardening the budget constraint to control inflation under the two track system', in Y.Y. Kueh, J.C.H. Chai and G. Fan (eds), *Industrial Reform and Macroeconomic Instability in China*, Oxford: Clarendon Press, pp. 232–46.

Chakravarty, S. (1987), *Development Planning: The Indian Experience*, Oxford: Clarendon Press.

Chand, S. and K. Sen (2002), 'Trade liberalisation and productivity growth', *Review of Development Economics*, **6** (1), 120–32.

Chen, Lanyan (1999), 'Expanding women's co-operatives in China through institutional linkages', *Development and Change*, **30**, 715–38.

Chen, N.R. and W. Galenson (eds) (1969), *The Chinese Economy under Communism*, Chicago: Aldine.

Chow, G. (1993), 'Capital formation and economic growth in China', *Quarterly Journal of Economics*, **108** (3), August, 809–42.

Clark, C. (1967), *Population Growth and Land Use*, London: Macmillan Press.

Clark, C. and K.C. Roy (eds) (1997), *Comparing Development Patterns in Asia*, Boulder, CO: Lynne Rienner.

CM (*China Market*), Hong Kong: Economic Information and Agency, various issues.

Coale, A.J. (1991), 'Excess mortality and the balance of the sexes in the population', *Population and Development Review*, September, 517–23.

Collins, S. and B. Boswarth (eds) (1996), 'Economic growth in East Asia: accumulation versus assimilation', *Brookings Paper on Economic Activity*, **2**, Washington, DC: Brookings Institution.

CP (*China Price*), Beijing: State Price Bureau, various issues.

Crompton, P.L. and G.R. Rodriguez (1992), 'Implications of recent trade and industrial reform in India', *Agriculture and Resources Quarterly*, **4**, 542–73.

Dasgupta, M. and Li Shuzhuo (1999), 'Gender bias in China, South Korea and India 1920–1990: effects of war, famine and fertility decline', *Development and Change*, **30**, 619–52.

DDZGGDZCTZGL (*Dangdai Zhongguo de Guding Zichan Touzi Guanli*) (*Contemporary China's Fixed Investment Management*) (1989), Beijing: China's Social Sciences Publisher.

Desai, P. and J. Bhagwati (1975), 'Socialism and Indian economic policy', *World Development*, **3** (4), 213–18.

DFAT (2001), *India: New Economy, Old Economy*, Canberra: DFAT.

Diamond, L. and R.H. Myers (2000), 'Introduction: elections and democracy in Greater China', *China Quarterly*, 162, 365–86.

Dollar, D. and A. Kraay (2004), 'Trade, growth and poverty', *Economic Journal*, February, F22–F49.

Dreze, J. and A. Sen (1989), *Hunger and Public Action*, Oxford: Clarendon Press.

Dreze, J. and A. Sen (eds) (2002), *Development and Participation*, New Delhi: Oxford University Press.

Eckhaus, R. (1995), The metamorphosis of giants: China and India in transition, *MIT, Department of Economics Working Paper*, **95**/22, Cambridge, MA: MIT Department of Economics.

Eckstein, A. (1966), *Communist China's Economic Growth and Foreign Trade*, New York: McGraw-Hill.

Eckstein, A. (1977), *China's Economic Revolution*, Cambridge: Cambridge University Press.

Economist Intelligence Unit (2001), 'The plot thickens', http://www.economist. com, accessed 31 May 2001.

Edwards, S. (1993), 'Openness, trade liberalisation and growth in developing countries', *Journal of Economic Literature*, **31** (3), 1358–93.

Encarnation, D.J. (1989), *Dislodging Multinationals: India's Strategy in Comparative Perspective*, Ithaca, NY: Cornell University Press.

Enke, S. (1971), 'The economic consequences of rapid population growth', *Economic Journal*, December, **81** (324), 800–811.

Evans, P. (1995), *Embedded Economy: States and Industrial Transformation*, Princeton, NJ: Princeton University Press.

Fan, S.G. and X.B. Zhang (2002), 'Production and productivity growth in Chinese agriculture: new national and regional measures', *Economic Development and Cultural Change*, **50** (4), 819–38.

Field, R.M. (1996), 'China's industrial performance since 1978', in R.F. Ash and Y.Y. Kueh (eds), *The Chinese Economy under Deng Xiaoping*, Oxford: Clarendon Press, pp. 88–125.

Gao, Xiaoxian (1994), 'China's modernization and changes in the social status of rural women', in C. Gilmartin, G. Hershatter, L. Rofel and T. White (eds), *Engendering China*, Cambridge, MA: Harvard University Press, pp. 80–100.

Gao, Z. (2003), 'Technology transfer in China's industrial development', unpublished PhD thesis, Brisbane: School of Economics, The University of Queensland.

Garnaut, R. (1996), 'Economic reform in India and China', *Journal of Asian Economics*, **7**/1, 29–47.

Garnaut, R. and K. Anderson (1980), 'ASEAN export specialization and the evolution of comparative advantage in the Western Pacific Region', in R. Garnaut (ed.), *ASEAN in a Changing Pacific and World Economy*, Canberra: Australian National University, pp. 374–410.

General Administration of Customs of the People's Republic of China (1998), *Chinese Customs Statistics*, Hong Kong: Economic Information and Agency.

Gillies, M., D.H. Perkins, M. Roemer, and D.R. Snodgrass (eds) (1992), *Economics of Development*, New York: Norton.

Government of India (GOI), *Economic Survey*, New Delhi: Government of India, various issues.

Government of India (GOI) (1956), *Second Five Year Plan*, New Delhi: Government of India.

Government of India (GOI) (1992), *India – a Reference Annual*, New Delhi: Government of India.

Government of India (GOI) (1996), *India Infrastructure Report*, New Delhi: Government of India.

Government of India (GOI) (1999a), *Ninth Five Year Plan, 1997–2002*, vol. 2, New Delhi: Government of India.

Government of India (GOI) (1999b), *First Report of the Committee on Empowerment of Women*, New Delhi: Government of India.

Granato, J., R. Inglehart, and D. Leblang (1996), 'The effect of cultural values on economic development: theory, hypotheses, and some empirical test', in M.A. Seligson and T. Passe-Smith (eds), *Development and Underdevelopment: The Political Economy of Global Inequality*, Boulder, CO and London: Lynne Rienner.

Gregory, P.R. and R.C. Stuart (eds) (1990), *Soviet Economic Structure and Performance*, New York: HarperCollins.

Grub, Phillip and Jianhai Lin (eds) (1991), *Foreign Direct Investment in China*, New York: Quorum Books.

Guisinger, S. (1989), 'Total protection: a new measure of the impact of government intervention on investment profitability', *Journal of International Business*, Summer, 280–95.

Haddad, L. and J. Hoddinot (1992), 'Household resource allocation and Cote D'lvore: inferences from expenditure data', in T.A. Lloyed and W.O. Morrissey (eds), *Poverty and Rural Development*, London: Macmillan Press.

Hanson, A.H. (1966), *The Process of Planning*, London: Oxford University Press.

Harding, H. (1987), *China's Second Revolution: Reform after Mao*, Washington, D.C: Brookings Institution.

Harris-White, B. (2004), 'India's informal economy: facing the twenty-first century', in K. Basu (ed.), *India's Emerging Economy: Performance and Prospects in the 1990s and Beyond*, New Delhi: Oxford University Press, pp. 265–92.

Harrison, A.E. (1994), 'Productivity, imperfect information and trade reform: theory and evidence', *Journal of International Economics*, **36**, 53–73.

Ho, P.T. (1962), *The Ladder of Success in Imperial China: Aspects of Social Mobility*, New York: Columbia University Press.

Hong Kong Trade Development Council (HKTDC) (1991), *China's Foreign Trade System*, Hong Kong: HKTDC.

Howe, C. (1971), *Employment and Economic Growth in Urban China, 1949–1957*, Cambridge: Cambridge University Press.

Howe, C. and K. Walker (eds) (1984), *The Readjustment in the Chinese Economy*, London: China Quarterly.

Howe, C. and K.R. Walker (eds) (1989), *The Foundations of the Chinese Planned Economy: A Documentary Survey, 1953–65*, Houndmills: Macmillan Press.

Hsieh, J.F.S. (2003), 'Democratising China', *Journal of Asian and African Studies*, **34** (4–5), 377–92.

Hunger, J. and J. Morris (1973), 'Women and the household economy', in R. Chambers and J. Morris (eds), *An Irrigated Rice Settlement in Kenya*, Munich: Welform Verlag.

International Monetary Fund (IMF) (2002), *International Financial Statistics Yearbook*, Washington, DC: IMF.

Ishikawa, S. (1983), 'China's economic growth since 1949: an assessment', *China Quarterly*, **94**, 242–81.

Ishikawa, S. (1986), 'Patterns and processes of inter-sectoral resource flows: comparison of cases in Asia', paper presented to a symposium celebrating the 25th anniversary of an Economic Growth Centre, Yale University on the Current State of Development Economics: Progress and Perspectives.

Jagannathan, R. and P. Guhathakurata (1991), 'The government: wanton ways', *India Today*, 30 April, 52–9.

Jalan, B. (1996), *India's Economic Policy: Preparing for the Twenty First Century*, New Delhi: Viking.

James, W.E., S. Naya and G.M. Meier (eds) (1989), *Asian Development: Success and Policy Lessons*, Madison, WI: University of Wisconsin Press.

Jefferson, G. and T. Rawski (1994), 'Enterprise reform in Chinese industry', *Journal of Economic Perspectives*, **8** (2), Spring, 47–70.

Jefferson, G., A. Hu, X. Guan and X. Yu (2003), 'Ownership, performance, and innovation in China's large- and medium-size industrial enterprise sector', *China Economic Review*, **14** (1), 89–113.

Jefferson, G., T. Rawski and Y. Zhang (1996), 'Chinese industrial productivity: trends, measurement issues and recent developments', *Journal of Comparative Economic*, **23** (2), Spring, 146–80.

Jiang, X. (1996), *Industrial Policy in the Transition period: An Analysis of the Chinese Experience* (in Chinese), Shanghai: San Lian Bookshop.

JJYJ (Jinji Yanjiu) (Economic Research) (in Chinese), various issues.

Jones, H.G. (1976), *An Introduction to Modern Theories of Economic Growth*, New York: McGraw-Hill.

Jonquieres, G.D. (2005), 'Challenges ahead for China's hi-tech', *The Australian*, 26 January.

Joshi, V. and I. Little (eds) (1994), *India: Macro Economics and Political Economy 1964–1991*, Washington, DC: World Bank.

Joshi, V. and I. Little (2004), *India's Economic Reform, 1991–2001*, Oxford: Oxford University Press.

Joskow, P. (1999), 'Regulatory priorities for reforming infrastructure sectors in developing countries', in J. Stiglitz and B. Pleskovic (eds), *Annual Bank Conference in Development Economics 1998*, Washington, DC: World Bank.

Kahn, H. (1979), *World Economic Development:1979 and Beyond*, Indianapolis, IN: Hudson Institute.

Kamath, S.J. (1993a) 'Promise and perils of development', *Policy*, Autumn, 21–6.

Kamath, S.J. (1993b), 'Promise and perils of India's economic reform', *Policy*, Autumn, 28–32.

Kandiyoti (1992), 'Women and rural development policies: the changing agenda', in C.K. Wilber and K.P. Jameson (eds), *The Political Economy of Development and Underdevelopment*, Singapore: McGraw-Hill.

Khatkhate, D. (1991), 'National economic policies in India' in D. Salvatore (ed.) *National Economic Policies*, New York: Greenwood Press.

Khatkhate, D. (1997), 'India's economic growth: a conundrum', *World Development*, **25** (9), 1551–9.

Kidron, M. (1965), *Foreign Investments in India*, London: Oxford University Press.

Krishnamurty, J. (1984), 'Country assessments: India', in H. Schubnell (ed.), *Population Policies in Asian Countries: Contemporary Targets, Measures and Effects*, Hong Kong: Centre for Asian Studies, University of Hong Kong, pp. 161–77.

Krusekopf, C.C. (2002), 'Diversity in land tenure arrangements under household responsibility system in China', *China Economic Review*, **13** (2–3), 297–312.

Kueh, Y.Y. (1984), 'Population growth and economic development in China', in H. Schubnell (ed.), *Population Policies in Asian Countries: Contemporary Targets, Measures and Effects*, Hong Kong: Centre for Asian Studies, University of Hong Kong, pp. 444–60.

Kuznets, S. (1966), *Modern Economic Growth: Rate Structure and Spread*, New Haven, CT: Yale University Press.

Lakshmanaswamy, T. (2002), 'Empowerment of women and household decisions', paper presented at the 3rd IIDS International Conference on Development, Bhubaneswar, India.

Lal, D. (1988a), *Hindu Equilibrium*, vol. 1, Oxford: Clarendon Press.

Lal, D. (1988b), *India – Country Study No. 5*, Panama and San Francisco: International Centre for Economic Growth.

Lal, D. (1995), 'India and China: contrast in economic liberalization?', *World Development*, **23**/9, 1475–94.

Lall, S. (2001), *Competitiveness, Technology and Skills*, Cheltenham, UK and Northampton, MA, USA: Edward Elgar.

Lall, S. and M. Abaladejo (2002), 'The competitive impact of China on manufactured exports by emerging economies in Asia', in C.A. Magarinos, Yongtu Long and F.C. Sercorich (eds), *China in the WTO: The Birth of a New Catching-Up Strategy*, Houndmills: Palgrave Macmillan, pp. 76–110.

Lardy, N. (1992), 'China's foreign trade', *China Quarterly*, **131**, 691–720.

Lardy, N. (1995), 'The role of foreign trade and investment in China's economic transformation', *China Quarterly*, **144**, 1065–52.

Lardy, N. (1998), *China's Unfinished Economic Revolution*, Washington, DC: Brookings Institution.

Laurenceson, J. and J.C.H. Chai (eds) (2003), *Financial Reform and Economic Development in China*, Cheltenham: Edward Elgar.

Lawrence, R.Z. and D.E. Weinstein (2001), 'Trade and growth: import-led or export-led?', in J.E. Stiglitz and S. Yusuf (eds), *Rethinking the East Asian Miracle*, Oxford: Oxford University Press.

Li, H.L. (2003), 'Economic reform in the urban land system in China', *Journal of Contemporary China*, **12** (34), 207–24.

Li, Lian Jiang (2002), 'The politics of introducing direct township elections in China', *China Quarterly*, **71**, 704–723.

Lin, Y. and T. Zhu (2001), 'Ownership restructuring in Chinese state industry: an analysis of evidence on initial organisational change', *China Quarterly*, June, 305–67.

Lin, Yifu and Y. Yao (2001), 'Chinese rural industrialisation in the context of East Asian miracle', in J.E. Stiglitz and S. Yusuf (eds), *Rethinking the East Asian Miracle*, Washington, DC: World Bank.

Lin, Yifu, Fang Cai and Zhou Li (eds) (1996), *The China Miracle: Development Strategy and Economic Reform*, Hong Kong: Chinese University Press.

Little, I.M.D. (1996), 'India's economic reforms 1991–96', *Journal of Asian Economics*, **7** (2), 161–76.

Liu, G. (1980), *Theoretical Issues in National Economic System Reform* (in Chinese), Beijing: Social Publishing House.

Liu, Zheng (1984), 'Country assessments: China', in H. Schubnell (ed.), *Population Policies in Asian Countries: Contemporary Targets, Measures and Effects*, Hong Kong: Centre for Asian Studies, University of Hong Kong, pp. 156–60.

Lu, D. (2000), 'Industrial policy and resource allocation: implications on China's participation in globalisation', *China Economic Review*, **11** (4), 342–39.

Lum, T. (2000), *Problems of Democratisation in China*, New York and London: Garland.

Ma, F.H. (1961), 'The financing of public investment in communist China', *Journal of Asian Studies*, **21** (1), 34–48.

Ma, Hong and Shangqing Sun (eds) (1981), *Zhongguo Jingji Jiegou Wenti Yanjiu* (*Studies in China's Economic Structural Problems*), 2 vols, Beijing: People's Publishing House.

Maddison, A. (1998), *Chinese Economic Performance in the Long Run*, Paris: OECD.

Maddison, A. (2001), *The World Economy: A Millennial Perspective*, Paris: OECD.

Mahalanobis, P.C. (1969), 'The Asian drama: an Indian view', *San Khya: The Indian Journal of Statistics*, Series B, **31** (3 and 4), 442.

Mahesh, R. (2004), 'Labour mobility and paradox of rural unemployment – farm labour shortage: a micro level study', *Indian Journal of Labour Economics*, **47** (1), 115–33.

Malenbaum, W. (1959), 'India and China: contrast in development', *American Economic Review*, **49**/3, 284–309.

Malenbaum, W. (1982), 'Modern economic growth in India and China: the comparison revisited, 1950–1980', *Economic Development and Cultural Change*, **31**/1, 45–84.

Mankiw, N.G. (2003), *Macroeconomics*, New York: Worth.

Mao, Tse-tung (1965), *Selected Works*, vol. 1, 2nd edition, Beijing: Foreign Language Press.

McClelland, D. (1983), 'The achievement in economic growth', in B.F. Hoselitz and W.E. More (eds), *Industrialization and Society*, Paris: UNESCO.

McKinsey and Co. (2004), 'India: from emerging to surging', McKinsey Global Institute, http:www.mckinsey.com, accessed 12 February 2004.

Mellor, J.W. (1976), *The New Economics of Growth: A Strategy for India and the Developing World*, Ithaca, NY: Cornell University Press.

Minami, R. (1994a), *The Economic Development of Japan: A Quantitative Study*, 2nd edition, Houndmills: Macmillan Press.

Minami, R. (1994b), *The Economic Development of China: A Comparison with the Japanese Experience*, Houndmills: Macmillan Press.

Ministry of Environment and Forests (MOEF) (1992), *Policy Statement for Abatement of Pollution*, New Delhi: Government of India.

Ministry of Environment and Forests (MOEF) (1997), *Minutes of the Consultative Committee of the Members of Parliament Attached to the MOEF* (held on 27 August), New Delhi: Government of India.

Ministry of Surface Transport (1993), *Pocket Book on Transport Statistics in India*, New Delhi: Government of India.

Mukherjee, A.N. and Y. Kuroda (2003), 'Productivity growth in Indian agriculture: is there evidence of convergence across states?', *Agricultural Economics*, **29** (1), 43–53.

Myers, C. (1958), *Labour Problems in the Industrialisation of India*, Bombay: Asia Publishing House.

Narayan, S. (1960), *Principles of Gandhian Planning*, Allahalsad: Kitabmabal.

Naughton, B. (1988), 'The third front: defence industrialization in the Chinese interior', *China Quarterly*, **115**, September, 351–86.

Naughton, B. (1996), 'China's emergence and prospects as a trading nation', *Brookings Papers on Economic Activity*, **2**, 273–344.

North, D.C. (1987), 'Institutions, transaction costs and economic growth', *Economic Survey*, **25**, 419–25.

O'Brien, K.J. and Lian Jiang Li (2000), 'Accommodating democracy in a one party state: introducing village elections in China', *China Quarterly*, **162**, 465–89.

OECD (Organisation for Economic Co-operation and Development) (1991), *The Transition to a Market Economy*, vols 1 and 2, Paris: OECD.

OECD (Organisation for Economic Co-operation and Development) (2002), *China in the World Economy: The Domestic Policy Challenges*, Paris: OECD.

Overdorf, J. (2004), 'Boom times – but no jobs', *Newsweek International*, **15** (5), 29.

Paranjape, H.K. (1964), *Jawaharlal Nehru and the Planning Commision*, New Delhi: Indian Institute of Public Administration.

Parikh, K.S. (1999), *India Development Report, 1999–2000*, New Delhi: Oxford University Press.

Parikh, K.S. and A. Shah (1999), 'Second generation reforms', in K.S. Parikh (ed.), *India Development Report*, New Delhi: Oxford University Press.

Perkins, D.H. (2001), 'Industrial and financial policy in China and Vietnam', in J.E. Stiglitz and S. Yusuf (eds), *Rethinking the Asian Miracle*, New York: Oxford University Press.

Perkins, D.H. and S. Yusuf (1984), *Rural Development in China*, Baltimore, MD: Johns Hopkins University Press.

Perkins, D.H., S. Radelet, D.R. Snodgrass, M. Gillies and M. Roemer (eds) (2001), *Economics of Development*, New York: Norton.

Pomfret, R. (1991), *Investing in China: Ten Years of Open-door Policy*, New York: Harvester Wheatsheaf.

Porter, M.E., H. Takeuchi and M. Sakakibara (eds) (2000), *Can Japan Compete?* Houndmills: Macmillan Press.

Posen, A.S. (2001), *Unchanging Innovation and Changing Economic Performance in Japan*, Washington, DC: Institute for International Economics.

Przeworski, A. (1991), *Democracy and the Market: Political and Economic Reforms in Eastern Europe and Latin America*, Cambridge: Cambridge University Press.

Pursell, G. (1992), 'Trade policies in India', in D. Salvatore (ed.), *National Trade Policies*, New York: Greenwood Press.

Rakshit, M. (2004), 'Some macroeconomics of India's reform experience', in K. Basu (ed.), *India's Emerging Economies: Performance and Prospects in the 1990s and Beyond*, Cambridge, MA: MIT Press, pp. 83–114.

Ramstetter, E.C. (1994), 'Employment-related characteristics of foreign multinationals in selected Asian economies', background paper for UNCTAD, *World Investment Report*, Geneva.

Rao, K.G. (2004), 'State-level fiscal reforms in India', in K. Basu (ed.), *India's Emerging Economies: Performance and Prospects in the 1990s and Beyond*, Cambridge, MA: MIT Press, pp. 115–50.

Rawski, T. (1975), 'China's industrial system', in US Congress, Joint Economic Committee (ed.), *China: A Reassessment of the Economy*, Washington, DC: US Government Printing Office, pp. 175–98.

Rawski, T. (1979), *Economic Growth and Employment in China*, New York: Oxford University Press.

Repetto, R. and M. Gillies (eds) (1988), *Public Policies and the Misuse of Forest Resources*, New York: Cambridge University Press.

Reserve Bank of India (RBI) (2001), *Report on Currency and Finance*, Mumbai: Reserve Bank of India.

Reserve Bank of India (RBI) (2003), *Report on Currency and Finance 2001–2002*, Mumbai: Reserve Bank of India.

Riskin, C. (1987), *China's Political Economy: The Quest for Development Since 1949*, New York: Oxford University Press.

Riskin, C. (1998), 'Several questions about the Chinese famine of 1959–61', *China Economic Review*, **9** (2), 103–9.

Roberts, D. (2003), 'The greening of China', *Business Week*, 27 October, p. 53.

Rodrick, D. (1995), 'Trade and industrial policy reform', in J. Behrman and T.N. Srinivasan (eds), *Handbook of Development Economics, Vol III*, Amsterdam: North Holland.

Rosen, G. (1992), *Contrasting Styles of Industrial Reform: China and India in the 1980s*, Chicago, IL: Chicago University Press.

Roy, K.C. (1986), *Foreign Aid and Indian Development: A Study from the Viewpoint of Peace and Development*, Ahmedabad: Gujurat Vidyapith.

Roy, K.C. (1988), *The Subcontinent in the International Economy 1850–1900*, Hong Kong: Asian Research Service.

Roy, K.C. and J.C.H. Chai (1999), 'Economic reforms, public transfers and social safety nets for the poor: a study of India and China', *International Journal of Social Economics*, **26** (1–3), 222–38.

Roy, K.C. and A.L. Lougheed (1979), 'The Green Revolution in India: progress and problems', *World Review*, **7** (4), 16–29.

Roy, K.C. and C.A. Tisdell (1993a), 'Technological change, environment and poor women: specially tribal women, India', *Savings and Development*, **17** (4), 423–40.

Roy, K.C. and C.A. Tisdell (1993b), 'Poverty amongst females in rural India: gender deprivation and technological change', *Economic Studies*, **31** (4), 257–79.

Roy, K.C. and Tisdell, C.A. (1996), 'Women in South Asia with particular reference to India', in K.C. Roy, C.A. Tisdell and H.C. Blomqvist (eds), *Economic Development and Women in the World Community*, London: Praeger.

Roy, K.C. and C.A. Tisdell (eds) (1998), 'Good governance in sustainable development: the impact of institutions', *International Journal of Social Economics*, **25** (6/7/8), 1310–25.

Roy, K.C., Tisdell, C.A. and R.K. Sen (eds) (1992), *Economic Development and Environment – a Case Study of India*, Calcutta: Oxford University Press.

Roy, S. (1984), *Pricing, Planning and Politics: A Study of Economic Distortions in India*, London: Institute of Economic Affairs.

Rozelle, S., G. Li, M. Shen, A. Hughert and J. Gilles (1999), 'Leaving China's farms: survey results of new paths and remaining hurdles to rural migration', *China Quarterly*, **158**, 367–93.

Rudolph, L. and S. Rudolph (eds) (1987), *In Pursuit of Lakshmi: The Political Economy of the Indian State*, Chicago, IL: University of Chicago Press.

Sen, A.K. (1981), *Poverty and Famines: An Essay on Entitlement and Deprivation*, Oxford: Clarendon Press.

Sen, A.K. (1986), 'How is India doing?', in D.K. Basu and R. Scisson (eds), *Social and Economic Development in India: A Reassessment*, New Delhi: Sage.

Sen, A.K. (1992), *Inequality Re-examined*, Cambridge, MA: Harvard University Press.

Sen, A.K. (1995), Economic development and social change: India and China in comparative perspectives, London School of Economics and Political Sciences Discussion Paper.

Sen, A.K. (1999a), *Commodities and Capabilities*, New Delhi: Oxford University Press.

Sen, A.K. (1999b), *Development as Freedom*, New York: Knopf.

Sen, A.K. (2004), 'Democracy and secularism in India', in K. Basu (ed.), *India's Emerging Economy; Performance and Prospects in the 1990s and Beyond*, New Delhi: Oxford University Press.

Shenoy, S. (1971), *India: Progress or Poverty? A Review of the Outcome of Central Planning in India 1951–59*, London: Institute of Economic Affairs.

Siebert, H. (1999), *The World Economy*, London: Routledge.

Simon, J. (1977), *The Economics of Population Growth*, Princeton, NJ: Princeton University Press.

Singh, M. (1982), 'Credit policy of the Reserve Bank of India', in *50 Years of Central Banking – Governors Speak*, Mumbai: Reserve Bank of India.

Singh, N. (2004), 'Information technology and India's economic development', in K. Basu (ed.), *India's Emerging Economies: Performance and Prospects in the 1990s and Beyond*, Cambridge, MA: MIT Press, pp. 223–62.

Sinha, M.N., N. Sangeeta and K.A. Siddique (1999), *The Impact of Alternative Policies on the Economy with Special Reference to the Informal Sector: A Multi-Sectoral Study*, New Delhi: National Council of Applied Economic Research.

Smil, V. (1993), *China's Environmental Crisis*, Armonk: M.E. Sharpe.

Solow, R. (1957), 'Technological change and the aggregate production function', *Review of Economics and Statistics*, **39** (August), 317–20.

Srinivasan, T.N. (2000), *Eight Lectures on India's Economic Reforms*, New Delhi: Oxford University Press.

Srinivasan, T.N., J.Y. Lin and Y.W. Sung (1993), *Agriculture and Trade in China and India: Policies and Performance since 1950*, San Francisco, CA: ICS Press.

Srivastava, R. and S.K. Sashikumar (2003), *Impacts of Internal and International Migration on the Indian Development*, monograph, New Delhi: Jawaharlal Nehru University.

SSB (State Statistical Bureau) (1984), *Guanghui di Sansiwu Nian* (*The Glorious 35 Years*), Beijing: China's Statistical Publishing House.

SSB (State Statistical Bureau) (1985), *Zhonggou Shehui Tongji Ziliao* (*China's Social Statistical Materials*), Beijing: China's Statistical Publishing House.

SSB (State Statistical Bureau) (1989a), *Zhongguo Nongcun Tongji Daquan* (*Comprehensive Statistics on China's Rural Economy*), Beijing: China's Statistical Publishing House.

SSB (State Statistical Bureau) (1989b), *Open Coastal Economic Areas Research and Statistical Data*, Beijing: China's Statistical Publishing House.

Statesman Weekly, The, Calcutta, various issues.

Strizzi, N. and R.T. Stranks (2000), 'China's environmental mess: implications for Canadian business', *Ivey Business Journal*, **6** (65), 73–80.

Sun, Haishun (1998), *Foreign Investment and Economic Development in China, 1979–1990*, Aldershot: Ashgate.

Sung, Y.W. and T. Chan (1987), 'China's economic reforms 1: the Chinese debate', *Asian-Pacific Economic Literature*, **1** (1), 1–24.

Swamy, S. (1973), 'Economic growth in China and India, 1952–70: a comparative appraisal', *Economic Development and Cultural Change*, **21**/6, pt 2, 1–84.

Swamy, S. (1989), *Economic Growth in China and India – a Perspective by Comparison*, New Delhi: Vikas.

Teja, R. (1992), 'Crisis recovery and transformation in India', *Finance and Development*, **29** (4), 31–3.

The Telegraph, Calcutta, various issues.

Thirlwall, A.P. (1989), *Growth and Development with Special References to Developing Countries*, 4th edition, Houndmills and London: Macmillan.

Tisdell, C.A. (1997), 'China's environmental problems and its economic growth', in C.A. Tisdell and J.C.H. Chai (eds), *China's Economic Growth and Transition*, Brisbane: The University of Queensland, pp. 1–4.

Tisdell, C. and J.C.H. Chai (1998), 'Unemployment and employment in China's transition', in UNCRD (ed.), *Challenges of Transformation and Transition from Centrally Planned to Market Economics*, Nagoya: UNCRD, pp. 31–46.

Tisdell, C.A., Roy, K.C. and G. Regoni (2000), 'Socio economic determinants of the status of wives within their family in rural India: analysis and empirical evidence', mimeograph, Brisbane: School of Economics, The University of Queensland.

UNDP (United Nations Development Programme), *Human Development Report*, various issues.

United Press International (2004), 'China confronts its environmental problems', http://web7.infotrac.galegroup.com, accessed 29 January 2004.

Van Ness, P. and S. Raichur (1983), 'Dilemmas of socialist development: an analysis of strategic lines in China, 1949–1981', *Bulletin of Concerned Asian Scholars*, **15** (1), 215.

Vyas, V.S. (2000–01), 'Agriculture: the second round of economic reforms', *Indian Economic Journal*, **48** (3), 24–33.

Walker, K. (1966), 'Collectivisation in retrospect: the socialist high tide of autumn 1955–spring 1956', *China Quarterly*, **26**, April–June, 1–43.

Weisskopf, T.E. (1980), 'Patterns of economic development in India, Pakistan, and Indonesia', in R.F. Dernberger (ed.), *China's Development in Comparative Perspective*, Cambridge, MA: Harvard University Press.

Wen, G.Z.J. (1993), 'Total factor productivity change in China's farming sector 1952–1989', *Economic Development and Cultural Change*, **42** (1), 1–36.

Wheeler, D. (2001), 'Racing to the bottom: foreign investment and air pollution in developing countries', *Journal of Environment and Development*, **10** (3), 225–45.

Wolf, M. (2005), 'India on its way to economic success', *The Australian*, 3 March.

Woo, M.Y.K. (1994), 'Chinese women workers: the delicate balance between protection and equality', in G. Gilmartin et al. (eds), *Engendering China*, Cambridge, MA: Harvard University Press, pp. 279–98.

World Bank, *World Development Indicators*, Washington, DC: World Bank, various issues.

World Bank, *World Development Report*, Washington, DC: World Bank, various issues.

World Bank, *World Tables*, Washington, DC: World Bank, various issues.

World Bank (1983a), *China: Socialist Economic Development*, vols 1–3, Washington, DC: World Bank.

World Bank (1983b), 'Health and nutrition in China', in J.C.H. Chai (ed.), *Economic Development of Modern China*, vol. 2, Cheltenham: Edward Elgar.

World Bank (1985), *China: Long-term Development Issues and Options*, Baltimore, MD: Johns Hopkins University Press.

World Bank (1988a), *China: External Trade and Capital*, Washington, DC: World Bank.

World Bank (1988b), *China: Finance and Investment*, Washington, DC: World Bank.

World Bank (1989), *India: An Industrialising Economy in Transition*, Washington, DC: World Bank.

World Bank (1996), *India: Country Economic Memorandum*, Report No. 15882IN, Washington, DC: World Bank.

World Bank (1997), 'Overview', in J.C.H. Chai (ed.), *Economic Development of Modern China*, vol. 2, Cheltenham: Edward Elgar.

World Bank (2001), *Engendering Development*, Washington, DC: World Bank.

Wrigley, E.A. (1988), *Continuity, Chance and Change: The Character of the Industrial Revolution in England*, Cambridge: Cambridge University Press.

Wu, Bangguo (2000), 'Chinese economy in the 21st century', speech at the World Economic Forum on 29 January in Davos, Switzerland, released by New China News Agency.

Wu, H. (2002), 'How fast has Chinese industry grown? Measuring real output of Chinese industry, 1949–97', *Review of Income and Wealth*, Series 48, No. 2, 179–204.

Xiao, G. (2004), 'Round tripping FDI in the People's Republic of China: scale, causes and implications', *Asian Development Bank Institute Discussion Paper No. 7*.

Young, K. (1978), 'Modes of appropriation and social division of labour: a case study of Oxxa, Mexico', in A. Kuhn and A.M. Wolpe (eds), *Feminism and Materialism*, London: Routledge and Kegan Paul.

Yu, Yonding and Bingwen Zheng (eds) (2000), *The Research Report on China's Entry into WTO: The Analysis of China's Industry* (in Chinese), Beijing: Social Sciences Documentation Publishing House.

Yusuf, S. and S.J. Evenett (eds) (2002), *Can East Asia Compete: Innovation for Global Markets*, Washington, DC: World Bank.

ZGGNSCTJNJ (*Zhongguo Guonei Sichang Tongji Nianjian*) (*China's Domestic Trade Statistical Yearbook*), Beijing: State Statistical Bureau.

ZGNCTJDQ (*Zhongguo Noncun Tongji Daquan*) (China's Comprehensive Rural Statistics) (1989), Beijing: Agricultural Publishing House.

ZGSYWJTJZL (*Zhongguo Shangye Waijing Tongyi Ziliao*) (*China's Commerce and Foreign Economic Relations Statistical Data*), Beijing: State Statistical Bureau.

ZGTJNJ (*Zhongguo Tongji Nianjian*) (China's Statistical Yearbook), Beijing: China Statistical Press, various issues.

Zhang, Fengbo (1988), *China's Macroeconomic Structure and Policy* (in Chinese), Beijing: China's Finance and Economics Publishing House.

Zhao, Suisheng (2003), 'Political liberalisation without democratisation: Pan Wei's proposal for political reform', *Journal of Contemporary China*, **12** (35), 333–55.

Zhou, Z.Y. (1997), *Effects of Grain Marketing System on Grain Production: China and India*, New York and London: Food Policy Press.

Index

Titles of publications are in *italics*.

administration, politicization of, India
  240–41
agency system, foreign trade, China
  112
agricultural taxation
  China 81–2, 161–2
  India 164
agriculture 68–85, 266
  deregulation, China 51
  funding industrial development 81–2
  growth rates 68–9
  pre-reform China 13–15
  pre-reform India 22–5, 35–40
  privatization, China 54–5
  reform, India 46–7
  subsidies, India 36–7, 60–61
air pollution
  China 226–7
  India 219
Albeladejo, M. 252
allocation of investment
  China 149, 150
  India 152–3
Athukorala, P.C. 42
atmospheric pollution, *see* air pollution
aviation, China and India 255–6

Bajpai, N. 47
balance of payments crisis, as reason
  for reform, India 42
banking system, China 53
Bardhan, P.K. 48, 195, 239, 240
Basu, K. 239, 240
Bhole, L.M. 174, 175
Bhowmik 177
biodiversity loss through deforestation,
  India 217–18
birth control policy
  China 169–70
  India 170–71

birth rate
  China 168–9
  India 168
bureaucracy, effect on economic
  reform, India 237
bureaucrats, influence of, India 236

capital allocation
  pre-reform China 33–4
  pre-reform India 39
capital goods industries investment,
  India 89
capital market development, China
  53–4
capital resources, pre-reform 8
cash crops, output 70–71
caste system, India 10–11
central planning
  as cause of economic crisis, India 42
  pre-reform China 32–3, 90
  pre-reform India 38–9
Chai, J.C.H. 228
Chand, S. 92, 107–8
chemical fertilizer, effect on crop yield
  74–5
China
  agricultural development 68–85
  democratization 242–9
  development strategy 12–20
  economic growth 180
  economic reform 41–2, 49–50, 51–9
  economic system, pre-reform 29–35
  environmental degradation 225–30
  foreign investment 133–9
  foreign trade 110–14, 117–20, 121–4,
    141–2
  and growth 127–30
  industrial performance 94–105
  industrial policy 86–9, 90–91
  industrial structure 181–2